ZAIRE '74

The Rise and Fall of Mobutu's Leopards

Neil Andrews

EMPIRE
PUBLICATIONS

EMPIRE PUBLICATIONS
1 Newton Street, Manchester M1 1HW
© Neil Andrews 2022

ISBN: 978-1-909360-97-6

Contents

For my three children, Owyn, Stanley and Gracie, who have all shared my love of football at some point, albeit to different degrees of participation.

In memory of my friend Jake, who made school far more tolerable with his entertaining conversations on various aspects of the game, and my grandad, who first sparked my interest in football all those years ago.

Acknowledgements

ISPENT FAR LONGER than I imagined writing this book. I originally started work on it back in 2008 but struggled to make any real headway for a number of years because real life got in the way on more than one occasion. Yet throughout that time there was one source of constant encouragement and I will be forever thankful to Nicola for her help and support in getting this across the finish line. By her own admission she could not suggest much in the way of insight into the football merits of the likes of Lobilo Boba and Mwepu Ilunga but she was always ready to listen and offer advice when I hit a wall.

I would like to thank my editor Ashley Shaw at Empire Publications for his help and support, not to mention his positive response when I first submitted my idea, and Andy Lyons at When Saturday Comes magazine for agreeing to publish so many of my articles over the past fourteen years, which helped hone and improve my writing style. Their feedback has been invaluable.

I would also like to thank Nick Hart, my one-time fanzine editor and podcast collaborator, who has always been willing to entertain my silly ideas over the years and gave me the freedom to write and talk at length on all manner of subjects. Thanks too to my old university mate Rob Hick, who unknowingly helped with the research of this book and provided some valuable leads when the trail had otherwise gone cold, my cousin Alan for his help with the photos, Merv Payne and Neil Fissler for their advice and suggestions, Francois Arnaud for his translations, Walburga Krebber for taking the time to respond to my questions, Willie Donachie, Roselly at Third World Newsreel, and the British Library for their help when I originally started researching this book.

Finally, I would like to thank Brendan Byrne, Ron Voce and Nity Raj for their football-themed friendship over the years, my Mum and Dad for encouraging my passion for the game at an early age, my siblings Sami, Tasha and Sean for putting up with my Subbuteo all over the carpet floor when we were kids, Aunt Jackie for keeping this a secret, Owyn and Gracie for being themselves and Stan for showing a great interest in the subject matter and offering his opinions on which photographs to use.

Author's Note

THE HISTORY OF the Democratic Republic of Congo is complex. The country's long, painful transition from being the private domain of a Belgian king to a truly independent state is a tale of greed, corruption and bloodshed, with the shadow of President Mobutu looming large over much of it. This book touches upon some of that history and the impact it had on those that travelled to West Germany in 1974 to compete in the World Cup finals, but focuses primarily on the rise of football as the country's national sport, from its early colonial beginnings through to the immediate aftermath of the team's European adventure.

During that time the country underwent a number of name changes, which have been documented along with the renaming of various cities, clubs and even the president himself where relevant. However, to avoid confusion and maintain a steady narrative, I have opted not to do the same with the players themselves, who were required by law to drop their European names and adopt new "African" identities as part of Mobutu's authenticité campaign that began in 1971. As such, those that took part in the 1972 African Cup of Nations and 1974 World Cup are referred to throughout by the names that were officially submitted to FIFA ahead of the tournament in West Germany and used by journalists, reporters and TV commentators throughout the competition (a quirk of which saw all twenty-two players of the Zaire squad identified by their original surnames). This includes TP Mazembe midfielder Martin Tshinabu, who was listed as Tshinabu Wa Munda but was sometimes referred to as Tshinabu Wamunda or Tshinabu Wa Munda by other sources.

Naturally there are some anomalies. Anderlecht defender Julien Kialunda, who was based in Belgium at the time, was not affected by the president's decree while TP Mazembe forward Leonard Saidi fell out of favour before World Cup qualification was achieved and disappeared from the international scene altogether. Yet where possible, the Zairean names of all those involved have been used for familiarity and consistency.

1. Grass Roots

NO ONE IS QUITE SURE when the first ball was kicked in anger along the banks of the River Congo. The former Belgian colony has enjoyed a long relationship with the game of football, stretching back to before the First World War. It boasts the second oldest association on the continent after South Africa and established one of the first competitive leagues in the region as long ago as 1916. Yet accusations of "African ignorance" were freely used by the likes of BBC commentator John Motson when Zaire graced the World Cup Finals in West Germany in 1974, displaying a lack of knowledge with regards to the evolution of the game in the country and the many hurdles that had to be overcome before the team lined-up against defending champions Brazil.

As with so many other African nations, the game's development in what is today known as the Democratic Republic of Congo is rooted in its colonial past. A sweeping land-mass situated in the heart of the continent, the DRC dominates sub-Saharan region of Africa. The territory was first charted by European explorers in the 1870s when Sir Henry Morton Stanley undertook an exploration of the region at the behest of King Leopold II of Belgium, who had long cast an envious eye over the region as he looked to expand his nation's - and his own - interests along the west coast of the continent. Leopold formally acquired the much sought after land at the Conference of Berlin in 1885, promptly named it the Congo Free State and made it his own private property in the process. He began to exploit the colony's rich mineral wealth for his own ends, making a fortune for himself and his associates through the booming rubber trade. However, his brutal methods and repressive control eventually attracted international condemnation following an investigation into the king's activities by a British committee of diplomats in 1903.

As a result of the committee's recommendations, the state was formally taken over by the Belgian parliament, who were at first reluctant to assume responsibility, and renamed it the Belgian Congo. Keen to distance themselves from the actions of Leopold, who still maintained his industrial interests in the region, the government abandoned the policies of forced labour and exploitation employed by their king and instead opted for a more traditional approach to ruling the colony. This included introducing European pastimes and activities as a way of "educating" the native population. It wasn't long before the first organised football matches took place in the capital Léopoldville in 1912, following the examples of South Africa and Egypt, where the first recognised clubs were formed as early as 1879 and 1907 respectively.

Deemed a perfect pastime for the colonial agenda, the game's popularity quickly spread and by the early 1920s African-run leagues began to emerge around the country. This new-found popularity was thanks largely to two very different bodies of Belgian colonial rule - the church and the army.

The army - or the *Force Publique* - was originally conceived by Leopold to terrorise the local population rather than defend territory. Now run under more conventional lines, Belgian officers were keen to promote European sports and went so far as to make football a compulsory requirement in the training of the indigenous rank-and-file. Outside the military, the many Roman Catholic missions that quickly sprang up throughout the colony helped spread the game further and in 1919 the country's first football association - the Association Royale Sportive Congolaise (ARSC) - was founded by the missionary Raphaël de la Kethule de Ryhove, commonly referred to as Father Raphaël, who would go on to be something of a driving force in Congolese soccer and later establish one of the traditional powerhouses in club football, Daring Club (later DC Motema Pembe).

Yet there was another factor behind football's rapid growth in popularity, one that the ruling colonial powers probably did not expect. The adaptability of the game to any surface combined with the relatively cheap costs of staging a match – familiar stories of games involving rags, paper and other types of makeshift balls abound – made the sport very attractive to the Congolese. The game may have been introduced in an effort to create a disciplined, efficient and healthy populace in true Imperial style, but it inadvertently provided the local population with the opportunity to freely express themselves, albeit within the constraints of the football laws, something that had not been possible in the colony until that point. Rather than conform, the game offered them the chance to rebel without fear of reprisal and many of the clubs that sprang up around this time became a focal point for local communities, similar in many respects to the way the game grew in Britain. As a consequence football gave the country a sense of national identity that helped hurry along independence from Belgium.

Due to the size of the territory and the logistics involved, there was no national league at this early stage. Instead regional competitions sprung up around the twin centres of Léopoldville (later Kinshasa) in the West and the industrial town of Elisabethville (later Lubumbashi) in the Katanga district in the south-east of the country. Football in Elisabethville centred around two independent associations - the *Ligue de Football de Katanga* (LFK), an organisation run for the benefit of white colonials, and the *Fédération des Associations Sportives Indigènes* (FASI), founded by a Benedictine missionary, Father Grégoire Coussement in 1925. The LFK was a relatively short-lived exclusive organisation, running a championship from 1936 to 1950. By comparison, the FASI had over 30 affiliated clubs in 1950, competing in four leagues divided over three divisions and with over 1,250 registered players.

Meanwhile in Léopoldville Father Raphaël's league was thriving, despite a number of European clubs having already been established by Belgian, Flemish, French and British colonists. With an initial roster of 35 teams, the competition was divided into five divisions and held its first championship in 1918 for clubs in and around the capital, with many of the sides involved later becoming dominant forces in the country's first national league.

The clubs were formed on partisan lines akin to their European counterparts, emerging from the various industrial, religious and colonial organisations in place around the country. Tout Puissant Mazembe, for example, were formed by Benedictine monks under the name FC St. Georges, who, like Father Raphaël and Daring Club, wanted their students to enjoy athletic pursuits alongside their studies, recruiting many of their players from the colleges they ran. Later renamed FC Englebert following a lucrative sponsorship deal with a popular tyre brand, the club would go on to win five African Cup of Champions titles and provide seven members of the squad of players that would travel to the World Cup. A Catholic club appropriately named Vaticano hailed from Elisabethville while F.C. Saint-Eloi Lupopo began life as the company team of the Katanga

Railroad. They were originally called Standard in honour of their founder's favourite team back home, Standard Liège, before adopting the name of St. Eloi, the patron saint of railwaymen.

They were one of the few company teams in the Elisabethville region that did not owe their existence to the Union Minière du Haute Katanga (UMHK), a copper mining corporation that recognised the benefits of encouraging their workers to take part in local matches. With a motto of "good health, good spirits and high productivity", UMHK played their part in the formation of Union Sportive Panda, Lubumbashi Sport and F.C. Kipushi. The corporation was a major footballing force in the region until the winter of 1941 when armed troops opened fire on striking miners on one of the many company-owned football pitches in the Lubumbashi region. Yet despite this incident, UMHK inspired several other big companies around the country to follow their lead.

In Bas-Congo, F.C. Inga were sponsored by a local electricity company and F.C. Cinat by the neighbouring cement plant while CF Sucraf owed their existence to the local sugar plant. Surprisingly, despite the military's active involvement in the original development of the game in the Belgian Congo, there were very few army teams - Union Sportive Militaire Saio in Elisabethville being one of the few exceptions - although several clubs such as AS Dragons in Léopoldville attracted many fans from the Force Publique.

Under the administration of the ARSC, which controlled the game in the western half of the country and would later become the national association after independence, teams began to venture further afield to take on rivals in the neighbouring French Congo. For many years the highlight of the football calendar was the Stanley Pool Championship and subsequent cup competition - named after the lake that separated the capitals of the two Congolese colonies. Between 1923 and until both countries gained independence in the 1960s, clubs from Léopoldville joined those from Brazzaville to compete in two competitions organised by the *Fédération de Football Association du Pool.* Teams from the Belgian side of the River Congo dominated both competitions - winning all but five of the league titles on offer and every cup competition bar one.

Following the end of the Second World War, football on the continent of Africa began to break down borders as teams travelled further afield to seek out new opposition and play matches. At the end of the 1949/50 season what is considered to be the first sub-Saharan African football championship took place when a representative FASI team from Katanga entertained a touring team from Johannesburg, South Africa at the Leopold II stadium in Elisabethville in front of 30,000 spectators. The home side enjoyed a resounding 8-0 victory but such was the success of the tourists' visit - the game was one of an eight-match tour of the African copper belt that culminated with a match in Bulawayo - that a series of friendlies were played by teams from the Belgian Congo against opposition from French Equatorial Africa, Angola and both North and South Rhodesia.

With standards improving - not only in terms of playing ability but also in facilities and equipment (some players were still competing barefoot as late as 1949) - new opposition was sought for the locals to test their mettle. The various associations around the country extended invitations to the leading Belgian clubs of the day and having recognised the success of other cultural exports to the colony, the authorities agreed to help fund any tours through Belgium's Colonial Office. The first to arrive were Beerschot AC of Antwerp, one of the leading Belgian clubs of the day, who were invited to play an exhibition game against a Léopoldville select XI to celebrate the inauguration of the 70,000-seat Stade Roi Baudouin (King Baudouin Stadium) that opened in 1952 and would later host the *Rumble in the Jungle* title fight between Muhammad Ali and George Foreman in 1974, although by then it would be called the Stade du 20 Mai, the first of many name changes the venue would undergo.

The visit proved to be something of an unexpected watershed on the domestic front, marking the beginning of the end of the dominance enjoyed by white "European" teams within the Congo. Beerschot comfortably beat their opposition, made up entirely of white colonials, 7-1 but several days later they were made to work by a side containing the best African Congolese players available - the first time a representative mixed team had taken the field - and scraped home with a 5-4 win. Contemporary match reports remarked on how well the Africans had played in comparison to their colonial "paymasters" and Robert Van Brabant, one of the leading coaches in the Belgian Congo who attended the match as an observer, suggested that the Antwerp club would have had struggled even further had the team been comprised entirely of native talent. 'It was not an experiment to be tried either,' he reflected. 'If Beerschot had been beaten, the defeat would have perhaps left the sporting framework'. Van Brabant's observation sat well with those seeking independence, and talk of forming a national side, composed entirely of African players, began to dominate conversation in footballing circles.

An unofficial international match had taken place in the Belgian Congo against Northern Rhodesia (later Zambia) in 1948 with the home side winning 3-2. However the game was played between two representative sides rather than national teams and it would be another two years before the idea of a Belgian Congo football team would become more concrete. The various associations that had a controlling interest around the country had begun to come together to form a more cohesive unit towards the end of the 1940s, but the traditional east/west split between Léopoldville and Elisabethville still existed. They were eventually brought together in 1955 not by football but by a tour of the country by King Baudouin that led to a tournament of sport in honour of the visit and a harsh lesson in how to play the game from none other than Belgian champions Anderlecht who were invited to play a Select XI from the various Leagues around the country and promptly won the game 9-1. Despite the result the match whetted the appetite of the Congolese authorities and by the time Standard Liège toured the colony the following year, the ARSC had already started laying the groundwork for the formation of a national team, making a tentative selection of players and nicknaming them "The Lions".

In 1957 two further events served to heighten a sense of national identity and helped further the colony's argument for independence. The first were the repercussions of a visit by Union Saint-Gilloise and a match against an ARSC representative team that ended in a riot. The tour began rather innocuously, with Union enjoying an emphatic 6-0 win against a mixed team of European colonials and indigenous players but two days later the tourists faced a tougher challenge, with slightly more than sporting pride at stake.

On Sunday, 16th June, they came up against a strong all-African representative side at Léopoldville's Stade Roi Baudouin in front of a crowd of over 60,000 spectators who were expecting to see their side triumph over the white Europeans. But things took a turn for the worse when the Belgian referee controversially disallowed two seemingly good goals for the home side, who slumped to a 4-2 defeat despite outplaying their professional opponents for much of the game.

A large section of the crowd, angered by what they saw as collusion between the match officials and the Belgian side, began throwing missiles at the players and tried to get at the referee before police moved in to try to quell the disturbances, a move that only served to fuel things further. The protests continued after the game and ended with 132 people injured, including the colony's director general of education, and over fifty cars damaged - but only ten arrests.

Daybreak the following morning marked the end of the first anti-white demonstration in the capital and the colony's ruling body were quick to try and prevent any further protests. Rather belatedly, the organisers admitted it was a mistake not to have had a neutral official but the local press were already pointing the finger of blame elsewhere. Recognising the perceived injustice of the native supporters, they identified the emergence of a growing nationalist movement as the root cause of the disturbances. *Le Courrier d'Afrique* went one step further and questioned whether such tours by Belgian teams should continue. 'These meetings are not appropriate,' they declared in an editorial shortly after the game. 'They assume a deeper meaning than just playing football.' By the time the article was published however, the boat had already sailed in more ways than one and several of the African stars who started the game that day were already eyeing moves overseas.

In May, a select team containing the very best players from around the colony embarked on a ground-breaking tour of Europe following an invitation from the Belgian FA to play a collection of games against some of the leading sides of the day. The 18-man squad, containing such talents as Paul Bonga Bonga and striker Leon "Trouet" Mokuna, who had already spent some time in Portugal with Sporting Lisbon and had the honour of being the country's first professional footballer, set sail for Europe with instructions from the ARSC to "prove the existence of a real Belgo-Congolese nation". They didn't disappoint with their performances as they took on the might of Anderlecht, Beerschot, Olympic de Charleroi and Standard Liège in the space of a fortnight. Bonga Bonga in particular caught the eye of many observers and so impressed the staff of Liège during the tourists' last game that they immediately tried to sign him after the final whistle. On that occasion the player refused but, not to be deterred, *Les Rouches* eventually got their man and, with a little help from a local football journalist, signed the 24-year-old later that year.

The powerful defender proved to be a big hit in Europe, helping Liège to the Belgian Championship in 1958 and 1961. Yet he is perhaps best remembered as the first African footballer to be selected in the *World Soccer Magazine* World XI alongside such luminaries as Tottenham Hotspur and Northern Ireland international Danny Blanchflower and Brazil's Nilton Santos the following year. But he was by no means the only player from the tour to make a name for himself and several of the squad went on to ply their trade overseas. Midfielder Henri Erumba became the first black player to play for Belgian giants Anderlecht, striker Maximilian Mayunga enjoyed several successful seasons with the Royal Daring Club de Bruxelles while Mokuna also carved out a career in Belgium after a second spell with Sporting in Portugal and was the league's top goal scorer in 1959, netting 19 goals.

They were quickly followed by the likes of Julien Kialunda, 'The Puskas of Léopoldville', who became one of the big stars of Belgian football after joining Anderlecht from Union Saint-Gilloise and would later play a small role in Zaire's footballing adventure in the 1970s. By 1960 around thirty players from the Congo were on the books of Belgian clubs, with ten of those turning out regularly in the first division.

These transfers would later have serious repercussions for the international game back home but at the time many in the sport, especially the administrators within the ARSC, saw it as an opportunity to make a quick buck. Indeed, the transfer of Leon Mokuna to Sporting Lisbon in October 1954 was initially blocked by the Congolese football federation who, in a letter to FIFA President Jules Rimet in October of that year, explained that they felt they were entitled to some form of monetary compensation. However, the players themselves quickly rebelled against this stance and in a telegram to football's world governing body two months later argued that it was rather rich for the association to seek compensation for an individual when they themselves were not paid for their services, let alone insured, a situation that would leave many if not all in dire straits if they were seriously injured during a game. In the end, the ARSC relented and Mokuna got his transfer but the increasing drain of local talent to overseas clubs left a bitter taste in the mouths of many and when independence was finally gained, the window of opportunity for footballers in the Congo was slammed shut.

The ARSC did finally manage to establish a national league in 1958, bringing together the various regional leagues under the collective name of the Linafoot (Ligue Nationale de Football) and placing them on a - albeit minor - professional footing. FC Saint-Eloi Lupopo walked away with the first national title but the haphazard nature of football in the Belgian Congo meant the next champions weren't crowned until 1963, some five years later. The cost of travel and the logistics involved in fulfilling fixtures hampered the league's progress in those early years, coupled with the internal strife suffered by the colony during its transition to a free state. As such, it suffered in comparison with the traditional regional championships that went before. Yet this did not stop the organisation from being ambitious in its outlook and at a congress held on March 20, 1959 the ARSC outlined its plans for football within the country. These plans included consolidating the league championship with a national cup competition, publishing the colony's first sports-specific newspaper, establishing training schools in the capital city and, most importantly, founding a national team to represent both the country and the association. This last point took on greater significance the following year when Belgium finally granted independence.

The independence movement had been growing since the mid-1950s but the riot following the game against Union Saint-Gilloise caught nearly everyone by surprise, particularly the Belgian government, and seemingly accelerated the colonials' cause. Events elsewhere, especially the independence of Ghana in 1957, added fuel to the fire and by October 1958 the *Mouvement National Congolais* (MNC) had established itself as a political force in the territory under the charismatic leadership of Patrice Lumumba, a former postal clerk and travelling beer salesman. In response to these protests and demonstrations, the politicians in Brussels began to debate the future of the colony with no real fixed agenda but before they could announce any meaningful timetables for possible independence they were overtaken by events in January 1959 when a political demonstration in Léopoldville turned violent, resulting in several hundred people losing their lives in heavy rioting that lasted several days as the authorities struggled to maintain order.

King Baudouin immediately declared that Belgium would work towards the full independence of the Congo "without hesitation, but also without irresponsible rashness" in a radio address. Yet the government's first response was to throw Lumumba in prison and charge him with incitement before proposing a woolly "transitional programme" for the colony without actually specifying a date for the handover of power. Nonetheless, when the king made his second visit to the Belgian Congo later that year, it became clear that the colony would not tolerate any more delays. Upon his arrival in Léopoldville he was pelted with rocks and stones by protesters angry at the imprisonment of Lumumba and the rest of his visit was marred by demonstrations wherever he went. Desperate to avoid being drawn into a colonial war like those experienced by their French neighbours, the Belgian government opted to give into the demands of the Congolese leaders who wanted independence sooner rather than later.

In January 1960 the Belgian government invited the leading politicians of the colony to Brussels to open discussions regarding the best route for independence for the Congo, including Patrice Lumumba, who was released from prison for the occasion. To the surprise of many, it was quickly agreed to grant the Belgian Congo full independence on June 30th of that year, with a general election to be held the month before. The Congolese delegation were praised for their efforts in achieving their aims so quickly, but the speed with which the Belgians granted independence and the lack of preparations for such an event created a multitude of problems that left the country in a very unstable state.

From the ensuing chaos emerged a man who would have a profound influence on the fortunes of the Democratic Republic of Congo as a whole and that of the national football team in particular, turning them from African minnows to World Cup finalists in less than a decade. That man was Joseph-Désiré Mobutu.

2. Enter Mobutu

IT'S FAIR TO SAY that had Joseph-Désiré Mobutu persevered with a career in journalism instead of becoming involved in the movement of independence, the likelihood of Zaire appearing in the 1974 World Cup Finals would have been very remote indeed. Under the president's patronage the country's football team went from no-hopers to two-time Continental champions and World Cup qualifiers in less than ten years. Yet this success was not driven by an overwhelming love of football, rather by a burning desire to avenge a defeat at the hands of the Black Stars of Ghana during Mobutu's inauguration celebrations.

The fact that he was president at all was remarkable in itself. Born on October 14, 1930 in humble, if not exactly poor surroundings, the future leader of the Belgian Congo had a habit of being in the right place at the right time throughout his early life and seemed blessed with an ability to turn any negatives that came his way into positives. Having received a very good education, he excelled academically but his mischievous reputation caught up with him towards the end of his school career when he attempted to stow away on board a boat to Léopoldville with a girl. The priests at his Catholic boarding school were not amused and enlisted him into the *Force Publique* for seven years as punishment. His spell in the colonial army would serve him well in later years when the opportunity arose and military life gave him the discipline that was seemingly lacking from his character. Moreover, he was able to continue his studies by borrowing books and European newspapers from the Belgian officers which, according to one biography, he would read while supposedly on sentry duty. Having passed an accounting course, he began to write articles for newspapers and magazines and eventually quit the army in 1956 to become a journalist full-time with *L'Avenir*, a daily journal in the country's capital.

It was while working as a journalist that Mobutu became actively involved in the movement for Congolese independence and befriended many of the prominent personalities involved. He grew especially close to its leader, Patrice Lumumba, who would later go on to become the country's first Prime Minister, and became his personal aide during negotiations with the ruling Belgian government that led to the country finally breaking free of colonial rule in 1960. However, just ten weeks after the Republic of the Congo was formed, the newly-established government's position was under threat after the military forces, upset at not being included in a decision to grant all civil servants a pay rise, mutinied against the remaining Belgian officers that had stayed behind to train the new army.

Although not a leading figure in the fight for independence, fortune was once again on Mobutu's side when he again found himself in the right place at the right time. With the country on the verge of chaos and relations with newly-elected president and political rival Joseph Kasavubu at breaking point, Lumumba turned to his trusted friend for help and appointed him Chief of Staff of the Congolese Army. It was a move that would dramatically backfire on him. Before the year was out, Mobutu had used his new-found influence over the country's armed forces for his own ends in what became known as the Congo Crisis and his dramatic rise to power was confirmed in September.

While the Nationalist Lumumba and pro-Western Kasavubu were comically trying to sack each other from their respective positions of office, Mobutu – ever the opportunist – was seeking American backing to put an end to the crisis and seize power. This duly arrived via the CIA, who were only too happy to offer assistance after Lumumba had turned to the Soviet Union to help suppress a Belgian-backed secessionist uprising in the southern state of Katanga. Mobutu overthrew his former friend and ally and placed him under house arrest following the American-sponsored coup, but kept Kasavubu on as president. The Soviet Union withdrew their advisors and in a move designed to curry favour with the United States, Mobutu accused Lumumba of being a communist (ironically, Mobutu would later turn to the USSR after America deserted him).

Nevertheless, it would be another five years before Mobutu took absolute control of the Congo. With the CIA calling the shots, Mobutu took something of a supporting role and set about strengthening his position. In 1961 he handed Lumumba, who had tried to flee the country, over to police in Katanga, knowing full well that the chances of him surviving were slim. Lumumba was duly assassinated and Mobutu, without a hint of irony, went and built the highest monument in Kinshasa in memory of his martyred "friend". He then sat back and let Kasavubu preside over a succession of failed governments – while at the same time annoying the CIA – before stepping in to seemingly rescue the country once again after another rebellion saw one of Lumumba's former ministers, Pierre Mulele, occupy two-thirds of the country before being defeated by his Congolese army in 1964. As a result, former American diplomat and journalist Smith Hempstone concluded that Mobutu was 'one of the weakest strongmen in history, a black Hamlet, plagued by indecision, unwilling to assume power himself.'

The following year Mobutu finally asserted himself and seized control of the state in a second, bloodless coup after Kasavubu was involved in another power struggle with his Prime Minister Moise Tshombe, who had led the Katanga uprising in 1960. From the start he made it crystal clear that the country would be ruled as he, and he alone, deemed fit. In one of his first speeches after assuming power, the newly appointed president addressed a large crowd in one of the capital's stadiums and told them that it had taken five years for the politicians to lead the country to ruin. As a result, a new approach would be taken. 'For five years there will be no more political party activity in the country,' he informed them. In a stroke Mobutu had established an unchallenged dictatorship that would last until 1997, where any whim would be adhered to, no matter how bizarre and his first such whim concerned the national football team.

Independence had done little for the state of the game in Congo-Léopoldville, as the country became known to avoid confusion with their French neighbours, but the indigenous population's enthusiasm for the game had not diminished. Despite the national league being curtailed by the ongoing disturbances, regional and local competitions carried on as normal, although one government minister was forced to reprimand Congolese players for taking the game a bit too seriously after one weekend of fixtures saw four broken legs, four broken feet and a number of dislocations. In a statement issued to the Associated Press in October 1961, Congo's Minister of Youth and Sport, Michel Mongal, condemned the lack of sportsmanship within the game and the violence that tarnished it. 'Referees, linesmen and even the players themselves are frequently attacked,' he declared. 'Some fans even go as far as to burn cars, houses and threaten people with death. It is no secret that the sporting instinct is lacking among many footballers and their supporters.'

On the international stage there was at least some progress. The ARSC was again seeking to become a fully fledged member of FIFA after their initial application fell by the wayside when a money order lapsed during the independence celebrations (this wouldn't be the last time an administration error would cause embarrassment to the country's football federation). Their second application was more successful and after being granted provisional membership in February 1962 they were welcomed to football's governing body in 1964, just in time for them to join a boycott of African nations from the 1966 World Cup qualifying competition.

By now Congo-Léopoldville had officially dipped their toes into international competition when they accepted an invitation to take part in the fourth instalment of the French African Games - *Jeux de l'Amitié* – that ran from 1960-64. Open to former French colonies on the continent, the 1963 tournament featured seventeen teams, including a strong France side, and was held in Senegal. The team found themselves drawn in Group D and on April 11th 1963, they played their first international match against Mauritania, winning 6-0. But the hectic scheduling of the tournament meant that they would play their remaining three games on consecutive days. Defeats to neighbours Congo-Brazzaville (2-1) and Ivory Coast (1-0) followed before they regained some honour by beating eventual finalists Tunisia 1-0 in their final match (Tunisia would lose the final to the hosts on corners, Senegal having won nine to their opponents four). The following year they were invited back and reached the final, losing 2-1 to Cameroon, but lacking their European stars, results against stronger sides left a lot to be desired. The team often yo-yoed between dishing out heavy defeats to the continent's weaker nations and being soundly beaten by Africa's best when it really mattered.

In November 1965, two weeks before Mobutu seized power, the Lions made their first appearance at the African Cup of Nations in Tunisia. Grouped with reigning champions Ghana and fellow debutants Ivory Coast, it proved to be a sobering experience. Thrashed 5-2 by the Black Stars in their opening match, they were all but eliminated from the competition when they went into their second and final game. Needing a win to keep their slim hopes of progressing alive, they slumped to a 3-0 defeat and returned home early. Ghana meanwhile would go on to retain their title, an achievement that was not lost on the incoming president of Congo-Léopoldville.

Mobutu's decision to invest time and money in both the country's domestic clubs and international team was heavily influenced by the policies of Ghana's first independent leader, Kwame Nkrumah. The Ghanaian president saw football not only as a rallying point for nation-building following independence but also a way of uniting Africa. Seeking change, he was determined to boost the standing of African football on the international scene, with Ghana at the forefront, and initially found great success. Funded by the country's rich resources, Nkrumah established the first domestic championship and slowly began to assert influence not only on the pitch with the Black Stars but also in the halls of the Confederation of African Football (CAF). In 1964 he personally bankrolled the first continental club championship to the tune of 250 guineas, following the organisation's hesitancy to press forward with a competition inspired by the European Cup. The move granted him a greater voice, which he subsequently leveraged to organise the aforementioned Pan-Africanist boycott of the World Cup in England that resulted in the continent being assured of a place at all future finals after FIFA backed down.

Having established Ghana as the dominant force in African football, it probably came as little surprise to Nkrumah when the team received an invitation to play the Lions as part of Mobutu's ongoing inauguration celebrations in June 1966. The new Congolese president had been busy since becoming leader the previous Autumn and had already begun to use football as a propaganda tool to consolidate his position and popularity. Although his motives were less altruistic than his counterpart, he too recognised the game's importance when it came to uniting a disparate population. Within days of assuming power he had organised a domestic tournament in his honour then ordered a match to be played on a company field where hundreds of local unionists had been murdered during the colonial uprising. A win against the mighty Black Stars would promote his cause further.

The Ghana team arrived in a country gripped by national fervour. Earlier that month, Mobutu had undertaken a campaign of authenticity to identify himself with the Pan-Africanism movement and had renamed several of the nation's cities, in an effort to wipe away any trace of Belgian colonialism. As part of his *authenticité* programme, Stanleyville became Kisangani, Elisabethville was renamed Lubumbashi while the capital Léopoldville was now known as Kinshasa and by turn, the country became Congo-Kinshasa. To add extra spice to the encounter, the match was to take place on June 30th, Independence Day, affording Mobutu the perfect opportunity to demonstrate his country's military might at the Stade Roi Baudouin as part of the celebrations. Yet the attempts to intimidate the opposition failed miserably. An excellent Ghanaian side outplayed their hosts to record a comfortable 3-0 win, much to the president's chagrin.

Humiliated, Mobutu wasted no time in overhauling the national side. All Belgium-based players, commonly referred to as *Belgicains*, were ordered to return home with immediate effect and the High Commissioner for Sport, Antoine Ngwenza, was sent to Europe to secure their release, regardless of the cost. Documents held by the Fédération Congolaise de Football-Association (FECOFA), which superseded the ARSC in 1968, revealed that on one occasion the organisation agreed to pay over 950,000 Belgian Francs on the president's behalf to free four players from their club contracts. Considering the sums involved, the teams in Belgium were only too happy to agree terms and Mobutu personally greeted the players on their return in July. 'I have called you back with the sole aim of forming a team befitting this great country,' he explained before revealing the true nature of the exercise. 'We must, each person in his own field, do the maximum to fittingly defend national prestige.'

The *Belgicains*, who included such talents as Freddy Mulongo, who won the title with Standard Liège in 1963, and Royal Daring Club striker Max Mayunga, strengthened the national team overnight and under the guidance of coach Emmanuel Elonga, a professor of Physical Education in Kinshasa, the new-look side took to the field for the first time the following month for a friendly against Central African Republic. As if to banish the failings of the past completely, they did so with a new name, Mobutu having dispensed with the Lions epithet in favour of the now familiar Leopards as part of his reforms. The new dawn of Congolese football was confirmed by a victorious 5-0 romp over the opposition.

Seemingly vindicated, Mobutu's financial sponsorship intensified, funded by the economic boom the country was enjoying as a result of copper and cobalt mining in the mineral rich province of Katanga. Hungarian coach Ferenc Csanádi was hired to bring a more professional approach to the side and the sport's infrastructure at club level was improved, together with better training facilities and equipment, all paid for with state funds. The president bankrolled a number of high-profile friendlies against overseas teams including Brazilian club sides Vasco de Gama and Santos, who included Pelé in their starting line-up, plus England's Stoke City, which earned the visitors a £500 fine and a year-long ban from touring from the Football Association. Overseas tours were also funded and when prompted to justify the expenditure, Mobutu simply replied 'Sport is just as important as the economy'. Nonetheless, the heavy investment began to return dividends as early as 1967.

On the international stage the Leopards overcame Sudan and Tanzania to qualify for the next edition of the African Cup of Nations, with Csanádi blending the talents of the *Belgicain* professionals and local amateurs to good effect. In the African Champions Cup, meanwhile, Tout Puissant Englebert were sweeping all before them on their way to claim their first continental title, albeit in controversial circumstances. Up against Ghanaian champions Asante Kotoko in the final, Englebert were expected to deliver. Fittingly for a club founded by Benedictine monks, the team were forbidden from consuming alcohol or indulging in dalliances with women before the first leg and interned in a military camp. They came away with a creditable 1-1 draw but for the return leg in Kinshasa, Mobutu again resorted to intimidation tactics in an attempt to influence the result, as Asante coach Carlos Alberto Parreira vividly remembers. 'The stadium had been packed with what seemed like 90,000 or 100,000 people for hours before the start,' he recalled. 'Then armoured cars would roll in and circle around the athletics track outside the pitch, with President Mobutu in the central one, waving to the crowd, with the guards pointing guns. The referee was so afraid. There were very few decisions that went our way.'

The show of military force failed to have the desired effect and the second leg ended 2-2, which meant a play-off on neutral territory was required. Opinions differ on what happened next. Official sources suggest that a mix-up in communications meant the Ghanaians were not told where the game would take place. The club, meanwhile, insist they were disqualified after they refused to contest the replay following the poor decisions in the away leg. Either way, Englebert pitched up in Cameroon for the match and were awarded a walk-over and the title by default. Asante would get their revenge three years later when the sides met in the final once again. During the second leg in Kinshasa, their enigmatic and slightly eccentric goalkeeper Robert Mensah, who typically wore a cloth cap when keeping goal, refused to leave the field with his teammates after Englebert were awarded a controversial penalty. Placing the ball on the spot, he dared the Congolese team to take the kick. Tshinabu Wa Munda accepted the challenge but failed to beat Mensah and Asante held on to win 2-1 against the odds.

Ghanaian and Congolese football would renew its increasingly bitter rivalry at the 1968 African Nations Cup in January held in Ethiopia. Drawn together in Group B, the Black Stars prevailed thanks to a late strike from future New York Cosmos striker Willie Mfum but the final whistle saw emotions boil over and Saïo Mokili was expelled from the tournament for attacking the referee. Despite the setback, wins over Senegal and neighbours Congo-Brazzaville earned the Leopards a place in the semi-final and a match against the host nation. Ethiopia had cantered through their group after winning every game but were given an early fright when Csanádi's side raced into the lead with goals from Kidumu Mantantu and Léon Mungamuni. The Leopards were pegged back by their opponents but deep into extra-time Mungamuni fired home the winning goal to set up a tantalising final against their old foes.

The final was something of an anti-climax. The heavy schedule, so typical of African football at the time, had clearly taken its toll on both teams, who played out a taut affair lacking in goalmouth action. Watching from the stand that bore his name, Emperor Hailé Sélassié sat motionlessly on a throne with a dog at his side and the trophy in front of him, occasionally resorting to a pair of binoculars to get a closer look at what action there was. There was very little to get excited about but the only goal of the game was a worthy winner. Winger Pierre Kalala produced a fine piece of skill to control a high ball from Pierre Kasongo inside the opposition box before firing a thunderous left footed shot into the roof of the net.

For President Mobutu, the goal was priceless. It had taken Congo's leader less than two years to change the country's footballing fortunes but his work was not yet done. He wanted everyone to know who had made it all possible and ensure that his presidency was synonymous with the team's triumph. Prior to flying the victorious squad back home from Addis Ababa, the president declared a national holiday to guarantee a sizeable crowd would be waiting at the airport to greet their new heroes. As the players emerged from the aircraft, the bond between state and sport was visibly demonstrated by their carefully choreographed attire. Dressed in full kit, every member of the team wore a replica of Mobutu's signature leopard-skin toque. The ridiculous ensemble was offset by a large white board that hung around their necks with their name emblazoned across it, allowing for easy identification for both the fans and, more importantly, the waiting officials on the tarmac. White boards aside, the tactic worked. As a motorcade carried the squad to an official reception in the city, where they would hand the trophy over to the president, hordes of well-wishers lined the streets chanting "Leopards! Mobutu! Leopards! Mobutu!". For the people of Kinshasa, the two were already indivisible.

Later that year, TP Englebert successfully defended their African Club Cup title in slightly more conventional circumstances, defeating Togo's Étoile Filante 6-4 on aggregate to complete a unique double for Congo-Kinshasa. However, they needed a reprieve from CAF to do so. Having initially been knocked out in the first round by Ivory Coast champions Africa Sports, the club were reinstated after it was discovered that their opponents had fielded no less than three ineligible players. Having defended their title once, they reached to the final again in 1969 but were denied a third successive triumph by Al-Ismaily of the United Arab Republic. It proved to be a watershed year for the club, who were dogged by controversy on the domestic front after groundsmen found a human skull buried in the centre circle of the Stade du 20 Mai (formerly the Stade Tata Raphaël) in Kinshasa. Having gone unbeaten at the stadium for a number of years, Englebert were accused of using juju and witchcraft to unfairly influence games. Whether there was any truth in the allegations is open to debate but the team failed to win another major trophy for seven years after the discovery, by which time they had been renamed Tout Puissant Mazembe Englebert, or TP Mazembe for short (the original *Tout Puissant* prefix, which means 'almighty' was added after the team's first title winning season in 1966, when they went the entire campaign undefeated).

Englebert's slump in fortunes was mirrored somewhat by the national team. Their African Nations Cup victory should have heralded a shift in power on the continent but a costly administrative error impeded the Leopards' progress. Farcically, someone forgot to post the team's entry forms for the upcoming World Cup in Mexico. Having missed the deadline, the Congolese football federation attempted to rectify their mistake but FIFA refused to budge and along with Guinea, they were forced to watch from the sidelines as the rest of the continent fought it out for Africa's guaranteed place in the finals.

The news was a crushing blow not only for the players but also for the coaching staff, who learned the news within days of being awarded *La Medaille d'or du Merite Sportif* from Mobutu in recognition of their achievement. With World Cup qualification no longer a possibility, Csanádi opted to return home to take up a position with Hungarian champions Ferencváros as reserve team manager, leaving behind a solid foundation for his successor to build upon. His eventual replacement was Frenchman André Mori, a former journeyman with a distinctly average playing career whose only coaching position of note was a brief tenure with a provisional club in the French Riviera. The appointment would ultimately end in failure, with most of the blame resting squarely on Mori's inexperienced shoulders. Yet his cause was not helped by the Congolese football federation who failed to plug the gaps left by the lack of competitive matches in the team's fixture schedule, leaving them ill-prepared to defend their African Cup of Nations title.

With automatic qualification for the next edition of the championships assured, the Leopards played very little international football after their cup win. Indeed, prior to their opening group game in February 1970, the team competed in just six full internationals in the intervening two-year period, with a ten-month break between fixtures on one occasion (To put that number into perspective, the Leopards had played 18 international matches in 1967). Regardless of the lack of game time, results on the pitch were encouraging and did not suggest a dip in momentum. While big wins over Senegal (4-0) and Nigeria (5-0) were impressive, the pick of the bunch was a 10-1 thrashing of Zambia, a scoreline that has not been bettered since by the national team. In between this run of games there was also an eye-catching 3-2 victory in an exhibition match against Pelé's

Santos during their second tour of Central Africa at the beginning of 1969 that attracted world attention. Although little more than a glamorous friendly, the result lured Congolese football into a false sense of security with regards to the Leopards' apparent invincibility.

Expectations were therefore naturally high when the team embarked for Sudan, with the defence of their AFCON title seen as a mere formality, but everyone concerned was given a rude awakening. The Leopards could only muster a single point from their three group games and were eliminated in the first round. The sterner tests afforded by Egypt, Guinea and their old foes Ghana had found them wanting and the team's failure on the pitch was compounded further by the Black Stars' subsequent march to the final.

Coach Mori bore the brunt of the criticism in the press back home and was scolded for his team selections and tactics. The Frenchman had made two bold decisions in the build up to the tournament in an ill-fated attempt to stamp his mark on the side. Eschewing the Leopards' natural attacking flair, he opted for a more defensive formation and restrained approach that was at odds with the nation's expectations. He had also dispensed with the *Belgicains*, preferring to build his team around the emerging talent from Congo's many domestic clubs, although his constant tinkering with the Leopards' starting line-up hinted that he had yet to settle on his strongest side. With one eye on the future, he had given debuts to many of the players who would later feature in West Germany, including Mwanza Mukombo and Kakoko Etepé, but this cut little ice with neither the press, Mobutu or the committee of FECOFA, who immediately sacked him, allegedly without pay, for failing to deliver a second title.

Recognising the limitations of Mori, who had been hired on the recommendation of Paris-based journalist Lucien Tshimpumpu Wa Tshimpumpu, the Congolese football association upped their game. The search was now underway for a coach with international pedigree, no matter what the cost. They did not have to look far to find the right man.

The Power and the Glory: President Mobutu shakes hand with Pelé before an exhibition game between Santos and the national team in June, 1967. The Brazilian side won 2-1 in front of 75,000 spectators.

Leopards captain Kidumu Mantantu swaps pennants with his opposite number, Zambia skipper Dickson Makwaza, prior to kick-off in the replayed final of the African Cup of Nations.

Kibonge Mafu enjoys a photo opportunity with Pelé. The midfielder would later use the image when running for political office.

3. An Unexpected Journey

HOW BLAGOJE VIDINIĆ ENDED up in Africa is a bit of a mystery. Having finished his playing career in the embryonic North American Soccer League (NASL), the former Yugoslavia international all but disappeared from the game for nearly two years before popping up as the surprise choice to lead Morocco at the 1970 World Cup. Undeterred by his lack of experience, the Royal Moroccan Football Federation (FRMF), or more pertinently associates of Prince Moulay Abdellah, offered Vidinić his first professional coaching job and immediately tasked him with avoiding humiliation in Mexico. It was a controversial move on the federation's part to say the least.

Qualification had been achieved under the stewardship of French coach Guy Cluseau but the team's progress to the finals had been far from conventional. Their first round tie against Senegal required a play-off because the referee had forgotten to play extra time at the end of the second leg in Dakar. Another play-off was called for in the second round following two goalless draws against Tunisia that led to the teams playing out a 2-2 draw in front of a sparse crowd in Marseille, who waited with baited breath for the announcement that the decisive coin toss had sent the Atlas Lions through to the final round. Having ridden their luck early on, Morocco burst into life in the final qualifying round and booked their place at the World Cup with a game to spare following home victories over Nigeria and Sudan in a three-team group format to determine who would represent Africa in the ninth edition of the tournament.

Having booked their place, however, their actual appearance at the World Cup was not assured until after the draw was made by FIFA in January 1970. With political tensions riding high, the Moroccan federation had warned the organising committee that they would withdraw from the competition if they were paired with Israel in the opening round of matches. It was no idle threat, with the association having withdrawn their Olympic team from the 1968 Mexico Games for the same reason, but to the relief of all concerned the luck of the draw kept the two teams apart.

Who would lead the team in Mexico was not so clear cut, however. Frustratingly for Cluseau, he would be denied the opportunity of leading his team in the finals having suffered a heart attack shortly after their final qualification game that forced him to take a sabbatical from coaching. He was initially succeeded by his assistant and former international Abdellah Settati, who was a popular choice among players and fans alike, but on the eve of the tournament he fell victim to the politics within Moroccan football.

Like many other African states Morocco had a rich benefactor in King Hassan II, who was willing to bankroll the country's best teams including the national side, publicly stating that the game was one of the few arenas 'which allows Morocco, a young and small state, to rub shoulders with the greatest world powers'. His love affair with football had been nurtured at a young age when he regularly attended championship matches while living under the French protectorate, sometimes disguising himself to do so, much to the chagrin of his generals. Following independence in 1956 the crown prince played a pivotal role in the country's successful applications for membership to FIFA and the African Football Confederation and two years later he founded his own professional club, Association Sportive des Forces Armées Royales (ASFAR), otherwise known as the Royal Army Club. As king, his passion and personal involvement in the national side intensified after Morocco's World Cup play-off against Spain in 1961 saw the Atlas Lions hold their own against one of Europe's footballing super powers. Although they lost, the performance reinforced the monarch's belief that the football pitch was where his nation could compete on equal terms.

Now, with the team about to make their debut on the world stage, the king's confidence had been shaken by Cluseau's sudden departure. The Frenchman was a coach he knew well and trusted. In his dual role as trainer of both the national team and Association Sportive, Cluseau had enjoyed considerable success, winning the league six times in nine seasons with ASFAR to complement reaching the World Cup. Although Settati had been part of that success, a run of poor results against European club sides in the early part of 1970, including a 5-1 thumping by Saint-Étienne, raised concerns about his suitability for the role. Determined to avoid embarrassment in Mexico, the king exerted his influence and Settati was removed from his position as head coach.

Seeking a more suitable replacement, Hassan turned to a political ally for assistance. At first glance, Morocco and Yugoslavia seemed improbable bedfellows but the latter had cultivated strong diplomatic links with a number of former colonies around the world in the aftermath of the Second World War, primarily out of necessity. Although a communist state, the country had become something of a pariah in Europe, having first been expelled from the Eastern Bloc by Josef Stalin before rejecting the overtures of the capitalist West, who had promised to prop up Josip Tito's regime with financial backing. Stuck between two ideologies the Balkan nation joined forces with Morocco and 23 other countries, predominantly from Africa and Asia, to form what became known as the Non-Aligned Movement in 1961. One of the ten binding principles of the movement was the promotion of mutual interests and cooperation and Yugoslavia did not shy away from its commitment. Doctors, teachers, engineers and many other professions travelled overseas to support education and health projects around the globe as member states looked to improve their facilities and infrastructures. Among them was a large contingent of football coaches who were dispatched on demand to meet requests from those keen to benefit from the talent on offer.

Football had helped cement relations in the early days of Tito's charm offensive, with Yugoslav teams undertaking a number of promotional tours to countries within the Movement, including visits to Egypt, Ethiopia and Indonesia. Although they typically won handsomely against their inexperienced opponents, the political propaganda victory was of far greater value and reciprocal trips would see state leaders accompany their own teams to the Balkans, generating goodwill, a sense of unity and a number of diplomatic agreements that benefited both sides.

Like Mobutu in Congo-Kinshasa, these leaders also understood the part football could play in bringing a newly independent nation together and so sought help from their European partner to improve matters on the field of play. Before long Yugoslavian coaches would be prominent figures in dugouts across Africa and the Middle East. The Egyptian football association had led the way, appointing Ljubiša Brocić to lead their national team as early as 1954 and he would be followed by no less than four of his countrymen in the mid-60s, all of whom had been sourced and supplied by the Association of Football Coaches of Yugoslavia (Savez Fudbalskih Trenera Jugoslavije, SFTJ), who had been tasked with fulfilling such requests by their government.

Demand quickly began to outstrip supply, however. The shortage was primarily caused by a hangover from the days of the old colonial empires, namely a lack of English and French speaking coaches, particularly for roles in Africa. When Sudan solicited eight qualified coaches from the SFTJ in 1968, they could only fill six of the positions due to language deficiencies, despite receiving twenty-five applications. Nevertheless, the establishment of the Non-Aligned Movement and the ever-growing reputation of Yugoslav football opened doors for those seeking new opportunities and the financial rewards that came with them outside of Europe. By 1969, the SFTJ had placed forty-seven of their compatriots into coaching roles across seventeen different countries, including five at international level, and there was no sign of the demand waning as the new decade dawned with Kenya, Algeria, Kuwait and Zambia all seeking assistance around the same time as King Hussain. The association was therefore well-placed to help their Moroccan counterparts in their search and within days of Settati stepping down, his replacement was installed as the new Head Coach of the Atlas Lions.

A flamboyant and charismatic figure who bore a passing resemblance to the actor Christopher Lee, Blagoje Vidinić's appointment was a statement of intent by the Moroccan federation who wanted to be seen as a modern, forward-thinking association. Although by no means the first Yugoslav to manage overseas, Vidinić retained a certain star quality, albeit slightly faded, and his media-friendly sound-bites ensured plenty of column inches in the international press which helped to raise Morocco's profile. His coaching methods and approach to the game differed from his predecessor too and his worldly perspective was in stark contrast to the more insular outlook of Settati. Yet he was humble enough to recognise his own shortcomings and the swift managerial turnaround took an unexpected turn when Vidinić appointed Settati as his assistant. It was a prudent move by the Yugoslav, who opted to retain some familiarity within the coaching set-up rather than unsettle his new squad any more than was necessary so close to the finals. His assistant's knowledge of the team would also prove valuable in bringing Vidinić up to speed on the strengths and weaknesses of each player as he prepared for upcoming games against West Germany, Peru and Bulgaria, who Morocco had beaten 3-0 in a friendly six months before. It was a trick he would repeat later in his career as coach of Zaire.

Vidinić's association with the Leopards and their World Cup infamy is such that it is often overlooked that he had enjoyed a very successful playing career before moving into coaching. A goalkeeper by trade, he was an exciting prospect in his youth having made his debut as a precocious 17-year-old with FK Vardar in his hometown of Skopje. His towering 6'6" frame belied an athletic agility combined with sharp reflexes that for a period saw him touted as one of the best keepers in the game, drawing favourable comparison to the great Lev Yashin. The two lined-up against each other in the first ever European Championship final in 1960, but it was the Black Spider who came out on top, with the Soviet Union prevailing over Vidinić and Yugoslavia in extra-time at the Parc des Princes, Paris. Despite winning Gold at the Summer Olympics in Rome the following September, to add to the silver medal that he had won at the 1956 Games, the Euro defeat would ultimately cut short Vidinić's time on the international stage as he was deemed to have been at fault for both of the opposition goals. He won his final cap in October the same year and was not called-up again.

Inconsistency and erratic performances, not to mention his penchant for a cigarette, ultimately blighted Vidinić's reputation but did not prevent him enjoying a career that spanned 17 years and saw him keep goal for seven clubs in three different countries. Free to venture beyond the confines of the Iron Curtain, Vidinić's wanderlust initially took him to the picturesque surroundings of the Bernese Alps and FC Sion, signing a three-year contract shortly before his 30th birthday. In his debut season he helped his new side win the Swiss Cup, the first honour in the club's history and the only silverware Vidinić would pick up in his domestic career, but the promise of a final big pay-day in the inaugural season of the National Professional Soccer League (NPSL) lured him to the United States in the summer of 1967. He joined the Los Angeles Toros, a team financed by sports entrepreneur and owner of the NFL's LA Rams Dan Reeves, who had turned his attention to association football after failing to secure a National Hockey League franchise following the 1967 NHL expansion. Having assembled a cosmopolitan roster including five Yugoslavs, three Germans and a hearty mix of South American talent, the Toros' debut season failed to live up to expectations and they finished bottom of the Western Division.

Within a year the team had relocated to San Diego following the merger of the NPSL and the United Soccer Association to form the NASL. Vidinić would only play four further games for the club and within weeks of the new season starting he was traded to the St. Louis Stars for what proved to be his last hurrah as a player. Professional football in America experienced a turbulent birth and the newly-founded league was on the verge of imploding at the end of the 1968 campaign. Disastrous returns on their investment led to a number of owners deciding to cut their losses, no longer able to justify funding large squads of expensive overseas players in the face of dwindling interest and low crowds. The Los Angeles Wolves drew an average of fewer than 2,500 spectators during their final season playing at the Memorial Coliseum, which had a capacity of 93,000. CBS's decision to cancel their television contract was seen by many as the death knell and the number of participants dropped from a relatively healthy seventeen teams to just five. The Stars survived but the decision was made to go part-time with a focus on cheaper, local talent and Vidinić, along with a number of his teammates, was released from his contract.

Although unrewarding on the pitch, the move to America was a valuable learning experience for the Yugoslav goalkeeper regardless. Something of a joker, he had always been a popular figure in the dressing room but his personality and approach to the game was well suited to the gimmick-heavy enclave of North American soccer. Vidinić possessed all the eccentricities associated with goalkeepers that endeared him to fans and media alike. He sang opera during matches, could speak five different languages fluently and smoked like a chimney, which gave him a quizzical appeal to the American press, who, unable to pronounce his name, called him Barney instead, a moniker that stuck throughout his stay in the States. This exposure, although comparatively tame by modern day standards, stood him good stead for the coaching career that beckoned and his press conferences would be entertaining affairs at both the 1970 and 1974 World Cup finals.

His good humour and ability to manipulate the media to his advantage became evident shortly after the Morocco squad had arrived at their base in León. While other teams did all they could to avoid the reporters camped outside of their hotels and training camps, Vidinić took a more relaxed approach and held daily press conferences in the market square. He also invited locals and journalists to dine with his squad as part of a wider charm offence, using the opportunity to tackle any preconceptions they may have held. 'Morocco's team is by no means made up of camel drivers and mutton-eaters,' he assured reporters at one such gathering. 'Our players are neither howling dervishes, nor dissolute men who mourn their harems at home.'

As it transpired, Vidinić's team proved to be men of the world after all and were easily tempted by certain attractions on offer in León. On the eve of their opening fixture, *The People* newspaper gleefully reported how some of the Moroccan players had become preoccupied by the traditional evening promenade by the local female population outside their hotel. Determined to stamp his authority on proceedings, the coach had no qualms in slapping a 9pm curfew on his team and was forced to remind his charges of their duty to the folks back home after they struggled to beat a local amateur team 4-2 in a warm-up game.

He had good reason to be concerned by the task ahead. Afforded very little time to prepare, Vidinić's options were limited to the extent that Morocco only took a squad of 19 players to Mexico rather than the allowed 22. A combination of injuries, loss of form and a lack of fitness prevented a number of fringe players from travelling, including Mohamed Sahraoui, Abdallah Tazi, Maâti Khazzar and Abdel Ali Zahraoui, all of whom had featured in qualifying. He therefore opted for a more conservative approach built on discipline and patience, eschewing the Atlas Lions' traditional game based on flair and attacking football in favour of a more defensive formation for their opening game against West Germany. To the bewilderment of a number of Moroccan observers and officials, Vidinić's plan was to simply soak up pressure and hit their opponents on the counter. They feared the worst but the tactic almost worked.

Up against such greats as Franz Beckenbauer, Uwe Seeler and Gerd Müller, Vidinić's charges gave the Germans the shock of their lives when Houmane Jarir opened the scoring in the 22nd minute, capitalising on a bad defensive mistake by Horst-Dieter Höttges to fire home from close range. As their coach puffed his way through an entire pack of cigarettes, Morocco visibly grew in confidence and they came close to doubling their lead after Said Ghandi rose highest at a corner only to be denied by an acrobatic save from Sepp Maier. At the opposite end of the field goalkeeper Allal Ben Kassou was in inspired form, repelling everything thrown at him, including a thunderous close-range effort from Müller, as their opponents frantically sought an equaliser.

Against the odds, they held onto their lead until half-time and threatened to repeat North Korea's heroics from 1966. Swept up in the euphoria of a potential giant-killing, King Hassan even sent word to the national broadcaster informing them of his intention to address the nation straight after the final whistle should Morocco hold on to their slender lead. Sadly there was no fairytale ending. West Germany drew level eleven minutes after the restart when Seeler finally broke the Atlas Lions' resistance with a snapshot that eluded the despairing dive of Allal. In the 78th minute Müller scored what proved to be the winner, reacting first after Seeler's header rebounded off the bar, but although they lost the match, Morocco left the field with their heads held high.

Three days later any hopes of progressing out of the group were dashed by Peru who comfortably triumphed 3-0 to secure their own qualification for the next round. The swing in fortunes was attributed by a number of players taking an unexpected day off from training, a decision taken by Vidinić after learning that the game was unlikely to go ahead. On the opening day of the tournament a massive earthquake had struck Peru killing an estimated 70,000 people, and the Peruvian delegation had announced their intention to withdraw from the competition and return home as a mark of respect, forfeiting their remaining matches. After much deliberation and coercion from the Peruvian government, the team decided to stay on and ultimately went all the way to the quarter-finals, losing to eventual winners Brazil. However the match still rankles with the African players who feel an opportunity was missed. 'We had a day off from training and lost the psychological edge,' recalled Ghandi ruefully in 2020. 'The team lost focus and we were thrown off balance.'

The Atlas Lions recorded a little bit of history in their final game - a goal from Maouhoub Ghazouani was enough to earn a 1-1 draw against Bulgaria and secure Africa's first point at the finals in an otherwise meaningless dead rubber played out before a sparse crowd at León's Estadio Nou Camp.

The Peru match notwithstanding, it had been a successful

tournament for Vidinić. Although an early exit was expected, he avoided the humbling many had predicted and enhanced his own reputation by fielding a side that could challenge the 1966 World Cup finalists. Individualism and a gung-ho inclination to attack in numbers had been jettisoned in favour of a more guarded approach complimented by a strong teamwork ethic and improved fitness levels, ably supported by Adidas, who provided the entire team with new boots for the World Cup. 'I don't know what we would have done without them,' Vidinić said of the German sportswear manufacturer, 'we received unbelievable support.'

However within months of the team returning home, the Yugoslav's pragmatism was being questioned. Vidinić quickly discovered that King Hassan's royal patronage of the national side went beyond that of chief cheerleader. In true African style Hassan began to assert his influence and started meddling in team matters. At one training session he demanded that the players wore neck braces because they were looking at their feet too much during matches and before long he had installed a direct line of communication to the dugout, as a former Moroccan international testified, albeit anonymously, to French magazine *So Foot*. 'On the bench there was a telephone and a switchboard operator,' revealed the informant. 'He was responsible for taking calls from the king and transmitting his instructions to the coach or to the players.'

Vidinić's position became untenable following the return leg of their politically-charged African Cup of Nations qualifier against Algeria in December 1970. Despite taking an early lead, Morocco had lost the opening game in Algiers 3-1 and the possibility of an early elimination at the hands of their neighbours and great rivals was a scenario that Hassan refused to contemplate. Taking matters into his own hands, he decreed that the stakes were too high to leave such an important decision as team selection to a humble football coach and before the game in Casablanca he sent one of his generals to the changing rooms to personally deliver the starting line-up to Vidinić. Whether the coach acquiesced to this royal proclamation is unknown but the Atlas Lions triumphed nonetheless, winning 3-0 after extra time to book their place in the next round. The following day, a newspaper aligned to the country's Minister of Sport wasted no time in manipulating the result for maximum propaganda impact, publishing a giant poster of the victorious players and attributing the result to the king's intervention rather than any tactical input from the team manager.

A 5-3 aggregate win over Egypt the following March secured Morocco's qualification for the 1972 edition of the African Cup of Nations but in a demonstration of his complete control over the country's footballing infrastructure, Hassan opted to sideline his Yugoslav coach. In a remarkable turn of events, ASFAR coach Sabino Barinaga was installed as the new boss of the Atlas Lions, leaving a vacancy with the Royal Army Club that was filled by Vidinić. The reasoning behind the switch is unclear. Barinaga, who famously scored the first ever goal at Real Madrid's Bernabéu Stadium, was an experienced football manager having coached Real Betis, Atlético Madrid and Valencia among others, but the Spaniard had failed to defend ASFAR's league title or make an impact on the continent's African Cup of Champions Club competition and had flopped in his brief stint in charge of Nigeria. Although a relative novice by comparison, Vidinić had impressed in his first year as a coach and some argue that Hassan felt the Yugoslav could translate his success on the international scene at club level. The two men were friends away from the football pitch but the continual interventions and intrusions were beginning to grate on the coach, resulting in conflict when he refused to back down. Whatever the thinking was behind Hassan's decision, it inadvertently hastened Vidinić's departure from Moroccan football.

Vidinić's stock had soared as a result of his team's performances in Mexico and among his many admirers was President Mobutu, who had been pro-actively searching for a coach who could propel the national team of Congo-Kinshasa to the next level and by turn consolidate his own position as head of state. Sensing the opportunity had arrived to make his move, the president flew journalist Lucien Tshimpumpu Wa Tshimpumpu, who had become the leader's chief football advisor, to Rabat with a suitcase full of cash to secure Vidinić's services. The Yugoslav was openly receptive to Mobutu's advances following his demotion to club football. Hassan had paid his footballing staff handsomely and may have gambled on his wealth being enough to keep the Yugoslav but Congo's booming economy, fuelled by copper exports that were at record prices, had furnished Mobutu with the necessary riches to fund any counter offer if required.

The strained relationship between the former goalkeeper and his king may have been the catalyst for Vidinić's decision to leave Morocco but it was the generous salary and signing-on bonus offered by Mobutu that convinced him to pack his bags and head south to Kinshasa. The starting wage of $1750 a month may suffer by comparison with the monies commanded by today's modern coaches but back in 1971 it eclipsed the salaries of England's World Cup winning manager Sir Alf Ramsey and the new Scotland boss Tommy Docherty, not to mention the contract offered by King Hassan. Yet in return for financial security and a swift return to international football, Vidinić inadvertently exposed himself to the foibles and whims of a dictator who would stop at nothing to get his way.

4. Three Falls and a Submission

VIDINIĆ GOT AN EARLY TASTE of Mobutu's autocratic vagaries in the most unexpected fashion. Within days of arriving in the capital to take up his new role as national team coach, the president had consigned the name of Congo-Kinshasa to the history books, rechristening the country Zaire as part of his ongoing *authenticité* cultural revolution. Ostensibly inspired by the Portuguese mispronunciation of the Kikongo word nzere, which roughly translates as "the river that swallows all rivers", Mobutu seized upon the new name during a dinner conversation with Belgian anthropologist Jan Vansina, who explained how the phrase had the same meaning in many of the country's local dialects. He became so enamoured with the term and its powerful definition that he also renamed the Congo River and the national currency Zaire too, collectively referring to them as *Les Trois Z—Notre Pays, Notre Fleuve, Notre Monnaie* ("The Three Zs: Our Country, Our River, Our Money"). The move reinvigorated his efforts to promote a more centralised and singular national identity in an attempt to unify the population of 21 million from more than 200 tribes and a raft of further changes were quickly introduced.

A new flag was adopted, together with a new national anthem, *La Zaïroise*. Then, in an act that would come to define his dictatorship, the country's population was ordered to change their colonial Christian names, which were typically those of popular saints, in favour of something more "Zairean", with priests warned that they would face five years' imprisonment if they were caught baptising a child with a European identity. Western attire was also later outlawed, with the male population expected to wear a Mao-style tunic known as an *abacost*, an abbreviation for the term à bas le costume or "down with the suit", and as the *Zairianization* of the nation continued apace, all Zaireans had to address each other as *citoyen*, or citizen, rather than the more traditional greeting of monsieur and madame. He even banned Santa Claus.

Leading by example and in accordance with his own decree, the president dispensed with his birth name Joseph-Désiré and assumed the more impressive, if hardly self-effacing epithet of Mobutu Sese Seko Nkuku Ngbendu Wa Za Banga, or "The all-powerful warrior who, because of his endurance and inflexible will to win, goes from conquest to conquest, leaving fire in his wake" to give him his full title. Yet the inflexible will to win led to Mobutu compromising on the very values he was trying to advance when he hired Vidinić but the leader was neither unrepentant or embarrassed by such blatant hypocrisy. He wanted Zaire at the World Cup and would do everything in his power to achieve that goal.

As it transpired, the Yugoslav was the perfect man to support Mobutu's aims. His approach to the job saw him ignore the tribal rivalries and prejudices that had dogged the game in Zaire, which in turn helped promote a sense of national unity, particularly outside the capital. He integrated players from the tribes of the Baluba, Lulua and Bangala into his squad and split his time equally between the country's two footballing hotbeds, Kinshasa and Lubumbashi, leaving no stone unturned in his efforts to seek out the very best talent to strengthen his side. Those that had fallen out of favour or had been discarded by the coach's predecessors were also given a chance to prove their worth, including a grateful Kibonge Mafu, who would go on to play a key role in the team's campaign. 'I lost my place in the team after a row with the previous trainer,' admitted the midfielder. 'But Vidinić brought me back and restored my confidence.'

Kibonge's redemption would come later in Vidinić's tenure. His first act as coach was to oversee a pre-planned tour to Belgium and the Netherlands. Travelling with an 18-man squad, the team played four matches in two weeks in what ultimately proved to be an eye-opening experience for the new manager. The opening three games went reasonably well, with the Leopards narrowly losing 2-1 to FC Groningen before fighting back from 3-1 down to draw 3-3 in a remarkable match against SC Cambuur that saw four goals scored in a crazy four-minute spell in the second half. Striker Freddy Kapata had made it 1-1 on the hour mark to cancel out Gerry de Jogne's opener before Johan Zuidema restored Cambuur's lead in the 61st minute then extended it straight from the restart. Kapata hit his and Zaire's second in the 63rd minute to complete the goal frenzy and went on to seal his hat-trick and earn a respectable draw in the last minute to round off a pulsating game. Five days later the Leopards produced another respectable performance in a 1-0 defeat against Royal Antwerp but the team's defensive frailties were cruelly exposed by Club Brugge in the last game of the tour. In fairness, the toll of playing so many matches in such a short space of time had led to fatigue within the Zaire camp but the Belgian side were not in a charitable mood and romped to a 9-1 victory that saw winger Kakoko Etepé netting a consolation for the tourists five minutes from time. The defeat, although harsh, proved to be a valuable learning experience for Vidinić. If the Leopards were to be successful, improvements needed to be made to the squad's fitness and the quality of domestic coaching.

On their return home the Yugoslav immediately set to work, travelling around the country to assess the coaching styles and fitness regimes of the local club sides. He was left unimpressed on both accounts, despite Mobutu's investment. 'I think he was rather horrified by what he saw, by our lack of proper training and method on the field,' remembers Leopards' captain Kidumu Mantantu, who had returned to the side for the trip to Europe after suffering a fracture against Tanzania earlier in the year. 'We had some fine players, but they simply didn't know what to do to make the best use of their skills. It was not really our fault. We had seen only our fellow Africans play, and we did not appreciate that the standards and styles were all that different elsewhere. Mr. Vidinić had coached all over the world, so he knew from his experience what was good and what was bad.'

The players' poor diets were an additional cause for concern for the new coach. Meals typically consisted of fufu, a porridge made from yams, and kassawa, a millet that was typically accompanied by either monkey meat or roasted snake, a combination that left many of the team undernourished and unable to complete 90 minutes. 'For two months I did nothing but study the social milieu of the players, especially their eating habits,' Vidinić confessed. '(But) a world championship tournament cannot be won with snakes'.

The fact that many had to hold down jobs in tandem with their football careers only compounded matters further. When Kibonge turned professional he had to take part-time employment to support the meagre salary offered by his club AS Vita, utilising his accountancy diploma to find work with the local water utility company and the Ministry of Territorial Administration. Striker Jean Tshamala was forced to find employment with the national railway company following his transfer to FC Lupopo while Ndaye Muamba similarly juggled his training commitments with a position as a teacher at a Protestant secondary school for a year before deciding to focus on his football career, despite the income it offered. Recognising the player's sacrifice, his club Union Saint-Gilloise provided him with a house, food and a small goal bonus that afforded him a relatively comfortable if frugal life.

An understanding employer, not to mention parent club, was essential for any player selected for the national team. So vast were Zaire's borders that players based in Lubumbashi had to journey over 1,400 miles just to reach the capital for home matches, the equivalent of flying from London to Kyiv, while the whole squad were often required to travel further afield to fulfil away fixtures and attend overseas training camps several times a year, resulting in lengthy absences for all concerned. Presidential patronage ensured no one questioned the players' availability.

'Everything in Zaire was secondary to the importance of the national team,' observed Belgian football journalist Marcel van Bergen, who covered the Leopards' visit to Europe in 1971. 'The clubs had no say. The only compensation for releasing players consisted of a small monetary payment or a promise from the association that the national team would one day come and play a game against the club. Then the not always unimportant receipts were handed over to the club.'

There was a significant increase in the number of trips undertaken by the squad in the immediate aftermath of the sacking of Vidinić's predecessor, André Mori. Displaying a distinct lack of faith in the qualities of Léon Mokuna, who was once again asked to take the charge of the Leopards on an interim basis, Mobutu made most of the country's immense wealth and natural resources to secure coaching sessions for the squad, who became a bargaining chip in diplomatic negotiations, particularly with those countries that possessed a strong footballing pedigree. Zaire's close links with Belgium were also exploited for the benefit of the team and regular coaching sessions were arranged under the tutelage of some of the country's leading football trainers, including national team manager Raymond Goethals, who received a personal request from Mobutu for help.

Goethals took charge of the Leopards for three weeks during a visit to Brecht in October, 1970 and left such an impression that the Congolese Football Federation made an official approach for his services on a full-time basis. He opted to stay with *Les Diables Rouges*, eventually guiding them to third place at the 1972 European Championship finals, but retained close ties with the African side, assuming an unofficial advisory role during Zaire's successful qualifying campaign for their own continental championship. He was therefore well placed to pass judgement on the strengths and weaknesses of not only Vidinić's new charges but also the administrative setup of Zairean football.

'I was curious to see the quality of the players who had not benefited from the supervision of Belgian clubs and to see how they behaved as a team,' he confessed, explaining the reasoning behind his original decision to offer assistance at the time. 'In terms of ball control, no Belgian player has anything to teach them. The ball sticks to their feet. They have a natural flexibility, an amazing balance and a strong shot, and the team is well organised. A major disadvantage of the team, however, is too much individualism. The players forget too quickly that they are part of the team and the same also applies from a tactical point of view. During the match there must be constant yelling from the side to make them stick to their orders.

'The only thing the players have complained about is the climate in Belgium,' Goethals revealed. 'They were frozen! They had not brought the appropriate equipment and most of them played in rubber trainers, unsuitable for our muddy fields. They also didn't have enough sports shoes and jerseys because they didn't assume that they would have to change twice a day. The Belgian Football Association had to provide them with the necessary equipment.'

When alerted to the situation, the Congolese Federation simply sent a telegram informing the administrative staff that accompanied the team to buy everything they needed in Belgium but the incident demonstrated the haphazard nature of such trips. Goethals, meanwhile, would be linked with the Zaire job once again, following Belgium's ill-fated bid to reach the 1974 World Cup finals despite not losing a game or even conceding a goal throughout the qualifying rounds. Although tipped by Dutch newspaper *Leidse Courant* to succeed Vidinić, he returned to club football where he enjoyed a successful, silver-laden career, which included winning the Cup Winners Cup with Anderlecht and the Champions League with Marseille.

How much involvement Goethals had in the Leopards' African

Cup of Nations qualifying campaign is open to question. Nevertheless, in February 1972, a little over two months after they returned from their brief European tour, the Leopards were off on their travels again, bound for Cameroon and the eighth edition of the competition. Still acclimatising to his new role, Vidinić did not deviate far from the 18-man squad that had accompanied him overseas, although he was denied the services of three key players - midfielders Kembo Uba Kembo and Kibonge Mafu and striker André Kalonzo. The trio, known affectionately in some circles as 'The Three Musketeers', were serving a suspension handed down by the Congolese football association before the Yugoslav's appointment for the 'unpatriotic act' of refusing to play an international fixture unless they received financial compensation. However, Vidinić did manage to spring one surprise by selecting Belgium-based defender Julien Kialunda.

A precocious talent, Kialunda was one of the first Congolese footballers to play professionally in Europe having joined Union Saint-Gilloise as a teenager in 1960. A move to Anderlecht followed and when Mobutu ordered the *Belgicains* to return home he managed to avoid being repatriated after the High Commissioner for Youth and Sports, Antoine Ngweza, failed to reach an agreement with his club who were reluctant to release Kialunda without substantial compensation and guarantees of the player's future. He made the most of his reprieve, albeit at the expense of his international career, winning the Belgian league title four times, the domestic cup competition twice and playing in the final of the Inter-City Fairs Cup against Arsenal in 1970. Celebrated for his skill on the ball and uncompromising tackling, he cut a popular figure at the club, captaining the side on a number of occasions, and even caught the attention of *The Guardian* newspaper who commented on how he 'ruled the Anderlecht defence' during a European Cup tie against Manchester United. Now, at the age of 31, Kialunda was set to make his debut for the Leopards and reinforce the team's defensive line. It was quite a coup for the Zaire coach but the defender's inclusion also increased expectations of those back home, who anticipated a triumphant return and another African title.

Drawn in the tougher of the two first round groups, all six games would take place at the Stade de la Réunification in the port city of Doula over the course of five days, with the matches reduced to a series of double headers. The opening encounter between Congo-

Brazzaville and Morocco drew a reasonable crowd of 15,000 who witnessed a cagey 1-1 draw but by the time Zaire kicked off their campaign against the reigning champions Sudan, the attendance had drastically fallen to just under 5,000 hardy souls.

The Sudanese had upset the odds to win the cup when hosting the competition two years earlier but were considered to be the weakest of the four teams nonetheless. As such, and in spite of Vidinić's warnings against complacency, many Zaireans saw the game as a mere formality and their confidence appeared to be justified when Mayanga Maku scored shortly after half-time to put the Leopards 1-0 up. When Hasabou El-Rasoul equalised for Sudan just two minutes later the celebrations and any thoughts of an easy victory were brought to an abrupt halt. The game ended all square, a result that left Group B delicately poised and the prospect of a potential elimination at the hands of their neighbours and fierce rivals Congo in their next match, a scenario that did not bear thinking about. 'Kinshasa's instructions were to win this match at all costs', remembers Leonard Saidi.

Thanks to the hectic schedule of the tournament there was little time to dwell on the situation and 48 hours later the Leopards took to the field to face the Red Devils of Brazzaville. Frustrated by his team's performance in the opening game, Vidinić opted to roll the dice and tweak his line-up, dropping midfielder Benjamin Mutombo and misfiring striker Pierre Ngassebe in favour of Kilasu Massamba and Jean Tshamala, who had earned the nickname 'Machine' at club level for his style of play. Tshamala certainly made an impact, albeit with the goalpost after seeing his header fly wide in the opening minutes of the game, but Congo had no answer to the new-found attacking flair of the Leopards and fell behind in the 16th minute when Jean Kalala N'Tumba rose highest in the box to steer his header past the desperate dive of Maxime Matsima. The striker scored again in the second half to seal a 2-0 victory and put Zaire in control of the group heading into the concluding round of fixtures.

The task at hand was now quite straightforward - avoid defeat against Morocco and top spot plus a place in the last four was guaranteed. Or so it seemed. Behind the scenes some of the players were grumbling about the promised bonus payments that had failed to arrive in Doula. Foreshadowing the revolt that would take place in West Germany, Vidinić had to quell a mini uprising ahead of the match against his former team.

'We were promised a $100 bonus for every game we won,' Saidi explained, recalling the events that took place at the team's hotel ahead of the match. 'But the guy from the sports ministry who was supposed to bring the money for our bonuses did not arrive. While we were waiting for him in Douala, he had taken our bounty money and gone to Paris!'

Crestfallen, the players were determined to establish the bonuses they could reasonably expect for qualifying for the semi-final, but when they tried to broach the subject they received short shrift from their coach.

'I asked him the question while he was talking about the game,' admitted Saidi. 'He got angry and curtly asked us to go get our bags and go to the stadium. So without our bonuses, we went and played and qualified for the next round.' The team ultimately received $900 for their efforts but Saidi is still resentful towards Vidinić, who he claims retained $150 from the prize pot with the rest split equally between the players. 'It was hard to understand why Vidinić failed to honour his bonus promise but the federation gave him his share and he was silent.'

The players were clearly still sulking when the match kicked off as Morocco took the lead after just three minutes. In a performance best described as "huff and puff", it took a strike from Mayanga to level the scores ten minutes before half-time and his reward was to be replaced at the break by Saidi in a tactical move designed to close out the game and secure the required draw. Elsewhere, Congo's 4-2 victory over Sudan left them level on points and goal difference with the Atlas Lions. As per the rules of the competition the drawing of lots was required to determine who would progress alongside the Leopards and it was their Sub-Saharan neighbours that ultimately prevailed at the expense of the North Africans.

Congo's reward was a tie with hosts Cameroon while Zaire would face unfancied Mali, who had reached the last four despite drawing all their group games. Mali's main attacking threat was the in-form Fantamady Keita, who already had three goals to his name in the tournament, but their defensive frailties were there for all to see, having squandered the lead in each match of the opening round including surrendering a 3-1 advantage to Togo. They would also be without their best player, Saint-Étienne's Salif Keïta, who had failed to recover from an injury picked up in the game against Kenya. The odds favoured the Leopards and when Congo pulled off a shock to knock out hosts Cameroon, a second continental triumph seemed like a foregone conclusion to many, including the players. As Saidi succinctly put it, 'In our heads we were already champions of Africa.'

As it transpired, the semi-final proved to be a classic that ebbed and flowed before delivering a sting in the tail for Zaire. All seemed to be going to plan when N'Tumba poked the ball home to give Vidinić's side the lead after just six minutes but a little over ten minutes later Adam Traoré levelled the scores, then Mali seized the initiative shortly after the interval when danger man Keita scored in his fourth consecutive game of the tournament to put the Eagles in front. Kakoko Etepé equalised for Zaire on the hour mark only for Bassidiki Touré to restore Mali's lead within minutes but a strike late on from the much-maligned Ngassebe, who had come on for the injured N'Tumba, sent the game into extra-time. Having shared six goals, this pulsating cup tie was finally settled by the seventh just two minutes after play resumed when Leopards keeper Kazadi Mwamba failed to keep out a long-range effort from who else but Kieta, who earned a move to French club Stade Rennais with his performances in the competition. It was a game that deserved a big crowd but only 2,000 spectators turned up to witness one of the all-time great AFCON matches, which paled in comparison to the 40,000 that watched the other, less dramatic, semi-final.

Although out of the competition, Zaire's involvement was not quite over. Vidinić rang the changes for the obligatory third place playoff against Cameroon, including giving reserve goalie Louis Pombi Litinda a rare start, but although they raced into an early lead thanks to goals from Kakoko and Mayanga, Zaire's tournament ended in a whimper. The Indomitable Lions scored four times in the space of eleven first-half minutes to restore some pride for the home nation and went on to record a convincing 5-2 victory. The following day Congo rubbed further salt into the Leopards' footballing wounds by triumphing in the final to claim their first continental title, giving the country's President Marien Ngouabi bragging rights over Mobutu in the process.

This time, unlike the failure of 1970, there was no knee-jerk reaction from either Zaire's president or the country's football federation in response to the team falling short. Vidinić's immediate future had already been assured, with World Cup qualification the only criteria on which he would be judged, so the press and public were denied their traditional sacrificial lamb on this occasion. However, while it was clear that everything in the garden was far from rosy, the tournament unfolded in such a bizarre fashion that it was difficult to judge what progress, if any, had been made. Morocco had been eliminated without losing a game while Mali had reached the final without winning one inside 90 minutes, bringing into question the format of the competition and the quality of the opposition. Zaire conceded just two goals in the group stages then shipped nine over the course of two games in the knock-out rounds, coming home with a less than impressive record of one win in five games despite finishing fourth. Yet that one victory was against the eventual champions, which left a bitter-sweet taste in the mouths of many Zaireans.

Still, there had been plenty of positives for Vidinić to build upon, most notably the performances of wingers Kakoko Etepé and Mayanga Maku. Both naturally left-footed, the two youngsters had been touted for great things from an early age but had unintentionally caused a selection headache for some of the Leopards' previous coaches, who would frequently rotate the pair on the same flank in alternate fixtures. Vidinić solved this little problem by moving the 23-year-old Mayanga to the right channel to great effect, leading to the pair being named in the AFCON Team of the Tournament alongside another emerging talent of the Zaire team, Bwanga Tshimen, who would earn the nickname *The Black Beckenbauer* due the resemblance of his playing style to the West German captain.

In spite of their relative youth, all three were already old hands at international football. Mayanga had been such a prospect that he made his international debut at the age of 17 before making his first senior appearance for his club and had been considered for the Leopards squad in 1968. His performance against Santos a year later earned him the nickname *Brazilian* (he became known as *Goodyear* in later years, after the brand of tyre, because of his 'all-terrain stamina') but although he was selected by André Mori for the 1970 tournament, the AS Vita Club player watched the débâcle unfold from the sidelines as an unused substitute. Mori had preferred his teammate and rival for the left wing berth Kakoko, who had established himself as the star of FC Daring, where fans referred to him as the *Football God*. Aged just 19, he was in the starting line-up for the defeats against Ghana and Egypt alongside Bwanga, who had followed his brother, goalkeeper Kazadi Mwamba, into the national side. He too was a prodigious talent but he had almost wrecked his chance of an international career by declining an invite to be part of the victorious 1968 squad.

'Just before the final phase, I was in Kinshasa with TP Englebert and I decided to accompany my teammates who had been selected to training,' recalled the defender with a wry smile. 'When we arrived, they introduced me to assistant coach Nicolas Nzoï, who asked me if I had my kit to be able to train with the national team. I didn't have it but despite this, he offered me a place on the squad. After due consideration, I decided not to accept the invite because I recognised there were players ahead of me and I would not be in the starting eleven. I didn't want to go as a tourist.' Luckily for the defender, a change of leadership and the persistence of Nzoï gave him a second bite of the cherry later that year. 'The strength of the Leopards at the time lay in the number of friendly matches they played and just after AFCON '68, Nzoï called me up for a friendly match against Guinea in place of Salomon Mange without having done a single training session with the Leopards. From then, I remained a starter until my international retirement.'

Together with Kazadi and midfielder Kidumu Mantantu, this trio of youngsters would form the spine of Vidinić's team going forward. The coach also benefited from a U-turn by the Zairean football federation (formerly known as FECOFA but now referred to as FEZAFA following Mobutu's *Zairianization* programme). Having come in for criticism and been accused of deliberately weakening the Leopards' chances in Cameroon, they saw the error of their ways and lifted the bans on Kembo and Kibonge, allowing them to return to the fold. André Kalonzo was also free to resume his international career but the internal squabbles and political machinations that blighted football in Zaire would rob Vidinić of the striker's services. Having scored one too many goals for his club TP Englebert against the railway-owned St Eloi Lupopo, his employers, the railway operator KDL, tried to blackmail the player into moving between the two teams. When he refused, they transferred him to a provincial side in Kananga out of spite so he hung his boots up and retired from the game.

Kalonzo wasn't the only loss. The classy Julien Kialunda had featured in all five games of Zaire's campaign at the African Cup of Nations but returned home to Belgium and international exile after those in charge failed to honour the commitments they had made to him before the tournament started. Striker Pierre Kalala Mukendi had already written himself into the country's history books after scoring the winning goal in the final of the 1968 African Cup of Nations but at the age of 33 time was against him and he bid a fond farewell to the international scene in the team's last game at the tournament. And Saio Ernest Mokili would also disappear from the picture, largely as a result of Mobutu's refusal to allow any player to leave the country.

In spite of the president's imposed self-isolation when it came to the nation's footballers, several top European clubs, particularly in France, were still prepared to try their luck, keen to tap into a cheap source of talent in order to compete. Mokili received several lucrative bids to return to Belgium and was approached by Greek side Panathinaikos while Saint-Étienne went so far as to offer contracts to both Mayanga and Kakoko. Yet despite assurances from the clubs involved - including offers to cover travel costs each time a player was called up on international duty - Mobutu refused to budge.

Mayanga still remembers the episode well. 'Saint-Étienne's manager came to the team hotel after a match. We went down and shook his hand and he said "Mr. Mayanga and Mr Kakoko, I came here to meet you for a little discussion" but President Mobutu completely refused and said "No, my players will stay here."'

For Saio Mokili, who was coming to the end of his career, it was a bitter blow. His club had already given their blessing and he had travelled to Greece to finalise the move but was denied the chance of a potential pay-day by the combined strength of the president and the football federation and received a ban from the national team for travelling without authorisation for good measure. Fifty years on the bitterness the player feels towards Mobutu has not receded. 'I just felt hatred towards him,' the player admitted, making no effort to disguise his anger. 'I felt contempt because he made me miss out on a career. I still hate him.'

It is often said that international management is far less stressful than being involved in the daily grind of running a domestic football club, more so with the high levels of financial investment in the modern game. Yet despite being a consistent narrative for a number of years, it is a very European outlook. In Africa, the performance of the national team has always outweighed the importance of club football by some margin. So while there is plenty of glory to be had, the financial rewards can only really be gained by moving overseas, which naturally creates a headache for the national coaches back home, who until recently, had to rely on the good grace of clubs in Europe to release their players for important fixtures. Such a scenario only exacerbated the problem that all international managers have faced at one time or another - knowing your strongest starting line-up for when it really mattered. At club level, a manager typically has plenty of competitive games in which to try and find the right formula, not so for their international counterparts, who may only have a handful of friendlies before a key game. In such situations African coaches have been forced to field experimental sides to plug gaps left behind by those stuck in Europe, beholden to their employer's whims. Mobutu's stance ensured such a situation would be avoided during Zaire's World Cup qualification campaign, even if it did create some short-term collateral damage in the process, but this approach also gave Vidinić a selection headache prior to the Leopards' first qualifier and heaped further, unnecessary, pressure onto his shoulders.

The road to West Germany was due to begin with a trip to Togo in June 1972, exactly three months after their last game, the meaningless third place playoff match against Cameroon, but the fixture list was empty for the intervening period. To aid their bid, FEZAFA had withdrawn the team from the qualifiers for both the 1972 Olympic Games and the 1973 Pan-African Games to ensure there were no unnecessary distractions from the main task at hand. It had been a collective agreement between coach, federation and president but recent events had radically altered Vidinić's first-choice line-up. With the game now looming the coach had to adjust to the loss of a couple of key players while integrating some new faces into his squad and risk sending out an "undercooked" team. By contrast, their opponents had played six fixtures before their encounter with the Leopards and recent form suggested they posed a real threat.

To aid their preparation, a friendly was hastily arranged against Spartak Moscow, who happily accepted an invitation from the FEZAFA to play two matches against the Leopards and AS Vita Club (city rivals Dynamo Moscow had accepted a similar invitation the year before, bringing with them a delegation of over 100 people). Under the watchful gaze of President Mobutu and wife Marie-Antoinette, Zaire won a competitive game 2-1 with goals from N'Tumba and a late Mayanga penalty. The only real surprise in Vidinić's line-up was his choice of captain. Leonard Saidi had only started one of the previous five games but now the midfielder had the distinction of captaining both his club, TP Mazembe, and country although he would only hold the honour for a matter of months.

The first leg of the double-header against Togo took place at the sparsely populated Stade Général Eyadema in Lomé and ended in a goalless draw. Keen to avoid defeat, Vidinić adopted a wary approach and opted to nullify the opposition's attacking threat through the deployment of man markers and an aggressive marking approach that at times bordered on violence. Nonetheless the coach's draconian tactics worked and the Leopards returned to the Stade du 20 Mai for the second leg with their clean sheet intact, although they rode their luck. 'We had a very tough first game,' said Kidumu, looking back on their opening match. 'The referee was very unpopular with the crowd for not giving the home side a penalty but we won the second-leg easily enough.' Home advantage certainly suited Zaire and they comfortably progressed to the Second Round, enjoying a comprehensive 4-0 victory thanks to goals from the recalled Kembo Uba Kembo, Kakoko and another brace from the in-form N'Tumba.

The Leopards completed their international calendar in July with a 6-0 drubbing of Guinea. At first glance, the decision not to take part in the Pan-African games appeared short-sighted, especially as the qualifying group stage, due to be held in neighbouring Congo, would have afforded Vidinić with at least five opportunities to experiment without the need to travel any great distance. Yet there was a degree of reasoning behind the decision. Had they qualified, the team would have been required to travel to Nigeria the following January, with the possibility of playing five further games over the course of eight days just weeks before the next qualifying round for the World Cup was due to take place. Moreover, TP Mazembe were making impressive headway in the African Cup of Champions Clubs and as part of his contract with the FEZAFA, Vidinić was required to travel with the team, acting as head coach for all inter-continental ties to help boost the standards and competitiveness of Zaire's domestic teams. Unfortunately their run would end in bitter controversy and bring Saidi's involvement with the national team to a premature conclusion.

The official reason behind the team's elimination from the competition was that Mazembe refused to play the second leg of their semi-final tie against Hafia FC of Guinea, having contested the eligibility of the referee assigned to officiate the game by CAF. Hafia were awarded a 2-0 walkover and progressed to the final, where they triumphed over Kenya's Simba FC 7-4 on aggregate. Having been left in the hotel lobby, dressed in their kits waiting for the team bus to arrive, the Mazembe players' recollection of events differ somewhat.

'It was at the time of good diplomatic relations between Mobutu and Guinea's president Sekou Touré,' explained Jean Tshamala, who had scored in the first leg, which the Zaireans had won 3-2. 'The cup we were contesting bore the name of the late President Nkwame N'krumah (Ghana's first independent leader and Vice President of Guinea who had died in April 1972) and the country was celebrating a national holiday in his honour on the day of the game. So Sekou asked Mobutu to let this game go as part of the celebrations.'

Saidi is in agreement. 'The Guineans weren't sure of winning against us on the pitch,' he asserts. 'This is why the Hafia committee made the request to their president, who hastened to make an arrangement with President Mobutu, who agreed to please his friend. Sports Minister Sampassa Kaweta Milombe travelled personally with us to Conakry as head of the Zairean delegation in order to carry out the plan.'

Whether it was by design or merely a coincidence, there was a change to the team's itinerary that added weight to the players' suspicions. The squad had been due to spend their entire stay at a hotel next to the stadium that typically accommodated visiting football teams and tourists alike, but after just two days they were inexplicably moved to lodgings some 25km away ('a hotel comparable to a prison' according to Tshamala). It was there that objections were first raised by the delegation about the match officials, receiving assurances that CAF-certified replacements were en route to take charge and instructions that any further complaints should be recorded with the competition organisers on the day of the game. However, come match-day, the entire Mazembe delegation were left stranded at the hotel when the team bus failed to show up.

'Vidinić came to see us, aware of the scheme,' Saidi continued, accusing the coach of being part of the plot. 'He asked us to put on our jerseys and be ready to go to the stadium. We were all prepared but there was no bus to take us to the stadium and time was ticking by. We called Sampassa to inform him of the lack of transport but he replied that he was too busy!'

'It was a teammate who was following the report on Guinean national radio, who noticed that the countdown was on while waiting for us to arrive,' remembers Tshamala. 'We learned over the radio that we had lost by default.'

Before the dust had time to settle, the team were dispatched in rude haste to Liberia to play two friendlies while the club's president flew to Cairo to lodge an appeal. It proved to be a futile exercise and CAF ratified the result of the match as a walkover, much to the chagrin of Saidi, who, feeling betrayed by Vidinić and Zaire's politicians, called time on his international career with immediate effect. The implications of the whole episode were also felt by defender Bwanga Tshimen, who was in the running for the African *Ballon d'Or* title after his performances at the African Cup of Nations and on the continent with Mazembe. He ultimately finished runner-up to Hafia's Chérif Souleymane, who scored three times in the final against Simba FC to swing the vote in his favour, but Bwanga's Silver Ball marked the first time a player from Zaire had made it onto the podium.

It was a bitter-sweet moment that encapsulated the year. Despite flashing moments of glory,

Zairean football had fallen short at the final hurdle at every level - club, country and individually. 1973 would prove to be a different story altogether.

5. The Sound of Munich

THE LEOPARDS ENTERED the New Year with World Cup qualification still uncertain and without their captain. Blagoje Vidinić moved quickly to address the latter, recalling midfielder Kidumu Mantantu and installing him as skipper in place of the disgruntled Leonard Saidi but getting to West Germany was a trickier proposition for the Yugoslav. There were still two knock-out rounds to navigate before a final pool of three teams battled it out for the right to represent Africa at the finals.

Before Vidinić could even contemplate that scenario there was a tricky tie against Cameroon to overcome. The Indomitable Lions had enjoyed mixed fortunes since the teams last met in the African Cup of Nations, having played three times as many matches as the Leopards in the intervening period but failing to progress in the qualifying tournaments for either the Olympics or the Pan-African Games. They came into the match with a record of just one defeat in their previous nine outings but this would be their first game of the 1974 qualifying campaign, having received a walkover in the first round after Gabon withdrew.

Vidinić opted to completely restructure his midfield ahead of the first leg in Douala at the beginning of February, bringing in the uncapped Mana Mambwene to play alongside the recalled Kidumu and Kembo Uba Kembo, who dropped back into his more familiar central role following a rare foray upfront against Togo. Jean Kalala N'Tumba spearheaded the attack once more, reliably supported on the flanks by the pace of Kakoko Etepé and Mayanga Maku, while goalkeeper Kazadi Mwamba lined up behind a settled defence of Joseph N'Dongala Lungwila, Mwanza Mukombo, Bwanga Tshimen and Kafula Ngoie. It proved to be a winning strategy with the Leopards producing a measured display of attacking flair balanced with defensive tenacity that kept the home side at bay. A spectacular second minute strike from N'Tumba was enough to give Zaire a precious 1-0 lead to take back to Kinshasa in a game that was also notable for the debut of Cameroon striker and future World Cup history maker Roger Milla.

A vociferous and expectant crowd of just over 46,000 gathered at the Stade du 20 Mai in party mood but the Indomitable Lions were not giving up on their own dreams of qualification just yet. The visitors dominated the first half as the Leopards put in an uncertain performance awash with unforced errors and, as the nerves started to creep in, Cameroon drew level on aggregate two minutes before the break when Paul-Gaston Ndongo beat three men before firing low and hard past a sprawling Kazadi. The half-time whistle was greeted by stunned silence from the disbelieving crowd but any hopes that the break would see an improved Zaire performance were quickly diminished when Cameroon continued to frustrate the home side's forward line. Throwing caution to the wind Vidinić hauled off the ineffective Mayanga and the misfiring Kembo in favour of Tshinabu Wamunda and Mbungu Ekofa but, although the changes finally added that much needed bite to the Leopards' attack, it failed to deliver the equaliser that would have seen the Leopards progress. In a progressively bad tempered affair it was Zaire's "bite" in the tackle that had the greater impact on the fixture, which left their opponents bemoaning the loss of goalscorer Ndongo and Jean-Baptiste Ndoga, both of whom sustained long-term injuries. It would become a familiar tactic in the Leopards' armoury, rolled out whenever they found themselves frustrated by the opposition.

With the scores level a play-off was required and Kinshasa once again played host to Cameroon two days later. 'We were lucky enough to win the toss to decide who should stage the play-off,' declared Kidumu Mantantu. The shock-waves of the second leg defeat were still being felt within the Zaire camp, resulting in a drastic change of personnel for the winner-takes-all clash. Defender André Mandiki, brought in to replace the injured Mukombo for only his second cap, was given such a torrid time by Daniel Eboue that not only was he dropped but he never played for his country again. Lungwila and Kembo were also left out of the starting line-up along with *Goodyear* himself, Mayanga Maku, who seemed to be testing the patience of his coach. Mwepu Ilunga and Tshinabu Wa Munda were all recalled in their stead along with debutants Kilasu Massamba and Ricky Mavuba Mafuila, who was often known as the *Black Sorcerer* due to his proficiency at dead ball situations, including being credited as the first Zairean footballer to score directly from a corner kick.

As in the first leg Zaire came out of the blocks quickly and caught Cameroon cold. Within three minutes they had taken the lead through Kakoko, who raised the roof at the Stade du 20 Mai by firing a left-foot volley past goalkeeper Michel Aka'a. The attacks continued and the visitors had Aka'a to thank for restricting the Leopards to a single goal. When Cameroon did manage to get out of their half they found their route to goal blocked by Mavuba, who was enjoying himself in the middle of the park. Everything seemed to be going to plan but the Indomitable Lions lived up to their nickname after half-time as Eboue, the nemesis of the unfortunate Mandiki, began to have an increasing influence on the game. Kazadi was called into action to deny the Cameroon centre forward after he turned Bwanga and Ngoie inside out, pulling off a save that brought a roar from the partisan crowd as though Zaire had scored a second. The Leopards' keeper then had to be at his very best to turn a goal-bound effort from John-Paul Akono around the post for a corner and as the visitors asserted pressure in search of an equaliser, Zaire's tackling and aggression grew in intensity once again as they looked to curb the threat of Eboue. Ironically, this rough-house approach only served to bring Bwanga's involvement in the game to a premature conclusion rather than their intended target.

As Eboue again raced through on goal, Bwanga and his defensive partner Ngoie tried to halt his progress by "sandwiching" him in a poorly executed pincer movement. Recognising the danger, the skilful striker executed an impressive turn of pace to glide past the pair and avoid the coming-together. Unfortunately for Bwanga, he crashed straight into Ngoie and ended up in hospital for his troubles. But it was Zaire who would have the last laugh. Two minutes from time substitute Mbungu Ekofa won a questionable penalty from Gabonese referee Francis Wolbert Anguiley, who had been well fed and entertained during his extended stay in Zaire's capital. Cameroon's protests fell on deaf ears and Tshinabu netted from the spot.

Soft refereeing decisions aside, Zaire were good value for their win and Vidinić must have been quietly satisfied with the performances of the four players he brought into the side. Tshinabu scored and the enormity of the occasion had not got the better of either Mavuba or the equally inexperienced Mwepu and Kilasu, who played their part in defence. Indeed Mavuba had been the stand-out performer, working well with Mana in midfield and taking the game by the scruff of the neck when required in a mature display that belied his youth.

Momentum was clearly building but it would be another six months before their decisive World Cup qualifier against former bête noire, Ghana.

Fortunately for Vidinić there was a second qualification tournament on the horizon. The opening round of the 1974 African Cup of Nations would begin in April and Zaire had been handed a tie against Upper Volta (now known as Burkina Faso), who had very little pedigree when it came to international football. The team's greatest achievement to date had been to qualify for the recent Pan African Games but they had lost all three matches in the final tournament, conceding ten times in the process, and hadn't even bothered to try to make it to West Germany. It was therefore a game Zaire were expected to win handsomely and they did not disappoint, beating their opponents 5-0 in the first leg in Ouagadougou. The coach kept faith with Mavuba and although the twenty-two-year-old scored his first international goal, it was his fellow midfielder and team captain Kidumu Mantantu who stole the headlines with a hat-trick. With Mayanga also finding the net, it was a convincing exhibition of football that rendered the return leg a mere formality. As such, the press back home in Kinshasa, conscious of the team's forthcoming qualifier against the Black Stars, implored Vidinić to rest key players for Upper Volta's visit with sports paper *Elima* running no less than two editorials on the subject.

There was no miracle at the Stade du 20 Mai for the Upper Voltese as the Leopards romped to another impressive victory, scoring four times to win the tie 9-1 on aggregate. Remarkably, they were paired with Cameroon once again for the second and final qualifying round, which threw up a notable curio. Since the two teams met in their dramatic World Cup clash there had been a change of personnel within the opponents' dugout. German Peter Schnittger had been replaced by another former Yugoslavia goalkeeper, the great Vladimir Beara, bringing Vidinić up against the very man he had replaced back in 1960. Beara got the better of his successor in the first leg with Cameroon winning 2-1 in Yaoundé but the return fixture in Kinshasa saw the Leopards prevail once more over the Indomitable Lions and secure their place in the finals in Egypt.

For newcomer Ndaye Mulamba the match was a double triumph, having scored the first international goal of his career in the 2-0 win. It had been a long time coming for the striker, who had been on the fringes of the first team for longer than he cared to remember. First called up by Ferenc Csanádi ahead of the 1968 African Cup of Nations at the age of seventeen, he had impressed the Hungarian in training but had not been selected for any of the warm-ups games and was ultimately cut from the 30-man squad that flew to São Paulo ahead of the finals for a training camp with some of Brazil's top coaches. Despite Csanádi's promises that his chance would come the player was left in the wilderness following the coach's departure until Vidinić offered him a route back into the national side. He was called up for consideration for the 1972 continental championship but despite making a good impression he again failed to make the final cut after the coach opted for familiarity and experience. Nevertheless, the Yugoslav did not forget the striker from Luluabourg and brought him back into the fold. Now, with a goal to his name and a couple of caps to boot, he was at the forefront of the coach's plans. And as the team celebrated their qualification, Vidinić sidled up to Ndaye during the post-match party and assured him he would have a seat on the plane to Egypt.

Not that Ndaye remembers much of the festivities. The team descended on a local Kinshasa nightclub just before midnight, where the alcohol flowed so freely that the next thing the player recalls is being bundled into the back of a taxi at 8pm the following evening. 'We didn't do anything. We just drank a lot…' was his honest answer when asked about the events of the night before, which had begun with an audience with Mobutu himself at the presidential palace where he outlined his expectations quite clearly to the team. 'He set us a mission to win the Cup,' revealed Ndaye. 'And promised "mountains and wonders" if we succeeded.'

Mobutu could certainly afford to gift mountains to those that pleased him. Copper prices were still rising and as the fifth largest producer of the metal, the *New York Times* surmised that Zaire's gross national product for 1973 would be close to $2.7 billion. This in turn led to increased overseas investment, despite the president's decision to press ahead with the nationalisation of foreign-owned agricultural and mining interests in the country. The earnings provided financial momentum for all government diversification efforts including industrial initiatives, power production, transport and agricultural development and also made a lot of people extremely rich. Those that benefited from the wealth did not have the tact to hide their good fortune either, with imports of Mercedes-Benz cars hitting an African record that same year.

For his part Vidinić received a small bonus for qualifying for the Cup of Nations as per his contract with FEZAFA but buying a new car was low down on his list of priorities. He still had the small matter of World Cup qualification to address and the showdown with Ghana was looming large.

The Black Stars came into the game a shadow of their former selves. Still reeling from their shock defeat to Sudan in the final of the 1970 Cup of Nations, they had enjoyed a miserable couple of years on the international stage. Having failed to qualify for the 1972 tournament, losing in the opening round to Togo, they would not be present in 1974 either having lost home and away to Ivory Coast. An appearance in the final of the Pan-African Games suggested an upturn in fortunes but their World Cup campaign to this point had been a mixed affair. Having enjoyed a comfortable 10-1 aggregate win over minnows Dahomey in the first round, their tie against Nigeria had been marred by crowd violence and controversy. Having gone 3-2 ahead in the opening game in Lagos, the match was abandoned five minutes from the end after rioting in the stands spilled over onto the pitch. The result was annulled by FIFA, who awarded Ghana a 2-0 victory, and the return leg ended in an incident-free 0-0 stalemate. Yet the Black Stars still held sway over the Leopards and demonstrated their determination to overcome their opponents by inviting Dinamo Bucharest and Romania's Olympic team coach Nicolae Dumitru to assist with preparations at their training camp in Winneba. They also had home advantage in the first match, something they fully intended to exploit.

A hostile welcome greeted the Zaire squad when they arrived in Accra, national fervour having been stoked by the Ghanaian federation, and a capacity crowd of 30,000 packed the national stadium to watch the drama unfold. The Leopards deservedly started the game as favourites. There was a nice, settled look about Vidinić's side with the right degree of experience running through its spine and they were clearly superior to their opponents in terms of skill and fitness but poor weather in the preceding days reduced the effectiveness of their passing game. Heavy rain left the pitch sodden and it cut up almost immediately, making ball control difficult as it bobbled off divots of grass and mud.

In a scrappy game of few chances, the winner came from the penalty spot. A collision between Mwanza Mukombo and Ghana's Mohammed Polo as they chased a through ball led to referee Gebreyesus Tesfaye to point to the spot after the striker was upended. Mukombo had cause to feel aggrieved at the decision. Polo, eyes firmly fixed on the ball, appeared to run into the defender while the ref was some distance away from the incident, having failed to keep up with play, but Zaire's protests were waved away. Kazadi guessed right but defender Akuetteh Amrah's kick had enough power to beat the goalkeeper and give the home team a slender advantage on a deteriorating pitch.

Those prone to melodrama were quick to declare that Zaire's dreams of reaching West Germany were now hanging by a thread and cursed the match official, who waved away subsequent penalty claims after N'Tumba was twice felled in the box. Vidinić, although disappointed by the defeat, was less concerned and took a more rational view. History was on the Leopards' side. Ghana hadn't beaten their opponents on home soil since 1966 and only one team had managed to do so in the intervening period, a run of 21 international games that the coach was confident of maintaining. Yet no matter how relaxed he may have appeared to the outside world, the typically cool, calm and collected Yugoslav must have felt a slight sense of trepidation when he learned that Mobutu himself would be attending the second leg. He made two changes to the team that started in Accra. With Mayanga absent through injury, Mbungu Ekofa came in for Tshinabu to support N'Tumba in attack while the more experienced Kembo replaced Mavuba, who had struggled in the Ghanaian mud. It was a strong line-up and one that signified Vidinić's intention to take the game to their opponents but as always, controversy threatened to overshadow the game before it even kicked off.

The Black Stars had been seriously weakened after four of their stars were called up to take part in an ill-timed Afro-Latinamerican football tournament in Mexico featuring a CAF representative team that was distinctly lacking in Leopards. When allegations of Machiavellian interference were levelled at the national federation, FEZAFA President Lokwa Bobandjola was forced to make a statement about the paucity of Zairean talent and dismissed the claims as 'baseless'. Nevertheless it added an extra dimension to an already intriguing encounter that was now threatening to boil over.

If fireworks were expected, the Leopards certainly delivered and wiped out Ghana's advantage in the opening minute of the match. Some clever interchanges between Kakoko and N'Tumba saw the ball spread wide to the winger who delivered an inch perfect cross for the striker to head home. It was the perfect start for the home side and one that delighted the watching Mobutu and his guest, President Moktar Ould Daddah of Mauritania. Nine minutes later it was 2-0 as Kakoko turned from provider to goalscorer, outpacing the Ghanaian defence to double the lead and put the Leopards ahead in the tie for the first time.

Having dominated the first half, Zaire were given a shock in the opening period of the second when Sam Yaw took advantage of confusion in a crowded penalty error to level the scores on aggregate and raise the possibility of a play-off. Any nervous tension that may have been permeating the stadium was eased by that man Kakoko, who delicately chipped goalkeeper Henry Lante France to restore the Leopards' two goal cushion on the night. Opposition hearts sank as Zaire slowly ran down the clock but there was still time for one more goal. Substitute Mavuba, on for Mbungu, was brought down in the box in the 89th minute and dusted himself down to score from the spot to seal an impressive 4-1 defeat over their old foes.

With only three teams left standing out of the original twenty-two African entrants, the fourth and final round of qualification was a straight shoot-out to determine who would go to West Germany. Each team would play each other home and away over a period of nine weeks and whoever notched up the most points would be declared the winner. Joining Zaire in this footballing triumvirate were Zambia and the very team Blagoje Vidinić led at the 1970 finals in Mexico, Morocco. Intriguingly, they would not meet until the last two games of the mini-championship.

There were remarkable similarities between the three teams - each had a rich benefactor who enjoyed basking in the reflective glory of their respective national sides and used such success to underpin their leadership. Moreover, these political leaders recognised the propaganda value an appearance at the World Cup offered and were keen to take full advantage. For King Hassan of Morocco it was the honour of appearing in consecutive finals to accompany their appearance in the Olympics that would reaffirm their ascendancy in

African football. For Zambia's Kenneth Kaunda and Zaire's Mobutu, it was the chance to become the first black African team to walk out as an equal partner on the game's biggest stage. There were other parallels too. While King Hassan had created a footballing dynasty based on personal wealth, Zambia's rise in the continental game mirrored that of Zaire's. Improvements in the nation's footballing infrastructure had been funded by the boom in copper prices under the premiership of Kenneth Kaunda, who came to power following independence in 1964, a year before Mobutu took office. Yet like Hassan, Kaunda was also an avid follower of the sport and would often turn up to watch lower league matches unannounced just for the thrill of a game. Likewise, he too had turned to Yugoslavia for help when his team hit a plateau and appointed Ante Bušelić in 1971, around the same time Mobutu poached Vidinić from Morocco, who coincidentally were now led by Blagoje's old assistant, Abdallah Settati. It made for a fascinating showdown.

The Atlas Lions had started qualification as strong favourites to make the trip to West Germany and were brimming with a confidence that bordered on arrogance going into their opening game. They had effortlessly navigated the knock-out phase without losing a game, and although their success had largely been built on impressive showings in the home legs of each tie, they were expected to brush Zambia aside when the two sides met in Lusaka at the end of October. Zambia were the surprise package of the tournament and their appearance in the final group stage was attributed to luck of the draw. The team had started the year without the necessary funds to meet the cost of their international commitments and had to rely on the state's generosity but like Morocco, they too had yet to taste defeat and had won all three home matches handsomely. Even so, they were still seen by some as mere cannon fodder and having seriously underestimated the strength of their opponents, King Hassan's men went into battle under-prepared and were walloped 4-0!

This shock result ensured that Vidinić would not take them so lightly when the Leopards paid a visit to the 7 April Stadium two weeks later, flying into Lusaka aboard Mobutu's own private jet. With N'Tumba unavailable, he had to rethink his attacking options and juggle his line-up, opting to play Kembo, whose nickname was *Mister Goal*, as the lone striker ably supported by Kakoko and Mayanga, who had recovered from injury, on the wings. Kibonge was recalled to the midfield while at the back youngster Lobilo Boba partnered Bwanga in the centre of defence. The coach's plan was simple but effective; stifle the opposition then hit them on the break. Roared on by a capacity crowd, the home side started brightly but failed to breach Zaire's defensive phalanx, becoming increasingly devoid of inspiration as the fruitless attacks mounted. Slowly the Leopards began to exert their own pressure and began to ask questions of the Zambia fullbacks who were struggling to cope with the pace and skill of Vidinić's favourite wingers on the flanks. By half-time the game was all but over with Zaire delivering a quick one-two: first Mayanga rounded off a fine counter-attack to open the scoring, then eleven minutes later Kakoko produced a sublime piece of skill to make it 2-0, flicking the ball over the head of a defender and volleying a brilliant curving shot past Joseph Chomba. Zambia's miserable first half was complete when the wonderfully named Brighton Sinyangwe blasted a stoppage-time penalty high over the bar, allowing Zaire to shut-up shop in the second period and claim two valuable points. That's not to say there was no further drama in the match.

Midway through the second half, the home fans stormed onto the pitch and rushed towards Kazadi Mwamba in the Leopards' goal, convinced that the keeper was using some form of witchcraft to protect his goal. They were eventually removed by police but not before Kazadi was searched. 'It was insane, unheard of,' remembers his brother and teammate Bwanga Tshimen, who still finds the incident amusing. 'I still wonder about the laxity of the referee and CAF. We saw a group of people, accompanied by the police, enter the field, approach Kazadi and start to frisk him! After an unsuccessful examination, they left without the referee flinching.'

Vidinić named an unchanged side for the first time in the competition when the teams met in the return match in Kinshasa a fortnight later. The Leopards' victory in Lusaka had sorely damaged Zambia's hopes and to have a realistic chance of claiming top spot the visitors had to avoid defeat. Even a draw would take automatic qualification out of their own hands. Another win for Zaire meanwhile would put them within touching distance of the finals. Bušelić had little option therefore but to go for broke and opted for an attacking 4-2-4 formation in order to take the game to his opponents in the very stadium where the team had lost 10-1 just four years before.

There would be no repeat of that outrageous scoreline but there would also be no miracle either. Zambia's four-man attack pressed heavily, particularly in the early stages of the match, but came up against a Leopards defence that simply soaked up the pressure. Zaire broke the deadlock in the 32nd minute through Kembo, his fourth goal in qualifying, to spark wild celebrations on the terraces of the Stade du 20 Mai but the party was brought to a rude halt less than a minute later when Obby Kapita fired home to level the scores and bring a deathly hush over the stadium. The game descended into a nervous, cagey affair, both sides caught between the rock of needing to score and the hard place of not conceding. As time ticked on Zambia slowly opened up but as they pounded forward in search of the goal they needed to stay alive their vulnerability to Zaire's pace on the counter-attack was exposed. With three minutes left, the Leopards surged forward and Kakoko's deft touch steered the ball past Emmanuel Mwape to seal the win and end the valiant effort of their opponents.

The Leopards could now almost taste the sauerkraut and steins of Dortmunder beer. Two points from their remaining two games would be enough to guarantee their place at the World Cup. The jubilation that now swept the country was downplayed by Vidinić, who was acutely aware that the first game against Morocco was only two weeks away. The punishing schedule of the 1973 football calendar had seen the team trek thousands of miles to compete on two fronts and the coach was conscious of the physical and mental demands being placed on his players. The last thing he needed was for his team to be distracted by premature festivities so close to the finish line.

'It wasn't easy because of the enormous travelling involved and the hostile reception one usually got,' admitted Kidumu, 'but fans are so partisan in Africa, they tend to get carried away with their enthusiasm. You can imagine our delight when Zambia beat Morocco, whom we felt were our more dangerous opponents. We managed to beat Zambia twice so we were very confident by the time Morocco arrived in Kinshasa for the decisive match. Perhaps a little too confident as it turned out.'

The Atlas Lions' 2-0 win over Zambia in Tétouan had reignited their campaign but did little to dampen the blind optimism in Zaire. The country was in no doubt who would win come match day but if the burden of expectation was already weighing heavy on the shoulders of the Leopards, it must have surely intensified immeasurably when an invitation to attend an evening aboard the president's three-decker riverboat arrived at their door. Unashamedly christened *President Mobutu*, the ostentatious craft was a cross between a yacht and a paddle steamer and was moored on the Zaire River in readiness to greet the team.

'We spent the whole evening with him,' remembers Mayanga Maku, 'and it was so he could give us personal motivation to win the game. He promised each of us a villa, a car and a trip for our families to anywhere in the world. We made the population happy. Life wasn't rosy for everyone but when the Leopards won the whole country was in euphoria. They forgot their problems and they forgot their miseries, all they thought about was the Leopards. To keep them happy, Mobutu had to bet on us. It was propaganda.'

The pressure on the team was relieved slightly with the news that the president would not be attending the game in person. He would be in Paris on the day of the match, en route to the United Kingdom for an official State visit that would lead to a diplomatic incident. Mobutu controversially smuggled his dog into the country, which upset H.M. Queen Elizabeth II after she discovered that the canine was with the president during his stay at Buckingham Palace. Nevertheless, they still had to go out and win the game. Any other result would reopen the door for Morocco and shift momentum back towards North Africa.

Although the official attendance for the match was recorded at just under 8,000, it was estimated that over 20,000 spectators crammed into the stadium the December afternoon. The sheer weight of numbers was captured by a press photographer as the national anthems rang out around the ground. The nervous tension is visibly etched on the faces of the Zaire players as they stand to attention against a backdrop of a crowded terrace behind the goalmouth at the far end of the stadium. The moment of truth had arrived.

An early goal would have been the perfect tonic to settle the jitters of everyone bar the Moroccans but Zaire's opponents had arrived with a simple yet very effective game plan. Happy to sit back and pack the defence, the massed ranks of the Atlas Lions had little trouble repelling the Leopards' attacks, denying them space and time on the ball, and as the half progressed, Zaire became increasingly desperate for a breakthrough. The anxiety that had risen exponentially on the terraces was now palpable on the pitch. Vidinić's men abandoned their initial approach of skill and flair in favour of one of brute force that proved equally futile. Morocco made it to the break with their goal intact.

Having initially paid heed to the idiom 'never change a winning team', Vidinić instinctively knew he had to tweak his line-up. The threat provided on the flanks by Kakoko and Mayanga that had been so fruitful in earlier games simply wasn't working. *Goodyear* was hauled off and replaced by the striker commonly referred to as *Volvo*, Ndaye Mulamba. The change in formation did not lead to a change in attacking style, however. Zaire continued to kick lumps out of Morocco, much to the chagrin of the opposition whose pleas for protection from the Ghanaian referee George Lamptey fell on deaf ears. The ferocity was such that Morocco's play-maker Ahmed Faras left the field injured after one crunching tackle too many. The substitution led to a temporary loss of shape and focus among the opposition ranks but it was long enough for the Leopards to pounce. Typically for a game of such high drama, the opening goal was shrouded in yet more controversy, with Kembo poking the ball over the line after an almighty goal-mouth scramble in the 58th minute. The Moroccan players were livid and surrounded the referee, claiming that goalkeeper Ahmed Belkoucrhi had been fouled in the build-up and the ball forced from his grasp, but Lamptey was unconvinced and waved away their protests.

Clearly shaken, the composure and discipline that the Atlas Lions had demonstrated throughout the first half suddenly deserted them. Three minutes later Kembo Uba Kembo struck again, this time in more orthodox fashion to make it 2-0, sparking wild celebrations among the crowd, the tension that had taken such a firm grip had now gone. With no way back into the game, the demoralised Moroccan team took their frustrations out on Zaire, hacking and elbowing their way to the final whistle. Star of the show Kembo was a clear target and denied the opportunity of a hat-trick by some vicious treatment at the hands, or rather boots, of the opposition, hobbling off injured twenty minutes from the end. Not that it mattered. His replacement Mbungu Ekofa scored the third and final goal to confirm victory and send Zaire to the World Cup. Cue pandemonium.

As the fourteenth team to make the finals, the Leopards' qualification received widespread coverage in the international press. Naturally, many newspaper reports focused on the bonuses the players were promised and the *Daily Mirror* ran a small report under the headline "It's great to be Zaire…" detailing the incentives offered to the team. German publication *Der Spiegel* noted that the rewards had 'aroused the envy of European stars' before passing comment on the fact that the houses would be made from bricks and mortar rather than traditional clay, signifying a step in class for many. The news of their bonuses even made it as far as Australia, with Melbourne newspaper *The Age* reporting on the president's decree to reward his victorious team. Back in Kinshasa, *Salongo* carried similar reports but with an altogether different angle that reverentially credited the victory to President Mobutu. Rather than honouring the manager or his players, the newspaper instead paid homage to Zaire's leader, printing a pre-arranged photo of Mobutu receiving the "match ball" from Vidinić while the team looked on, heads bowed in respect. It was a fine piece of political propaganda. The fact that the president was in Europe at the time was totally inconsequential.

A telex from the Zairean Federation to FIFA declare the result as a 'day of glory for the Republic of Zaire' but the champagne was back on ice before the week was out. Still seething over the performance of the referee and his leniency towards Zaire's physical play, the Royal Moroccan Football Federation, supported by the Under Secretary of State for Youth and Sport, sent their own communiqué to FIFA in the form of an official protest. The federation questioned the impartiality of the match official, the validity of at least two of the goals and demanded the game be replayed. They also requested that the scheduled return fixture between the two sides, due to take place just before Christmas, be postponed until FIFA had ruled on the legality of the result in Kinshasa.

'We saw no reason for the Moroccans to protest as much as they did,' observed Kidumu when asked about the controversy over the opening goal ahead of the finals. 'It was shoulder-to-shoulder and the referee gave a goal. They sent a film of the match and demanded that it should be replayed. In the meantime they refused to meet us in the second leg but we sent a team to Morocco to show FIFA that we were willing to play. Although we had already qualified, with so many protests circulating from Chile and Russia, and then from Morocco, we didn't want to take any chances.'

Contentiously, the Moroccan federation alluded to the rivalry between Arabs and black Africans as the reasons behind the refereeing decisions, an argument that failed to impress FIFA. Their complaints were thrown out and Secretary General Helmut Käser delivered a damning response, stating 'Zaire scored three goals, so at least one was valid.' Furious at the judgement, Morocco threw their toys out of the pram and refused to play the last group game. Zaire were awarded a 2-0 walkover as a result and ended the final qualification round with a 100% record.

When Mobuto learned about the success of his Leopards in Paris, he telegraphed his congratulations and confirmed the first of the promised bonuses. Each member of the squad received a VW Passat and a newly built house in the chic commune of Lemba in Kinshasa but not at the direct expense of the president himself. The cars were supplied by Volkswagen while the houses were simply commandeered by the state from a private construction company but Lobilo Bobo, the young defender who had cemented his place in the starting line-up during the campaign, believed there was more to the gifts than simply honouring a pledge. 'The president had matched the promise made by King Hassan to the players of the Moroccan national team,' he recalled. 'After we won, Mobutu called us and gave us these presents, but it was not for participation in the World Cup or the African Championship. It was quite simply out of a burst of pride.'

The president had good cause to stand proud. A week after their heroics against Morocco, a number of the Leopards were back in action with AS Vita Club in the final of the African Cup of Champions Clubs against Asante Kotoko of Ghana. Trailing 4-2 from the first leg, the Zairean club overturned the two-goal deficit with a double from Mayanga and a third from Kembo to claim the club's first continental title. There was individual recognition too, with TP Mazembe's Bwanga Tshimen crowned African Footballer of the Year by *France Football* magazine, beating his older brother and goalkeeper Kazadi Mwamba into second place by just five votes. Zaire soccer was clearly in the ascendancy and the country had no reason to believe that it would come to an end anytime soon.

'That was definitely Zairean football's greatest year, the year when we swept aside everything in our path,' asserts Ndaye. 'But as they say, it's easy to reach the summit; the difficult bit is to stay there.'

Leopards on Tour: the squad listen to the advice offered of Belgium national team coach Raymond Goethals during a trip to Brecht in 1970.

AS Vita Club defender Lobilo Bobo became an integral part of the team following their disappointing performance at the 1972 AFCON tournament.

A nation expects. A nervous-looking Zaire side stand on the brink of history ahead of their World Cup qualifier against Morocco at Kinshasa's Stade du 20 Mai.

Depuis Paris où il se trouve en séjour privé

Le chef de l'Etat a offert à chaque "Léopard" une maison, une voiture et 15 jours de vacances

à la suite de la victoire du Zaïre sur le Maroc (3-0)

(Informations en pages 2, 13, 14 et 16)

SALONGO

Lundi 10 décembre 1973
2me année N° 147
Prix : 5 K à Kinshasa 6 K à l'intérieur

Les Léopards ont réalisé hier la promesse faite mardi 4 décembre dernier (notre photo) au chef de l'Etat en obtenant leur visa pour Munich. (Photo « SALONGO »).

The Salongo newspaper celebrates the team's success over Morocco with a pre-staged photograph of Mobutu receiving the "match ball" from coach Blagoje Vidinić. The president was in Paris on the day of the match.

6. The Dark Horses of Africa

THE DRAW FOR THE 1974 FIFA World Cup finals took place on January 5th in Sendesaal des Hessischen Rundfunks, a music hall and former television studio in Frankfurt that had previously played host to the 1957 *Eurovision Song Contest*. Unlike the razzmatazz show-pieces of today, the event was a more modest affair back then and the draw was completed in just fifteen minutes. Yet despite the relative brevity of proceedings, the draw still commanded an estimated audience of 800 million worldwide, eager to discover the fate of the 16 competing nations and the make-up of the four groups.

In the absence of an official FIFA World ranking, controversy surrounded the decision-making behind the seeding of the teams. As hosts and holders respectively, FIFA and the local organising committee agreed that West Germany and Brazil would be top seeds in Groups 1 and 2 but there was some debate as to who would join them. Following a vote, Italy and Uruguay were selected by virtue of their performances in Mexico four years earlier (although an unnamed delegate alluded to their status as previous winners as the real reasoning behind their seeding). It was expected that the remaining teams would then be "graded" based on previous performances but it was decided that none of the four South American nations should face each other in Round One. As a consequence, the teams were divided into pots based on their geographical region - Western Europe, Eastern Europe, South America and Rest of the World.

As Africa's sole representatives, Zaire naturally found themselves in Pot 4 alongside fellow debutants Australia and Haiti, who had made the most of home advantage to overcome Mexico in the final CONCACAF qualifying group. Surprisingly, the fourth spot was reserved for Sweden, who must have been left scratching their heads at the decision. Having finished third in 1950 and runners-up in 1958, the Scandinavians had competed in Mexico four years earlier and had a vastly superior record in the competition to both the Netherlands and Scotland, who found themselves in Pot 1, not to mention debutants Poland and East Germany, who were placed in

Pot 2. With Spain and Yugoslavia yet to meet to decide the sixteenth and final vacancy, it was hard not to feel some sympathy for the Swedes, but they ultimately fell victim to political bargaining behind the scenes. Sensitivities around the participation of the East Germans was a persuasive factor in the argument for regional divisions and there are indications that FIFA President Sir Stanley Rous had applied pressure to the seeding committee to keep Scotland out of the bottom group if grading were applied.

To underline the Spartan nature of the occasion further, the draw was made by Detlef Lange, an 11-year-old choirboy from Berlin who, together the Schöneberger Sängerknaben choir, would release the single *With a Little Tactics, With a Little Luck, We'll Bring the World Cup Back* on the back of his new-found fame in the build up to the tournament. He managed to inadvertently cause a sensation when he paired the two "German teams" together in Group 1, leading to audible gasps within the auditorium when the match-up was announced by Rous. As the enormity of the fixture sank in, there was a brief awkward silence, followed by a rapturous round of applause. Despite only being halfway through proceedings, the pick of the first round had been made.

The young chorister did Zaire no favours, however. Drawn in Group 2, the Leopards were handed the daunting prospect of facing reigning champions Brazil and would kick-off their campaign against a strong Scotland team. On learning his side were to play the Leopards, their manager Willy Ormond joked that he 'didn't know there was such a place' but his counterpart Blagoje Vidinić knew exactly what he was up against and seemingly relished the challenge handed to him. 'When the draw was made people expected me to be downhearted,' he told the *Daily Mirror*. 'But I was delighted! We have been grouped with such powerful nations as Brazil and Scotland and I welcome the opportunity for Zaire to show their skills alongside those of Brazil,' he continued. 'People ask me if I worry about the prospect. To them I always say that those teams will be more worried because they do not know what we can do.'

Published under the dubious headline "Watch the really dark horses go!", the Yugoslav coach offered an Anglo-centric view of this squad, likening the team's playing style to that of the Manchester City side of the age and, with a touch of hyperbole, favourably comparing his goalkeeper Kazadi Mwamba, whose grandfather was a highly decorated Zulu chief, to Gordon Banks. But his closing gambit would eventually come back to haunt him, when he ended the interview with an assurance that his side would not be in West Germany to simply make up the numbers. 'Zaire are going to give the whole world a new respect for African football,' Vidinić promised. 'We are going to surprise a lot of people and shall not be disgraced.'

The pairing with Scotland led to a number of enquiries with regards to possible friendlies against club sides from both north and south of Hadrian's Wall, all hoping to exploit Britain's new-found fascination with the Leopards and the exotic mystery they offered. For his part, Vidinić was keen to expose his inexperienced side to the type of football they were likely to face in their opening game against the Scots. Two weeks after the draw, *The Guardian* reported that Scottish First Division side Dumbarton had been in contact with the Zaire Embassy in London with an offer to play the African team at Boghead Park in a friendly as part of the club's centenary celebrations. 'The people at the embassy seem most hopeful and anxious that the game should take place', revealed managing director Alex Jackson but they faced a major obstacle in their efforts to secure the fixture. Under Scottish FA rules, a club side could not compete against an international team.

Perhaps recognising the benefits such a game would have for their own preparations, the SFA cautiously welcomed the idea. Assistant Secretary Ernie Walker confirmed 'If Dumbarton were to field a select side which was given the approval of our association then there would likely be no objection.' However, the inference that the governing body was willing to waive the rules emboldened others to try their luck. Hibernian Chairman Tom Hart was hopeful of snatching the fixture away from their rivals after securing his own meeting with Zairean representatives while East of Scotland FA secretary Sandy Jack announced that he too would be seeking to arrange a match against a regional Select XI. *The Times* meanwhile reported that officials from Queens Park Rangers had flown to Kinshasa and made arrangements to play a series of friendlies at Loftus Road in London against the Leopards in May.

After much negotiation, Zaire eventually accepted Sandy Jack's invitation of a challenge match against the best East of Scotland had to offer in the same month they were due to meet QPR. However, for reasons unknown, neither game took place and a friendly against fellow qualifiers Haiti also failed to materialise. In the end, Vidinić opted to take his squad to the Alps, preferring to play a series of fixtures against club sides from Switzerland and Italy, while QPR jetted off to enjoy a tour of Jamaica instead.

Those that wished to take a closer look at the Leopards at first hand did not have long to wait, however. On February 17th, the team left Zaire bound for Egypt and the ninth edition of the African Cup of Nations. With Zairean football riding high on the crest of success, expectations back home soared and Vidinić's team were anticipated to triumph with ease, despite the hosts being favourites to lift the trophy. Privately, doubts had begun to creep into the minds of the players, who were becoming overwhelmed by the weight of the nation's hopes on their shoulders, but the events of the previous tournament and their newly acquired status of World Cup qualifiers meant pride was becoming an increasingly important factor.

'Before going we were not sure how far we could go,' confessed defender Mwepu Ilunga. 'The important thing for us was to participate because we had already qualified for the World Cup'.

'In 1972 our slogan was "the podium or nothing",' added Mana Mambwene, 'but we finished at the foot of the podium in a competition won by our brothers on the other side of the Congo River. All the teasing that followed had revolted us; we really wanted to go far in this competition in Egypt and reach the final.'

The coach opted to keep faith with the core group of players that had served him so well over the course of the previous year and there were few surprises in his 18-man squad, but it would be a tournament played under a cloud. On the day the team arrived in Damanhour, where they were to contest their first match, tragedy struck at an exhibition game in Cairo between Dukla Prague of Czechoslovakia and local side Zamalek when a crowd of 80,000 tried to gain access to a stadium with a capacity of less than half that number. A gate collapsed and the stampede that followed resulted in the deaths of at least 48 spectators, with many more injured. In response to the tragedy, Egyptian newspapers encouraged people not to attend the competition in protest at the mismanagement of the situation and many fans heeded the advice, opting to stay away.

As a result, fewer than 3,000 spectators were present to witness Zaire's opening match against Guinea at the Ala'ab Damanhour Stadium, a venue that held ten times that number. Those that did attend saw the Leopards labour to an unconvincing 2-1 victory under a basking sun, thanks to a goal in each half from Ndaye Mulamba, the second of which was an impressive strike from the edge of the 18-yard box. Among the crowd was Scotland boss Willy Ormond, who took the opportunity to run his eye over the Leopards for the first time and duly left the stadium unconcerned by what he observed. 'I thought Zaire were quite good in attack,' he remarked. 'All four could play a bit. But at the back they were loose marking man-to-man and lacking pace. I did not see anything to give me a sleepless night.'

Regardless of the quality of the win, many enjoyed a sleepless night back in Kinshasa. Having telephoned home to share his news, match winner Ndaye, who only made the starting line-up due to Kembo Uba Kembo falling ill, struggled to hear his wife over the noise in the background as fans who had gathered to either watch the game on one of the few television sets in the city or listen to it on the radio, celebrated the result. The honking of car horns mixed freely with the chants of the revellers on the streets, hailing the goalscorer who was now struggling to be heard. But the premature party came to a crashing halt two days later when Zaire faced neighbours Congo in Alexandria.

To say that the match was a highly charged affair is something of an understatement. With the capital cities of the two countries just a mile apart at their closest point, not only was national pride at stake but also the egos of the respective leaders, who cordially hated each other. Victory was not only expected but also demanded by President Mobutu, who did not want to lose face to his counterpart Marien Ngouab for a second time, especially after his extensive investment in the nation's football team. Moreover, the game pitted the reigning African champions against the very team that planned to usurp them of their crown and a crowd of over 7,000 assembled to watch the drama unfold in Africa's oldest stadium. Yet despite taking a first-half lead through Mayanga Maku, Zaire lost 2-1, their first defeat in over six months, thanks to a late winner from Congo's Noël Birindi Minga. All three goals were spectacular strikes from distance that would have graced any international tournament but it was Minga's thirty-yard thunderbolt after a burst through midfield that was the pick of the bunch. Needless to say the quality of the goals did little to placate Zaire's leader.

Mobutu was furious. A telephone call from a triumphant Ngouab only intensified his anger further and he wasted no time in contacting Vidinić. In a portent of what was to come, Mobutu issued a chilling threat to the coach and his players - if they did not improve, they would end their lives in prison. With only one group game left to play, there was no room for error.

The Leopards knew they needed to beat their final opponents Mauritius to have any chance of progressing but the table was finely balanced. If Guinea overcame Congo in the other remaining fixture, it would all come down to goal difference to decide who went through to the next round. Vidinić, having been vocal in his criticism of some of the team in the press, sought a response from his players and he was not disappointed by their reaction as they bounced back from their midweek defeat to crush *Les Dodos* 4-1 in front of another sparse crowd at the Ala'ab Damanhour Stadium. Goals from Ndaye and Mayanga all but settled the match as a contest after twenty minutes and winger Kakoko Etepé added a third shortly before half-time to increase their advantage. Mauritius scored what proved to be a consolation on the hour mark but Mayanga ensured there would be no comeback when he netted his second of the game fourteen minutes from time. The result ensured Zaire finished runners-up in Group B and set up a mouthwatering semi-final clash against the hosts.

The hectic scheduling of the tournament plus home advantage gave Egypt the slight edge over their opposition. Remarkably, the semi-final would be the Leopards' fourth match in seven days, leading to concerns around the team's fitness levels. Indeed the coach made four changes for the game against Mauritius as he tried to keep his defence and midfield fresh for the challenges that lay ahead. Up front, Vidinić had no worries about his strike force, and in Ndaye Mulamba he had a forward in the best form of his life. In November, the player had scored twice in the second leg of the African Cup of Champions Clubs Semi-final, a double that secured a 4-3 aggregate win over Léopard Douala of Cameroon and propelled AS Vita Club to their first continental title, and his performance that day rocketed him to superstar status in Zaire. Legend has it he spent three hours signing autographs after the final whistle and had to seek medical treatment for a wrist injury as a result. But it was a domestic game just before the Leopards' departure in February that cemented his new found fame when the striker scored seven goals in an 8-1 victory over FC Saint-Éloi Lupopo. Having previously been garnered with the nicknames *Volvo* and the *Assassin of Katanga*, the following day's newspapers afforded Ndaye with the new and rather dubious sobriquet of *Hitler* on the pretext that he had "behaved like a dictator on the pitch and destroyed the opposition's defences".

Although a hero back home, the striker attributed his success at the championships to the fact that very few people had heard of him outside of Zaire. Recalling his conversations with Vidinić and his backroom staff, Ndaye revealed the reverse psychology employed to leverage his relative anonymity for the benefit of the team. 'They told me I was not well known across Africa and instructed me to make the most of it as I was not famous like Kakoko, Mayanga and Kibonge because they'd played so many times. "They don't know you, take advantage of it", so I followed all the advice I was given.'

As the undoubted star of the show, it was little wonder then that the coach chose to take his striker to the pre-match press conference at the team's hotel in Cairo where, together with Kakoko, he offered his views on the upcoming game against the hosts. 'We have played in empty stadiums since the start of the competition but on Saturday we will play at the Nasser Stadium. A representative of the Egyptian Football Association told me that all the tickets have been sold so there will be seventy-five thousand noisy fans cheering on the Egypt team. We are going to have to be in good shape and focus for the next two days. After dinner everyone will go to bed and rest.'

Ndaye and his teammates had good reason to take the match seriously and the motivation behind the squad's determination was revealed to the room by the striker. 'Mobutu called me this afternoon. He will be there on Tuesday for the final. He has changed his entire schedule to come and cheer us on. So we have no choice. We have to beat Egypt on Saturday then win the cup and bring it back to Kinshasa.'

Just how many fans attended the match is up for debate. The attendance was recorded as 50,000 but the terraces behind each goal were at best sparsely populated. Not that there was much to cheer about. The only action of note in the first 40 minutes of the match was a 20-yard drive from Zaire captain Kidumu Mantantu that goalkeeper Hassan Orabi acrobatically tipped over the bar. Nonetheless, despite having posed little threat to the Leopards' goal, Egypt went into the break 1-0 up, having benefited from a mistake by Mwepu Ilunga that bordered on comedy. Attempting to clear Ali Khalil's skewed shot, the right-back swung wildly at the ball at the back post, missed his kick and could only watch in horror as the ball deflected off his standing foot into the back of the net, triggering a wave of noisy celebration in the Nasser Stadium. It got even better for the Egyptians nine minutes into the second half when Aly Abo Greisha struck a low drive past the sprawling dive of Kazadi to put the hosts 2-0 up and seemingly book their place in the final.

Perhaps conscious of the fate that awaited them if they did lose, Zaire suddenly sprung into life and reduced the deficit straight from the restart. Collecting a cross from Kafula Ngoie, Ndaye turned sharply and slotted the ball under the sprawling Orabi, to the visible delight of his teammates. Six minutes later they were level when Kidumu bravely rose to head Lobilo Boba's high ball into the box over the on-rushing Egyptian goalkeeper, who came off worse from the challenge. With the momentum now firmly with the Leopards, Ndaye sealed a stunning fightback when he smashed the ball into the roof of the net from close range past the hapless Orabi, who left an inviting gap at his near post, to silence the partisan crowd. Zaire had scored three goals in little over fifteen minutes to turn the tie on its head and resurrect their title hopes in ruthless style.

'It was terrible for the Egyptians,' recalled Mana. 'Imagine you are the host country, you lead 2-0 and then…'

Back home, Mobutu was quick to capitalise on the victory and declared a national holiday in honour of the squad's achievement, an occasion made all the sweeter by the fact that Congo surprisingly lost to Zambia in extra time in the other semi-final. Their elimination removed the need for the president to show his face at the final and in a telephone call to the team hotel, he revealed he would not be in attendance after all. 'Matters of the utmost importance for the future of the country will keep me at the palace in Kinshasa,' he informed the squad, yet he promised to send his presidential aeroplane to collect the squad from Egypt and bring them home. Although this grand gesture did have one important caveat: 'With the Cup, otherwise, don't come home'. With a gallows sense of humour, Vidinić reaffirmed the threat and the situation facing everyone connected with the team if they did not win. 'We absolutely must bring the Cup back to Kinshasa,' he half-jokingly told the squad. 'Otherwise we will travel back in the hold of the presidential plane.'

Three days later, Mobutu's Boeing 707 duly landed at Cairo's International Airport but its departure was delayed by events on the football field rather than off it. After 120 minutes, the two teams could not be separated and a replay was required the following Thursday.

In truth, Zaire should have won it at the first attempt, having already beaten their opponents twice in World Cup qualifying. Staying loyal to the players that had hauled the team into the final in such dramatic circumstances, Vidinić named an unchanged side but once again they were slow out of the blocks and fell behind to an effort from Simon Kaushi, who volleyed Zambia into the lead from the edge of the six-yard box in the 40th minute. The second half was one-way traffic for the most part and the Leopards almost drew level when Zambia's goalkeeper Emmanuel Mwape was forced to scramble across his goal-line to keep out a long-range drive from Mavuba Mafuila. Eventually the pressure told and it was that man Ndaye Mulamba who again rescued Zaire with a low shot into the bottom corner after playing a one-two with Kibonge. Yet try as they might, they could not find a way past Mwape and could have lost it altogether right at the death but for an impressive double-save by Kazadi in the Zaire goal. An extra 30 minutes were required and for at least one person in the Nassar Stadium, it was all proving too much.

Vidinić could not disguise his frustration when the teams returned to the changing rooms at the end of normal time. Raising his voice, he warned his players that if they lost, he would not be getting on the presidential plane with them and would abandon them to the mercy of Mobutu. The rollocking and threats seemed to work. With barely three minutes left on the clock, Ndaye scored what looked like the winning goal from a free-kick. The strike certainly cheered up the Leopards' coach, who rose from the bench and informed his players that there was only a minute left before holding both arms aloft and making V for Victory signs. But the celebrations, like those in Kinshasa the week before, were premature. With just ten seconds left on the clock, Zambia equalised.

Vidinić's opposite number and fellow Yugoslav Ante Bušelić could claim it was the result of a tactical masterstroke on his part. Having previously played every game, Brighton Sinyangwe was dropped for the semi-final victory over Congo but restored to the fold for the big occasion and repaid his coach's faith by beating Kazadi at this near post to force a replay for the first time in the tournament's history and go someway to making amends for the penalty he missed during the team's World Cup qualifier in Lusaka back in November. It was an entirely avoidable goal but not for the first time in the competition, Zaire were punished for a defensive lapse.

The reported attendance for the final was 50,000 but just as in the previous rounds, the terraces around the stadium were sparsely populated once again. Yet when the Leopards turned up two days later, they were astonished to find the ground pretty much deserted, to the amusement of Mavuba who quipped 'Well, guys, there's no crowd. With any luck, perhaps the Zambians won't come too.' The truth of the matter was even more farcical. As the team prepared for the match, a well-dressed but clearly embarrassed functionary from the Confederation of African Football (CAF) entered the dressing room and addressed the players. He informed them that there had been a mix up in communications between the federation and the Egyptian press, who had failed to provide any details of the fixture to their readers. 'It turned out that they had only sold 300 tickets,' recalled Ndaye in 2010. 'They invited staff from the Zaire and Zambian embassies to come along and left the stadium doors open and allowed any spectators who showed up to enter free of charge.' As a result, the official crowd for the replay was a mere 1,000.

The news came as a blow to the players. Footballers feed off the atmosphere provided by the supporters and the Leopards were no different. To play a final in front of so few was demotivating in the extreme and Vidinić was conscious of the drop in morale in the dressing room. In an uncharacteristic move, the coach abandoned his typical pre-match team talk, which usually consisted of last minute instructions and tactical pointers, and spoke from the heart, referring back to his own experiences at the 1960 Olympic Games in Rome. 'When I was goalkeeper for Yugoslavia, we played a game against Turkey that held little interest for the Italians,' he informed them. 'Football, for me, is entertainment and if there are no spectators, there is no show and I can tell you frankly, it upset me. But Tirke (Aleksandar Tirnanić, Yugoslavia manager at the Games), our coach, reminded us that wearing the national jersey meant we have to put on a show for those who support us, who would like to be there, but who are at home and follow the match on the radio or television. So this afternoon, you guys are going to play for your fathers, your mothers, your brothers, your sisters, your friends. Even though there are three hundred people in the stadium, there are thirty million Zaireans behind you.'

The speech was as stirring as it was unexpected and galvanised the players and refocused their minds. When they emerged from the tunnel and walked across the running track to line up for the national anthems, they were indeed greeted by blocks of grey concrete behind either goal but the main stands had filled out a little after the federation opted to leave the gates open. The handful of supporters of each team that were in attendance were doing the best to create an ambience of sorts while the VIP area, which sat just above a rather large advertisement for Marlboro cigarettes, was suitably filled by well-dressed dignitaries, including FIFA President Sir Stanley Rous, and one very special guest - former World Heavyweight Champion Muhammad Ali, who would claim a title of his own in Zaire later that year.

Both coaches may have been tempted to ring the changes in light of the energy-sapping schedule of the previous fortnight yet neither took the opportunity to do so. Zambia named the same starting eleven while Vidinić merely shuffled his defence, opting to drop Ngoie in favour of Mukombo. In a sprightly opening half, the first real chance fell to the Copper Bullets, as Zambia were known due to their distinctive all-orange kit (although for unexplained reasons they wore black shorts in the second game). Picking the ball up thirty yards from goal, the unmarked Boniface Simutowe turned and hit a shot that Kazadi did well to tip onto the woodwork but with the Zaire goalkeeper stranded, Sinyangwe could only balloon the rebound over the bar. It would prove to be their best opportunity of the game.

On the half-hour mark, the Leopards opened the scoring. Taking over the goal kicking duties from his goalkeeper, Zambia captain Dickson Makwaza failed to find significant distance with his punt down field and played it straight to his opposite number Kidumu in the centre circle. The midfielder headed the ball back into the path of Ndaye, who, taking advantage of Zambia's deep defensive line, had positioned himself on the edge of the 18-yard box. Skilfully evading a desperate challenge of the on-rushing Makwaza, the striker raced into the penalty area and fired a low, left footed shot past the stranded Mwape.

Forced to chase the game, Zambia's attacking threat wilted from thereon. Their forays into the opposition half were easily repelled by a rejuvenated Zairean defence that showed little sign of the frailties that had earlier blighted them in the competition. At the back, Zambia were a bit more resolute and kept the Leopards at bay until fourteen minutes from time when Ndaye added a second to make the tie safe. Playing a clever one-two with Mayanga that split the opposition defence wide open, the *Assassin of Katanga* drilled the ball through the legs of Edwin Mbaso and beyond the outstretched hand of the goalkeeper before circling away to celebrate his ninth goal of the tournament, a record that stands to this day.

The shrill of the final whistle confirmed Zaire as champions of Africa but it was also a liberating relief for many of the players. Sinking to his knees in exhaustion, match winner Ndaye Mulamba disappeared under a swarm of bodies as those on the substitutes' bench invaded the pitch and pounced on him in celebration. It had been a hard-fought victory in many ways but a popular one among the neutrals within the Nasser Stadium and the Cairo newspaper *Al-Ahram* described the victory as 'certainly well deserved' in their report the following day. All that remained was for the squad to collect their medals and the Cup from Egypt's Deputy Prime Minister, Dr. Mohamed Abdel Kader Hatem, but for captain Kidumu Mantantu it was a moment of both triumph and embarrassment. As he held the trophy aloft in front of the gathered photographers and television cameras, the top fell off and smacked him on the head.

7. Frigid Air

AS THE BOEING 707 approached N'djili Airport, the stewardesses on the aeroplane were fighting to seat the passengers. 'Sit down, gentlemen, sit down. Otherwise, we'll take you back to Egypt,' one of them threatened, only half in jest. It had been a long, raucous flight and the patience of the air crew was wearing thin. The Zaire squad, dressed to a man in matching yellow and green tracksuits, had behaved like naughty school children on the back seat of a bus for the entire journey and after four-and-a-hours of mayhem, Mobutu's own private jet had lost its presidential airs and graces. The team had partied hard the previous evening, victorious guests of the organising committee of the African Cup of Nations, and despite the early departure from Cairo, they were still in celebratory mood.

Order was eventually restored with a stern, headmasterly word from their coach and mentor, Blagoje Vidinić, who not only told them to be silent but also correct their attire, ensuring they were presentable once the plane had landed and the doors opened. They did well to heed the instruction. It was only as they descended that they realised just how many people had turned up to welcome them home.

Mercifully, unlike the returning heroes of 1968, the newly-crowned Leopards of 1974 did not have to wear placards bearing their names. Thanks to increased television and newspaper coverage, the new generation of stars were instantly recognisable to the crowd that cheered their arrival and roared in approval when Kidumu raised the trophy for all to see, keeping the lid firmly in place as he did so. At the foot of the passenger stairs a line of dignitaries, composed of politicians, diplomats, military generals and other assorted officials, stood expectantly in order of importance waiting to shake the hands of each player. So great was their number that it took the team over half-an-hour to meet the assembled luminaries and reach the VIP reception lounge where President Mobutu sat patiently, awaiting an audience with Zaire's favourite sons.

It was rare for anyone to keep the country's leader waiting but for once Mobutu tolerated the delay. He was in jovial mood, having received a congratulatory telegram from Kenneth Kaunda, leader of Zambia, following the victory. In return, he had sent a message of thanks laced with hubris that was printed unabridged by the *Times of Zambia*. Thanks to the Leopards' labours, one-upmanship had never tasted so good but the president ensured he was standing on a small podium when greeting the team to remind them of their place in the grand scheme of life in Zaire.

'I asked you last week by phone to bring the cup home and you did,' he reminded his audience as they gathered before him. 'I will know how to remember it.'

As the procession of players shook hands and reverently bowed their heads, Ndaye Mulamba got the shock of his life when the Head of State paused to single out the nine-goal hero for special praise. 'Thanks to you, the whole world will know that Zaire, in addition to being the best nation in African football, also has in its ranks the best goalscorer on the continent,' Mobutu informed the now blushing striker. 'You are an example for the youth of our country.'

It wasn't the only surprise the president had in store. As the flash bulbs of the assembled press photographers popped brightly, Mobutu moved across the stage to a row of microphones to deliver a speech celebrating the team's achievements that was broadcast live on radio across the nation. Nearing a conclusion, he invited the people of Zaire to 'contribute to rewarding our Leopards for their victory and help them prepare with dignity for the football World Cup,' warning them that a national collection, or Soccer Tax as it became to be known, would commence the following day so that 'everyone can participate in this moment of national solidarity and help our brave team grow and carry the colours of our nation even higher.' The announcement was met by a thunderous round of applause from Mobutu's gathered acolytes and served to reignite the jubilant mood of the team, who could not hide their obvious delight at being named the beneficiaries of this financial incentive. It was the highpoint of their relationship.

'Mobutu treated the Leopards like his children,' explained Congolese journalist Kabulo Mwana Kabulo. 'He spared no effort, pulled out all the stops. The players were very motivated and they didn't want to disappoint him. He was like a father to them.'

In a repeat of the scenes of 1968, a convoy of military Jeeps carried the team away from the airport, along the dusty streets and through the city of Kinshasa towards the presidential palace of Mont Ngaliema. Again the streets were filled with well-wishers desperate to catch a glimpse of the team and the trophy and as their numbers grew, their armed escorts from the Republican Guard had to disembark to clear a path through the crowd. A reception awaited them at the palace, where they were to be decorated with the country's highest honour, the prestigious *Order of the Leopards*, before sitting down to dinner with Mobutu himself. It was the start of a week of festivities that saw a nationwide tour of the trophy before the team returned to the capital for the official celebration party at the Stade du 20 Mai the following Sunday, where they were once again treated like kings and paraded before an adoring crowd. The party ended prematurely for Vidinić, however, as he was forced to make a diplomatic retreat from a situation that saw him inadvertently usurp the president in terms of popularity. 'I left the celebrations early, saying that I was tired,' he recalled in later years. 'Because there were all these delirious people chanting my name, which is a little awkward when you're standing next to Mobutu!'

In reality the festivities could not have ended sooner for the coach. He had a World Cup to prepare for and could do without any distractions. To achieve this aim, the entire squad retreated to the idyllic surrounds of Virunga National Park, where they stayed at one of the president's many residences on the picturesque shores of Lake Kivu. Originally conceived by Belgian colonists as a science-oriented nature reserve with the aim of studying and preserving wildlife, it was later declared a UNESCO World Heritage Site but for the Leopards of 1974 it provided a safe haven away from the glare of the public eye. For two weeks an army of servants catered for their every need in a world of luxury that previously would have been beyond their imagination. It was an experience that brought the squad closer together and helped strengthen the bond between them. 'There was a competitive element between us,' explained Mayanga, 'between those from Lubumbashi and from Kinshasa, who had a real rivalry through their clubs, Tout Puissant Englebert and AS Vita Club. But as a national team we'd mostly been together since the beginning of about 1971. One of Vidinić's greatest strengths was that he had been able to make us like a big family over those years. Mostly, that's how we were.'

The two-week stay in Virunga allowed the team to recuperate

and recharge their batteries after their efforts in Egypt and the draining media circus on their return but it also left them ill-prepared for the intensive fitness regime Vidinić had planned on their return to the capital. A punishing six-week training camp, with sessions thrice daily, awaited them in Kinshasa. Their friend and coach had been replaced by a hard-nosed authoritarian, stubborn to the core, who confined the team to barracks and refused to let them leave to see loved ones, let alone have a beer or three. Despite temperatures hitting the 40 degree mark before midday, they would train in the morning, afternoon and evening, no matter how hot the sun beat down on them, repeating drills in a disciplined approach until they satisfied Vidinić's high standards. All the while he would repeat the same mantra until they heard it in their sleep. "We are African champions and we have a status to defend at the World Cup," he would cry as the players lapped the pitch or repeated ball control drills. "The whole world is waiting to see if we know how to play football."

At the end of the day the coach would gather them together and translate articles from foreign newspapers that criticised Zaire's participation at the forthcoming championship, pulling no punches as he read aloud the scathing words that barely concealed the contempt most had for FIFA's qualification system. A report in *The Times* bemoaning England's absence from the finals was a shining example of such opinion and summed up the attitude of many when questioning why 'nations of little or no football tradition or distinction should be in the final line-up while the pioneers of the game should be on the outside looking in.'

It wasn't just the media that were questioning the Leopards' presence. West German captain Franz Beckenbauer, potentially playing up to the crowd when interviewed by the same newspaper, weighed in with an equally dismissive statement. 'For me, a World Cup without England is not a real World Cup at all,' he told *The Times*. 'For Haiti, Australia and Zaire to be coming and not England does not make sense.' The mind tricks had a tendency to produce the desired effect however with the players redoubling their efforts the following day.

Any doubts they may have harboured about the veracity of Vidinić's claims were dispelled when a French television crew turned up unexpectedly to do an in-depth piece on the Leopards. It was fronted by acclaimed filmmaker Claude Lelouch, who had been so intrigued by Zaire's rise on the football pitch during a TV debate in France that he decided to fly to Kinshasa to find out for himself the secret behind their success. Against a backdrop of players practising their keepy-uppy skills and fulfilling the demands of a practice drill, Lelouch lazily repeated the well-worn views synonymous with European journalists, speaking of the 'qualities inherent in black players' namely virtuosity, pace and flair while criticising their defensive capabilities. Kakoko, Mayanga and Kidumu were all happy to be interviewed but did not play along with an increasingly terse Lelouch's request for pre-match predictions. The report also painted a rather harsh picture of the coach as a mean-spirited individual who refused to let the players off their leash, patronisingly stating that he 'did not know how to create the warm atmosphere which must reign within a football team'. It was a cold description at odds with the popular image of Zaire's trainer, but the reasons behind the character assassination quickly became clear, with the film ending on a bad-tempered Vidinić refusing to grant Lelouch a few words after one too many interruptions to that afternoon's training session.

Amid the negativity there was one positive piece of news from Europe. UK toy manufacturer Waddingtons released the first Zaire Subbuteo team, along with Australia and Haiti, as part of their table football offering in readiness for the World Cup. Numbered 176 in the company's catalogue, schoolboys in Britain could acquire their own version of the Leopards for the princely sum of 50p, blissfully unaware that it would become a collectors item in later years, with original sets in pristine condition selling for around £150 at auction today. Ironically events elsewhere in Africa in the Spring of 1974 almost conspired to consign the Zaire Subbuteo team to an historical anomaly and propel its modern day value even higher when a proposed continental boycott of British sport threatened the team's place at the World Cup.

A heated argument had been brewing over a proposed tour of South Africa and Rhodesia by the British & Irish Lions rugby union team, who had accepted an invitation against British government advice to play a test series against the Springboks that summer, despite worldwide condemnation of the country's apartheid regime. South Africa had become an increasingly isolated figure on the world stage following the Olympic Committee's decision in 1964 to exclude them from all future games and the United Nations had declared apartheid "a crime against humanity" the previous November. Their decision provoked a fierce reaction around the world and several players made themselves unavailable as the pressure grew in the media for the tour to be cancelled.

Six weeks before the first game was due to be played, *The Guardian* newspaper reported the increasing possibility of a total boycott of British sports by the Supreme Council for Sports in Africa in protest against the Lions' tour, which received immediate support from many quarters on the continent. At the end of April a resolution was adopted by the council during an emergency three-day session in Tunis appealing to the British government to cancel the tour in the 'interests of sport' and resolved to invite all members of the Council to suspend their sporting relations with the country if it went ahead, sending telegrams to Prime Minister Harold Wilson and Foreign Secretary James Callaghan for good measure. Having been drawn in the same group as Scotland at the World Cup, Zaire suddenly found themselves at the centre of a political squabble.

The situation deteriorated further when five countries - Kenya, Malawi, Tanzania, Uganda and Zambia - announced their intention to snub any sporting contest involving British athletes at the beginning of May. With the Commonwealth Games having already concluded in New Zealand and with no other major sporting event involving African nations on the horizon, the prospect of the Leopards being the first casualty of any embargo was now very real and all eyes turned to Zaire to see if they would support the boycott. Yet even as senior officials at their embassy in London were informing *The Guardian* that they had received no confirmation concerning the team's involvement in West Germany, diplomatic efforts behind the scenes saw the possibility of any withdrawal recede dramatically.

Seeking to avoid further embarrassment and in an attempt to quickly repair relations, particularly with those nations who were members of the Commonwealth, the UK Government publicly distanced themselves from the rugby team, refusing to let their staff or officials attend any of the games on the tour. Access to key facilities were withdrawn and it was made clear by the British Minister for African Affairs, Joan Lestor, on an official visit to Kenya and Zambia, that the tour was not endorsed by the government nor reflective of their stance on apartheid, a move which helped avoid a more widespread protest. Consequently, on May 16th, a day after the British and Irish Lions played their first game and a month before Zaire's match against the Scots, the Secretary General of the African Football Confederation, Mourad Fahmy, formally confirmed that the AFC had no plans to instruct its members to support the boycott, finally removing any lingering doubts about the Leopards' participation, much to the relief of FIFA President Sir Stanley Rous.

Back in Kinshasa, Vidinić refused to be distracted by the drama unfolding in the background, remaining steadfast in his focus on the task ahead. His boot camp was coming to an end and the time had come to name his squad for the finals. Of the eighteen players that travelled to Egypt back in February, only AS Vita Club midfielder Taty Mbungu failed to make it onto the roster for West Germany (coincidentally, he was the only member of the squad not to feature in any of the games in Egypt either). The combative Kilasu Massamba was recalled in his stead and there was also a place for Jean Kalala N'Tumba, despite the striker not being fully fit, having undergone surgery in an attempt to repair a troublesome knee injury. TP Mazembe reserve Kalambay Otepa pipped AS rival Pombi Litinda to the last goalkeeper berth while Kabasu Babo and Mwape Mialo were brought in as cover for the defence. It was a squad dominated by players from the big two clubs of the day, who accounted for fifteen of the twenty-two man party, ably supported by a peppering of representatives from CS Imana and FC Bilima plus one from FC Nyki, the aforementioned Mwape. With the exception of Julien Kialunda, still in self-imposed exile in Belgium, and possibly Saio Ernest Mokili, it was arguably the strongest squad at Vidinić's disposal, albeit one lacking real experience on the world stage. Only Kidumu had any previous experience of playing overseas and even that was as a student while studying in Belgium.

In an attempt to remedy this shortcoming, a trip to the Alps had been arranged that included five warm-up games against club sides in first Switzerland then Italy. Before they left for Europe, however, the squad had once again received a cordial invitation to spend an evening with the president at his palace in Nsele. Situated 40km east of Kinshasa on the banks of the Zaire River, the flamboyant estate, which stretched over a thousand acres, was personally commissioned by Mobutu and took the form of a replica imperial Chinese garden with a dash of Art Deco and Baroque architecture thrown in for good measure. An Olympic-size swimming pool could be found in the recesses of the compound and along the river was the riverboat *President Mobutu*, where the team had been entertained by their leader. A hospital ship, similar in appearance, was moored alongside - *Mama Mobutu*. It was designed to impress and it certainly had the desired effect of wowing the Leopards, many of whom had grown up in poverty. 'Meeting Mobutu was like meeting a god,' Mwepu Ilunga recalled many years later. 'He had his own zoo and beautifully manicured gardens, a fleet of Mercedes-Benz cars and minibuses, and the buildings were all made of amazing white marble. They reflected the sun and if you looked at them for too long you were almost blinded. It didn't seem to occur to us that whilst he was living a luxurious life many Zaireans, including some of our families, were starving. He was very much the African chieftain.

'He spoke of how the World Cup would be a show-piece for the new Africa and how proud he was that Zaire would be the first ever team from black Africa to appear at a Finals. What really impressed us was when Mobutu started speaking about our yellow shirts. "Yellow looks beautiful on black skin. You'll feel like 11 Pelés when you play football." Somehow he convinced all of us that we could do very well at the finals. He had this incredible galvanising influence.'

To spur them to greater heights, Mobutu dangled the usual financial carrots in front of the team, promising them great rewards if they performed well at the World Cup, including an outrageous bonus if they achieved the impossible and actually won the competition, plus further money on their return. In the meantime, the whole team would have access to a generous expense account during their stay in West Germany. 'To be offered wealth like that was unheard of in Zaire. Most of us left Nsele feeling giddy,' admitted the defender.

Despite the lavish promises, the players had no real reason to dispute the president's sincerity. On their return from Egypt, each player had received a $1000 bonus directly from Mobutu and many of them had visited the housing complex in Lemba where their new homes were being built, complete with gardens, running water, electricity and paved streets. The Volkswagen cars were en route and the team received first-hand reports from their own families and friends that the collection for the 'Leopards Fund' was well underway. But as their departure for Europe loomed ever larger, several members of the team began to question when they could expect to see the first payment, especially those who had already spent a large majority of that first payment on furnishings for their new houses and gifts for friends and family.

Seeking assurances that the money would be paid, Vidinić accompanied team captain Kidumu Mantantu on a visit to see Zaire's Minister of Sport, Sampassa Kaweta Milomb, in his offices in the capital. The minister refused to commit to a date but vaguely promised that they would receive payment before they left for Europe. When the money failed to materialise, doubts began to creep into the heads of the players with at least one confessing to an impending sense of doom when the squad boarded the plane to Geneva at the beginning of May.

Having trained in the sweltering, dusty tropical heat of Kinshasa for six weeks, the players got a bit of a shock when the cabin doors opened at Genève-Cointrin airport, where the temperature was struggling to hit 15 degrees Celsius. It was even cooler higher up in the mountains thanks to an unexpected cold-snap that had hit the region and as the team bus slowly climbed into the foothills of the Alps, all that the passengers could see as they peered out of the windows was the unwelcoming sight of a gloomy landscape covered in mist and rain.

Their headquarters for the duration of their stay in Switzerland was the mediaeval town of Willisau. Nestled in the Lucerne landscape in the shadow of the Napf Mountain, it was more famous for its fledgling jazz festival than its love of football but provided a suitable base for Vidinić to acclimatise his team to the milder climes of Europe. The Yugoslav did not have to wait long to test their mettle and within days of their arrival, Zaire lined-up to face FC Lucerne, who had just won promotion back to the top flight of Swiss football from Nationalliga B. To add a bit more bite to the encounter, the home side had been granted permission from Grasshopper Zurich to field their international midfielder Bigi Meyer. Meyer, who originally hailed from the area and had played for Lucerne before earning a move to the top flight, had turned out for Switzerland in a friendly against Belgium earlier in the week and his presence, combined with the locals natural curiosity towards Zaire, helped attract a crowd of nearly 3,000 for the encounter, despite unfavourable weather conditions.

The Leopards, dressed in a white kit with red stockings, had not played a competitive game of football since their 2-0 win over Zambia back in March and their lack of match practice was evident throughout as they slumped to a heavy 4-1 defeat at the Stadion Allmend. The bitter cold and a poor playing surface made treacherous by rain played their part in the loss but after a bright opening half-an-hour, where future Swiss international Karl Engel was by far the busier of the two goalkeepers, Vidinić's side simply ran out of steam in the pouring rain. The turning point came shortly before the interval when Mayanga contrived to blast a penalty over the bar, a miss that was duly punished two minutes later when Wildhaber netted the opening goal. After the break Lucerne added a second and although they pulled one back through Kembo Uba Kembo, who made no mistake from the penalty spot second time around, Zaire struggled with their opponent's effective offside trap. With their long sleeves pulled down firmly over their hands, the Leopards looked increasingly disinterested the longer the game went on and were finally sunk by a couple of late strikes from Wildhaber, who completed his hat-trick in the process.

The coach adopted a pragmatic stance after the game and was not too dismayed by the result, admitting that his team had been caught cold, in more ways than one, by a sprightly Lucerne team whose speedy attacks made the Zaire defence look vulnerable. 'Since we arrived here, we have not had much practice and the situation was not realistic since we had not played for two months,' he told journalists after the final whistle. Swiss Newspaper *L'Express* was less than convinced by the performance, however. Their match reporter admired Zaire's skill on the ball and ability to attack with pace but even taking the weather into account, more was expected from the international side. 'Without the excellent goalkeeper Kazadi, a real cat, the score would have been higher,' they wrote. 'If Zaire manage to glean a single point at the world championships, it would be a surprise.'

A week later the Leopards made the short trip to Aarau, who also played in Nationalliga B, and again came unstuck. By their own admission the players were still struggling to adjust to life in Europe, not only with the chillier Alpine temperatures but also the rich food, which upset their digestive systems and made the triple training sessions that were still part of their daily routine even more arduous than before. At least the rain had stopped, encouraging a crowd of 4,000 spectators to gather at the Stadion Brügglifeld. They witnessed a sluggish first half performance that was notable only for the opening goal from Srđan Čebinac, who, in one of life's little ironies, was a former Yugoslavia international. He added a second from the penalty spot shortly after the interval but it was a much better performance from Zaire in the second period, who grew into the game as it progressed. Mana Mambwene scored the best goal of the evening five minutes from the end but some shoddy finishing denied the Leopards a draw that would have done wonders for their confidence.

They did enjoy other morale-boosting experiences during their stay in Willisau and, snappily dressed in purple Adidas tracksuits, they became popular figures around town when Vidinić allowed them out of the hotel. 'The reception was fantastic,' recalled Ndaye. 'Zaire, a black team, was exotic. People came to touch us or have their picture taken with us. But it was expensive and we couldn't afford to buy anything. In Lucerne, I exchanged a football shirt for a pack of cigarettes!'

On the field, there were signs of improvement when the squad travelled to Italy for a match against Fiorentina, the first of three games against Serie A clubs. Having just finished the Italian season in sixth place, *I Viola* were arguably the strongest side the Leopards would face as they looked to sharpen their claws but, having struggled in Switzerland, Zaire looked a different team in Florence and more than held their own in what proved to be a competitive match. They took the lead following a crisp interchange of passes that allowed Bwanga Tshimen to burst through the opposition defence and square the ball to Ndaye who, like all good poachers, was ready and poised just outside the six-yard box. His original effort was well blocked by the on-rushing Franco Superchi in the Fiorentina goal but the ball fell kindly to the striker and he was able to force it home at the second attempt.

Unfortunately the Leopards were unable to hold onto their lead for long. Stung into action, Fiorentina levelled within three minutes when Walter Speggiorin headed home from a free-kick having been left unmarked in the penalty box, with the bounce deceiving the unsighted Kazadi Mwamba. And despite producing a more energetic display, Zaire were condemned to their third straight defeat in Europe when Speggiorin stooped low at the far post to head home the winner in the dying stages. Yet on this occasion they could consider themselves unlucky as the ball only looped up towards the onrushing Italian striker after Kazadi had pulled off a tremendous one-handed save to deny Giancarlo Antognoni. It was harsh on the goalkeeper, who deserved a bit more fortune, but overall the Africans had impressed their hosts with their attacking pace, individual flair and collective enthusiasm, even if they were a little naive tactically.

Of all the games Zaire played in the build up to the World Cup, the result against Fiorentina was arguably the most impressive. While much has been made of the team's defeats at the hands of club sides in both Switzerland and Italy, a little context is needed for the encounter at the Stadio Comunale. Remarkably, the Italian club played friendlies against no fewer than four different World Cup participants in the space of little over six weeks and won them all, outperforming the Azzuri in the process. Along with their victory over the Leopards, they also defeated Poland, who would go on to finish third, Argentina and Uruguay, conceding just that one goal scored by Ndaye along the way. By contrast, the national team, which did not contain a single Fiorentina player, lost to both the Poles and Argentina in the group stages and were eliminated, costing Ferruccio Valcareggi his position as head coach.

Four days after their trip to Florence, the Leopards arrived in Rome to play a fixture that was effectively a farewell testimonial for Roma's Francesco Scaratti, who would be donning the *Giallorossi* shirt for the last time. A crowd of 20,000 turned up at the Stadio Olimpico to watch the home side trounce Zaire 3-0, with Scaratti crowning his final appearance with a 30-yard drive for the third. It was the highlight of a game described by Italy's communist newspaper *l'Unità* as "mediocre", although from a historical perspective it was also notable for a rare appearance for Roma by a young Claudio Ranieri. In a performance underpinned by yet more poor defending and profligacy in front of goal, the newspaper singled out Kakoko and Mayanga for their willingness to attack the Roma goal but summed up Zaire as 'a very modest team overall' with a poor grasp of zonal marking. Reflecting upon the games in later years, Mayanga did not disagree with *l'Unità's* viewpoint but alluded to other mitigating factors that were now having an impact on the players. 'Some matches went quite well,' admitted the winger, 'but we found the training very hard, very intense. There had been some fatigue after the Nations Cup and now we were training three times a day.' Vidinić had focused primarily on the players' fitness levels since their victory in Egypt and with good reason. He may have been striving to install a more professional approach in order to meet the challenges ahead but the energy-sapping training drills and adverse weather conditions combined to leave his squad cold, tired and miserable.

The short tour ended on something of a high with a 1-1 draw against Cesena. Two days later they departed for Frankfurt, not entirely ready for the big event. The coach was astute enough to recognise this dip in confidence and began to steadily play down his team's chances in his press interviews as results went against him, as if priming them for the worst. 'We are drawn in one of the strongest groups,' he told a gathering of journalists at the team's hotel in Willisau after the defeat against Aarau. 'Yugoslavia, Brazil and Scotland are marvellous teams so you will not find us boasting about what we might achieve. We will do the best we can, but we know our limitations.'

Back home, things had taken a turn for the worse for Mobutu. Six people had been killed during a week of unrest and protests in Kinshasa and during a political rally at the Stade du 20 Mai, which was attended by over 100,000 people, the president paraded 48 "assassins" who were to be hanged for treason. The AZAP (Agence Zaire-Presse) news agency also reported that another 500 had been arrested and sent to work on the country's nationalised farms. What Mobutu needed now was a good news story to divert attention away from the rising poverty and unemployment levels, brought about by his decision to seize control of foreign-owned firms that forced European investors out of the country. All eyes therefore turned towards West Germany and the Leopards, in the full expectation that they would deliver a much sought after distraction.

8. Basecamp

ON THE FIRST DAY OF JUNE, two weeks before their opening match against Scotland, Zaire's vivid yellow and green Mercedes-Benz bus arrived in the small, secluded town of Ascheberg to be greeted by a traditional German oompah band and a crowd of curious but friendly well-wishers, eager to catch a glimpse of their exotic visitors. Situated in the lush Westphalian countryside, it offered convenient access to both Dortmund and Gelsenkirchen, where they would play all three of their group games. Yet on this occasion the coach struggled to navigate the short distance to the squad's base for the tournament, the Hotel Jagdschlösschen, such was the size of the welcoming party.

Delays had been a recurring theme for the delegation from the moment they touched down the day before at Frankfurt Airport on a Boeing 747 that had been specially chartered by President Mobutu for the team. As the aircraft taxied to a halt, it was met by a detachment of heavily armed police officers, who were there to provide protection to the team. Security was understandably tight. Two years earlier terrorist action by members of the Black September faction of the Palestine Liberation Organisation had led to the death of eleven Israeli athletes who were taking part in the 1972 Olympic Games in Munich. The West German authorities had been roundly criticised for the ease with which the terrorists had accessed the Olympic village and were determined that there would be no repeat of the atrocities at that summer's World Cup.

Back on the aeroplane, the Zaire squad, who had earlier enjoyed a splendid in-flight meal courtesy of their esteemed leader, peered through the windows and watched as the police established a perimeter before they were allowed to disembark the craft. Once inside the terminal building, they were ushered through passport control with such haste that Herman Joch, head of the World Cup organising committee who was there to officially greet the players and officials, struggled to get past the assembled mass of security men to fulfil his duties before they climbed aboard their distinctive bus.

It was a three-hour trip to Ascheberg from the Esso Motel Hotel in Frankfurt that accommodated the team overnight. By the time the party finally arrived at the hunting lodge, which had been decorated with Zairean flags, Blagoje Vidinić's patience was wearing thin. As the waiting pack of journalists pressed him for a quote for the following day's newspapers, he finally snapped, offering a terse 'We are not here as tourists' before scurrying off into the hotel foyer. His players, however, seemed to enjoy their new-found fame as eager young autograph hunters held out a varied array of notebooks, team photos, trading cards, sticker albums and other assorted World Cup memorabilia that had been on sale in local shops and petrol stations in the run-up to the finals for them to sign.

Despite the manager's outburst, the mood remained jovial and the hotel's proprietor, Herr Hubert Reher, received his new guests with a stirring if somewhat unpatriotic short speech. 'I hope that you will feel comfortable with us,' he told the team, 'and wish that you will become World champions.' Herr Reher was well versed in greeting dignitaries, having previously welcomed such prominent figures as Helmut Kohl, Uwe Seeler and Frank Zappa to his establishment, and rolled out the red carpet accordingly. The hotel was one of the finest in the district and the accompanying restaurant was renamed in honour of the team for the duration of their stay. As a consequence, Reher was reluctant to cook the traditional Zairean delicacies that the party had brought with them and wanted them to sample the local specialities instead. 'Once you've tasted it, you'll forget about monkey goulash,' he informed them, seemingly unconcerned about causing offence. Six containers of Podoho (smoked meat), Mohaba (chicken), Maccajobo (salt cod) and the yam-derived porridge Fufu went untouched as the hotelier served Westphalian venison and suckling pig with Pils, much to the players' delight.

The team's apparent penchant for monkey meat was a recurring theme in the foreign press, with even the most liberal publications guilty of reinforcing African stereotypes ahead of the start of the competition. New York's *The Village Voice* for example was quite adamant that the squad trained on fresh rations of their favourite meal daily and accepted 'no substitutes', having already explained to their readers that there were no facilities for cooking such dishes in West Germany, let alone the opportunity to purchase monkey meat at the local delicatessen. It's doubtful whether the claims that officials had demanded 'the right to fly three plane loads of tasty primates to

The electrical shops of Ascheberg were a magnet for Zaire's players.

Deutschland' and the proper pots 'to roast the little rascals right up' held any validity, but it made for a good story.

Once they had settled in, the Zaire entourage wasted little time exploring their new surroundings *en masse*, accompanied by their security detail consisting of uniformed officers from Lüdinghausen and plain clothes detectives from Münster. Having already lavished gifts on the team after qualification was secured, Mobutu ensured they had plenty of pocket money when they arrived in Germany and the two electrical outlets in the town proved to be of particular interest to players and officials alike and an unexpected bonus for Ascheberg's Mayor, Walter Bose, who owned one of the businesses.

'The small electrical shops certainly had a good time,' recalled local resident Walburga Krebber, who witnessed the team's shopping spree first hand. 'The players bought many electrical appliances, including televisions, stereos and washing machines, even though they did not know if they could use them in their homeland!'

Walburga's involvement with the team's adventure in West Germany was a happy accident. Her husband Manfred, a Bundesliga linesman since 1969 and respected figure within the local football community, was assigned to assist the Zaire delegation by the official organising committee during their stay. Through his duties the couple were granted intimate access to the squad and formed a close bond with the players, who in turn treated them as one of the team despite a noticeable language barrier. 'There were interpreters', explained Walburga. 'Otherwise we communicated through gestures, looks, demonstrations, writing and laughs – we just understood each other!

'My husband had a friendly relationship with everyone. If there was anything to discuss or to organise, he took care of it immediately,' she continued. 'In the evening, when I was there, it was like being in a big family. We all sat and dined together – the players, the coach Vidinić' and his wife, the physio, everyone.'

With Manfred staying with the team at the Hotel Jagdschlösschen, Walburga became a frequent visitor, not only to see her husband but also to act as an unofficial courier for the players. The purchase of camera equipment from one of the local shops sparked an unexpected interest in photography amongst the squad as they looked to relieve the boredom between training sessions. 'They took a lot of photographs. They took pictures like World Champions. Money did not matter,' remembers Walburga, who spent her evenings delivering the developed photos from the previous day to the players after finishing teaching at school in a nearby village. 'The photo lab agreed to have the prints ready for collection so I was greeted with "Wally photo!" almost every night!'

Defender Mwepu Ilunga was certainly impressed by his stay in Ascheberg. 'The facilities and surroundings were amazing,' he told author Jon Spurling in his book on the darker side of the World Cup, *Death or Glory*. 'Many of us had never been to Europe before so the neon signs and the sheer affluence of Germany took our breath away, as did our training centre.'

The aforementioned training facilities were located ten miles away in the nearby town of Seppenrade and twice a day their coach would make the twenty-minute trip to the modest non-league ground that belonged to SV Fortuna Seppenrade. While small in stature, the newly laid pitch suited Vidinić's needs, as he looked to hone his team's fitness ahead of the tournament.

Initially there was talk of a warm-up match between the hosts Fortuna and Zaire but the idea was scuppered by the Zairean Football Association, much to the disappointment of the home team. As team captain, Franz-Josef Löbbert was due to lead his side out to face their international opponents and later reflected on what would have been the biggest match of his career. 'This was a huge event for the players of Fortuna Seppenrade', he explained. 'But the long-awaited friendly against the national team was vetoed by association officials.' The team were not completely frozen out, however, and Löbbert revealed they were allowed to take part in the coaching sessions. 'We stood in for any missing players from Zaire and watched them train.'

The truth of the matter was that Zaire had accepted an alternative invitation, one accompanied by a financial incentive, to play a friendly against another team. Officials from VfB Oldenburg, a regional side from Lower Saxony, had visited the training camp in Seppenrade in the hope of arranging a fund-raising benefit match at their stadium. They secured the fixture by agreeing to pay a fee of $10,000 after negotiations with members of the Zairean delegation, which was to be handed over on the day of the game. As a consequence, Blagoje Vidinić and his squad made the two-hour journey in their colourful team bus to the Marschweg Stadium to face Oldenburg three days after arriving in West Germany. And while the players and coaching staff were treated to a pre-match meal of veal schnitzel and lettuce with lemon dressing, officials from the teams met in an adjoining room. There a metal case containing the agreed fee was handed to Zairean representatives, who duly checked the authenticity of the dollar bills as if they were playing out a scene in a Hollywood movie.

Shady backroom dealings aside, the game afforded Vidinić an opportunity to tweak his side in more hospitable conditions than the cold Alpine air that had greeted them in Switzerland. The fixture also drew a respectable crowd, with the match played in front of 10,000 spectators, a figure undoubtedly boosted by the sunny Whitsun Monday weather. They were entertained by a local brass band from the nearby town of Bösel, who added an international feel to the occasion by playing the respective national anthems of the two teams before the match kicked off.

If Vidinić was expecting an easy ride, he was given a jolt early in the first half when Oldenburg, wearing an all-blue strip, took an early lead through winger Dieter Wegner, whose low left-foot shot evaded Kazadi Mwamba in the Zaire goal after going through a crowd of players in the box. The Africans, again wearing their unfamiliar colours of white shirts and shorts with red socks, hit back shortly before half-time when Kidumu Mantantu netted from close range following a slick passing move that split open the Oldenburg defence. Before the referee had a chance to bring the opening half to an end, Zaire took the lead as Bwanga Tshimen found himself in acres of space with plenty of time to pick his spot and slot the ball home past goalkeeper Albert Voß.

Zaire assumed control in the second half with a goal that would not have looked out of place in the World Cup, a 25-yard thunderbolt from Kabasu Babo that dipped over the despairing dive of Voß. Mayanga Maku made it 4-1 with a fine left foot strike from just inside the edge of the area before Oldenburg pulled a goal back when Rainer Struckmann scored from the penalty spot, although Kazadi was unlucky not to save it after getting a firm hand on the ball. The German defender was also involved in Zaire's fifth and final goal, when he was unable to keep out Mana Mambwene's long range effort and deflected the ball into his own net to give the visitors a comfortable 5-2 victory and their first win in Europe.

For VfB Oldenburg the gamble had at least paid off. They recouped more than enough from the game to buy the boxing department of the sports club a new team bus and laid on a gala buffet for their visitors as a token of their appreciation before they returned to Ascheberg that evening. In return, Zaire got another taste of how the game was played in Europe. While the level of football on display was somewhat below international standard, Vidinić was relatively pleased with his team's performance, particularly in attack, having seen his side score five well-taken goals. At the back, however, the defence looked suspect at times, with left-back Mwanza Mukombo in particular guilty of making a rash challenge that was as cumbersome as it was crude in the build-up to the opening goal of the match. Yet such was the tempo and nature of the game that it lacked the necessary bite to really test the African side or offer any fresh insight into how they would perform in the upcoming tournament. When summing up the match, Horst Hollmann, sports editor of *Nordwest Zeitung*, neatly put the result into perspective. 'The Zaire national team has three things to fear in the World Cup: Brazilian ball art, Scottish hardness and Yugoslav tactics. VfB displayed none of these virtues today.'

While Oldenburg may have fallen short when it came to imitating the traits of Zaire's forthcoming opposition, Vidinić could take comfort from the fact that the very same exponents of ball art, hardness and tactics were experiencing their own problems, both on and off the field of play. This wasn't the Brazil side that had dazzled the world in Mexico four years earlier, the reigning champions were in a state of transition. Pelé had decided to call time on his international career and the team would be without the midfield talents of Tostão,

Gerson and Clodoaldo through injury, the latter ruled out just ten days before the *Seleção*'s first game. To compound matters further, they had not played a competitive fixture since the final against Italy in 1970.

To prepare his squad for the defence of their title, coach Mário Zagallo embarked on an ambitious itinerary of nine international matches in just six weeks, hoping to instil something of a club mentality into his players. Despite home advantage, the plan backfired somewhat and their form going into the finals was far from impressive. A 1-1 draw against Mexico was followed by laboured victories over Czechoslovakia (1-0), Bulgaria (1-0) and Romania (2-0), although there was some respite when they thumped Haiti 4-0. However, this proved to be something of a false dawn and a week later Zagallo's side were held to goalless draws by an unfancied Greece side and Austria. They rounded off the series of fixtures with unconvincing wins over the Republic of Ireland (2-1) and Paraguay (2-0) but they continued to struggle upon arrival in Europe and were held to a 1-1 draw by French club side Racing Strasbourg just days after narrowly beating a Select XI German Regional side 3-2.

Yugoslavia were also struggling for form ahead of the tournament, having failed to win any of their three warm-up games against international opposition. A 1-0 loss to a strong Soviet Union side, who would miss the finals after refusing to contest a play-off match against Chile on political grounds, was followed by a calamitous 3-2 defeat against Hungary in May after they had been 2-0 up at half-time. Their final game saw them take on a much-changed England side still reeling from the shock of their own failure to qualify and under the caretaker management of Joe Mercer following the sacking of Sir Alf Ramsey. Yet once again the Yugoslavs failed to hold on to a lead and were held to a 2-2 draw thanks to a late Kevin Keegan equaliser. Once in Germany Miljan Miljanic's team thumped local side Neu-Isenburg 9-2 in a picturesque stadium on the outskirts of Frankfurt but the game offered very little tactical insight. To confuse any rival spies and observers that may have been in attendance, the mischievous Miljanic opted to field a weakened side, playing many of them out of position with no numbers on the back of their shirts.

Scotland meanwhile appeared to be doing their best to destroy their chances before even setting foot in Germany, with their preparations rocked by not one but two drink-related scandals involving key members of the team. The first incident, which took place at the team's hotel in Ayrshire following a victory over Wales and just days before they were due to play England in a Home Championship clash, saw winger Jimmy Johnstone rescued by the coastguard after he stole a rowing boat following a drinking session and drifted out to sea. Although the episode has since become part of Scottish footballing folklore, the story dominated the news headlines for days afterwards and there were calls for Johnstone to be dropped from the squad. A superlative performance in a splendid 2-0 win against the "auld enemy" quickly saw the player forgiven. Unfortunately for manager Willie Ormond, the press seemed determined to undermine his squad. A week later the team found themselves splashed all over the front – and back – pages of the newspapers once again following a 2-1 win over Norway when a small group of players broke a curfew and spent a 'debauched drunken evening' with students in their hotel in Oslo. Johnstone was again involved, along with captain Billy Bremner, and came close to being sent home but while both players admitted their guilt, they felt the incident had been blown out of proportion, leading to a frosty relationship between the Scotland squad and journalists throughout the tournament. Yet the Scottish players found an ally of sorts in Blagoje Vidinić who, when asked to comment on the drunken antics by the *Sunday People* newspaper, simply joked 'Only the good players drink. The bad ones don't.'

With Scotland the sole British representatives in West Germany, Zaire's presence in the same group generated a great deal of media interest in the United Kingdom. With Vidinić happy to hold open training sessions, television crews and journalists descended on the towns of Ascheberg and Seppenrade, eager to get a story about one of the competition's more colourful participants. The tabloids in particular took great delight in recounting such tales of how winger Kakoko Etepé once ran down a zebra while captain Kidumu Mantantu was only too happy to pose for photographs dressed in a kilt, albeit worn over his tracksuit, ahead of the clash against Willy Ormond's men. Occasionally more meaningful insight was offered, including from none other than pundit Jimmy Hill, who was looking forward to seeing the team in action, telling readers of the *Radio Times World Cup Special* that 'Zaire will prove to be the most talented of the three mystery "underdog teams" at the World Cup'. However, Jack Rollins, esteemed editor of the *Rothmans Football Yearbook*, offered a more cautionary opinion to the same readers. 'European football is almost a total mystery to the Leopards,' he warned. 'Vidinić knows that his big problem is to prepare his exuberant players to meet the sophisticated tactics they'll face in the finals.'

Perhaps the most honest judgement came from reporter Gerald Sinstadt who enjoyed greater access to the players than most as part of ITV's World Cup presentation team. Having spent the morning getting to know the squad over breakfast, he travelled on the team bus to the training ground and watched from the stands as Vidinić put his charges through their paces. He described the squad as 'serious and a bit withdrawn' and judged Zaire as a team 'more sophisticated in its approach and preparation than many of us had perhaps expected.' Stereotypes about African football aside, whether Sinstadt was seriously expecting something more amateurish is unclear but he was not alone in exclaiming surprise at the level of skill on display from the smartly dressed African players. Wearing the latest Adidas boots and looking resplendent in their dark green, yellow trim Adidas tracksuits with *ZAIRE* emblazoned across the back in large letters, the squad certainly looked like a football team in waiting, airing their party tricks and attempting ambitious bicycle kicks for the cameras. Yet tellingly, Sinstadt felt that although the side had one or two outstandingly gifted individuals, he believed they lacked the collective strength to compete with their upcoming opponents in Group Two.

Privately Vidinić agreed with Sinstadt's sentiments. His willingness to play the role of bombastic cheerleader for African football in public belied his astuteness when it came to the international game and the limitations of his squad. While he was prepared to play up for the cameras, allowing photographers to snap staged training routines of the players leaping over show jumping fences, the Yugoslav was under no illusion of the task that lay ahead. In a rare unguarded moment, he admitted that Zaire lacked the strength in depth other teams could call upon and cast doubt on his team's ability to cope on the greatest stage of all. 'I admit I have no real reserve power,' Vidinić candidly revealed on the eve of the tournament. 'The eleven men I send out are the ones that have to do the job. We have never played in a contest at such a sophisticated level before. It is difficult to tell how my players will react.' Vidinić would not have long to wait before finding out. However, before a ball was even kicked in anger in Germany, he would play a key role in changing the face of world football forever.

Coach Blagoje Vidinić and team doctor Mambu Moura cast their eye over proceedings at Seppenrade.

Jumping for joy: Vidinić takes advantage of the facilities at the team's Seppenrade training ground to put his forward line of Kakoko Etepe, Ndaye Mulamba and Mayanga Maku through their paces.

The son of the founder of Adidas, Horst Dassler (pictured here in front of a portrait of his father) played a key role in ensuring victory for João Havelange at the FIFA Congress that preceded the 1974 World Cup. Adidas sponsorship helped transform the World Cup and the game in Africa and Asia.

9. Kingmaker

IT IS ALMOST IMPOSSIBLE to imagine a World Cup without the blanket media coverage that almost suffocates a global audience every four years. In 2018, over one billion people tuned in to witness France beat Croatia to claim their second title in Russia and over half the world's population watched some part of the tournament. Not only were fans able to view the matches in Ultra HD, but some media organisations even offered a virtual reality app that allowed the audience to get closer to the action. Back in 1974 the relationship between the various broadcasting networks and FIFA was still in its infancy but football's governing body was quietly confident of attracting an audience of one billion across the entire competition.

It had been a mere eight years since television covered every match of the 1966 tournament in England. Thanks to the advent and widespread use of communication satellites, the 1970 World Cup in Mexico offered live coverage of games throughout the developed world, with the added attraction of transmissions in glorious Technicolour for those with the latest television sets. The finals in West Germany would affirm football's status as a global product. To this end, a media army of broadcasters and journalists descended in unprecedented numbers. There were an estimated 132 commentators alone, ready to fill the gantries at the nine official venues, supported by 2,000 technicians from 180 television and radio stations. Although England would be absent, the BBC dispatched a team of seventy to cover the tournament, a far cry from the mere ten they sent to Chile in 1962, while ITV sent forty, both keen to align themselves to Scotland's cause in the process.

In addition to the various television companies, over 1,000 accredited journalists and photographers would also be in attendance. Crucially for FIFA, they would offer insight on events behind the scenes between games, reporting on the injury worries for certain managers or conducting lightweight interviews with the players, ensuring the competition remained in the public consciousness over their breakfasts. Yet on the eve of the tournament, it was the organisation itself that was providing the headlines for the morning newspapers.

As delegates assembled at the ruling body's 39th Congress in Frankfurt, the main topic of conversation was the forthcoming FIFA presidential election, which had generated an unexpected buzz around the proceedings. Incumbent Sir Stanley Rous, who had held office since 1961, was facing an aggressive challenge from International Olympic Committee member Dr. João Havelange, and was in danger of being voted out on a wave of anti-European sentiment that had been partly stirred up by his opponent.

Havelange, who had represented Brazil in the swimming pool at both the 1936 and 1952 Olympics, had undertaken an ambitious three-year tour to drum up support for his candidacy, visiting 86 countries despite a fear of flying. He spent an estimated $400,000 in the process, often travelling with Brazil's national team and Pelé to help the charm offensive. He appealed mainly to football's developing nations by promising increased funding, an expanded World Cup Finals and a youth edition that could be potentially hosted in such nations.

Rous, by contrast, was very much a Eurocentric traditionalist who believed in preserving the status quo. Despite the number of teams entering the qualification stage almost doubling between 1962 and 1974, during Rous's reign the World Cup had retained a rigid 16-team format dominated by the traditional powerhouses of Europe and South America. Sir Stanley had courted controversy too. His refusal to guarantee Africa a qualifying place for the 1966 tournament led to 31 members of the Confédération Africaine de Football boycotting the competition while his support of the South African Football Association in the 1960s almost led to a complete withdrawal from FIFA by the confederation. Yet the former Suffolk schoolmaster's opinions were by no means unique within the upper echelons of the game. At a UEFA meeting in May, several associations had expressed their anger to the FIFA president that weaker nations such as Zaire, Haiti and Australia were set to compete in the World Cup at the expense of more established nations including England, Czechoslovakia and Hungary.

'There was a strong sense across a lot of the football world that the game was a European venture and that FIFA should really operate in the interests of the European game and the European football nations,' wrote Paul Darby in his book *Stanley Rous's 'Own goal': football politics, South Africa and the contest for the Fifa presidency in 1974.* 'There was a desire to ensure that that remained the case. Any time the African nations sought to use FIFA or world football as a vehicle for registering their presence on the international stage, they were met with resistance. They were met with narrow European self-interest.'

The outdated, old school colonial stance embodied by Rous therefore gave Havelange the leverage he needed. Recognising the sense of frustration felt by the continent's footballing nations and the ill-disguised racist undertones behind some of the organisation's decisions and actions, the Brazilian centred his bid around Africa, promising riches to national associations who often struggled to pay their $150 annual FIFA membership fee. Clearly understanding the nuances of the forthcoming election better than his opponent, he appreciated the equal value of each member's vote and lobbied CAF president Yidnekatchew Tessema in the hope of securing the backing of the federation. His candidacy was duly endorsed but Havelange still had a number of obstacles to overcome if he was to dethrone the president.

Any appetite for change was countered by threats of a break away by the European Bloc if their interests were not satisfied. Rous had outmanoeuvred his opponent by sanctioning a proposal from the South American confederation, CONMEBOL, to increase the number of participants for the 1978 World Cup to twenty teams and there was a concern that under the Brazilian's leadership, only one of the extra four places would go to UEFA. The rest, reported *The Guardian* newspaper, would be divided between Asia, South America and Africa to fulfil Havelange's election promises. 'It will be surprising if UEFA are content with this,' opined David Lacey. 'And therein lies the great threat to the next World Cup, with European nations breaking away to concentrate on their own competition.' The prospect of such a devaluation of the tournament, which in turn would risk the future of the organisation, concerned a number of FIFA members and threatened to undermine Havelange's own platform. As it transpired, although the proposal was accepted by delegates, the finals in Argentina followed the same 16-team format that was employed in West Germany.

Delegates therefore had a simple choice: slow and steady reform or radical change. Rous was the steady ship who had transformed the World Cup into a global spectacle and built a solid foundation for further growth. Havelange offered the Third World the same kind of administrative influence they enjoyed within the Olympic movement and a larger presence at the finals. Yet his plans to transform the footballing infrastructure within the developing countries who vowed to back him would require considerable financial investment. To this end, he hoped to fulfil his promises by maximising FIFA's revenues from corporate sponsorship deals and other commercial opportunities to help fund his ambitious plans. Part of Havelange's strategy was to cultivate relationships with potential investors to secure long-term financial backing for the World Cup and among his targets were such giants as Coca-Cola and Adidas, who were already a major commercial partner for the 1974 tournament. The only problem was that Horst Dassler, the face of the sportswear manufacturer and heir apparent of the company, was a close ally of Rous.

Alarmed by whispers of the success of his rival's overseas lobbying, the FIFA president had sought Dassler's help to shore up his own campaign following his impassioned plea to the members of UEFA for their backing. Dassler, still irked by Havelange's decision to reject Adidas's offer to kit out the Brazil national team, was only too happy to support his friend, believing his endorsement would ultimately be beneficial for all concerned. Using his influence as the head of the company's French subsidiary, the businessman actively engaged with a number of association representatives on Rous' behalf and was quietly confident of victory when he retired to the Steigenberger hotel the night before the election. That confidence was shattered by his guest for the evening, Zaire coach Blagoje Vidinić, who quietly informed Dassler that he was backing the wrong man over a drink in the bar.

Dassler had no reason to doubt Vidinić's view. The two men had formed a close friendship after the Adidas executive had come to the Yugoslav's aid when he was coach of Morocco. Keen to establish his company's brand in Africa, Dassler sent boxes of equipment, including boots and kit, free of charge to Vidinić, who had been struggling with resources in the build up to the World Cup in Mexico. It was a calculated move, rather than pure altruism on Dassler's part, who hoped to increase his influence within FIFA, but when the two met in Mexico City after Morocco's elimination, he told Vidinić "From now on, your family and mine shall be friends."

Their relationship was duly cemented when the Yugoslav became coach of Zaire. Needing a kit that reflected the country's new identity, Vidinić turned to his new friend, who was only too happy to oblige, producing the iconic shirts that the team would wear in West Germany. Now it was time to return the favour.

Dassler sat and listened as Vidinić told him of the little gifts Havelange had presented to his hosts during his various visits to the continent and how the football federations had convened behind the scenes at the African Cup of Nations in Egypt to privately endorse the Brazilian. Havelange's commitment to exclude South Africa from FIFA until apartheid was abolished, a stance in stark contrast to that of Rous, had secured their support. Faced with the prospect of Adidas being left out in the cold, Dassler pondered his next move. Vidinić encouraged proactivity. "This is Havelange's room number," the Yugoslav confided to his friend. "Tell him that you were supporting Stanley Rous but that from now on, it is available to him." Dassler took his advice, met with Havelange and returned with a bottle of Champagne for Vidinić, having secured his company's interests in the event of a Brazilian victory the following day.

According to author Andrew Jennings, Vidinić had good reason to believe the African vote would swing the election. The coach had been paying cash for votes to elect Joao Havelange President of FIFA. It was a policy hastily adopted by Dassler following his change of heart, with Jennings asserting in his book *Foul!: The Secret World of FIFA* that the Adidas chief bestowed gifts of cash to any association official still holding out to encourage them to vote for Havelange. Little effort was seemingly made to disguise their actions. Writing in the *Sunday Times* a few days after the election, Keith Botsford spoke of 'little brown envelopes being passed around with such fraternal sentiments as "if that's not enough, please tell me".'

Their cause was boosted by France's delegation, who chose not to support Rous. Gripped by a dose of patriotic fervour, the Fédération Française de Football let age-old prejudices blind their judgement and they backed Havelange simply because he was not English. France's influence within FIFA and the IOC, two institutions founded by Frenchmen, had been on the wane for some time. It hit a nadir when Lord Killanin defeated Count Jean de Beaumont for the presidency of the Olympic committee prior to 1972's Summer Games, leaving both organisations in the hands of Knights of the Realm. 'There was a big fight between the French and English speakers,' recalls Christian Jannette, a member of Adidas' international relations team. 'French had been the first language at the IOC and English second. Now it was reversed.'

It was an unpalatable situation for the French, who sought to redress the balance by supporting a Francophone candidate with little admiration for the English game (Havelange had been an outspoken critic of the 1966 tournament, repeatedly claiming that it had been fixed in favour of the hosts and cited Brazil's early exit as evidence of the alleged collusion). Moreover their influence spread beyond Europe's borders to the former colonies of the French empire, who, without a hint of irony, were reminded of Rous' outdated colonialist stance towards Africa. Again, such behaviour did not go unnoticed. 'I saw a lot of African diplomats in Frankfurt,' continued Botsford in his article for the *Sunday Times*. 'Some of them the cream of the French education system, not necessarily voting but influencing their delegations.'

Yet despite the machinations of Dassler, Vidinić and the French association, nothing was guaranteed when the representatives of a record 122 national football federations, including Zaire's own deputation led by the Minister of Sport Sampassa Kaweta Milombe, finally assembled in Frankfurt's neo-Baroque Kongresshalle. There were other matters on the agenda to discuss, including the admittance of China to the club at the expense of Taiwan, that could prove vital come the final reckoning in the presidential race. As the congress progressed, Havelange, ever the politician, circled the auditorium, meeting and greeting delegates while his opponent carried out his official duties on the podium. But although he polled more votes, winning 62 to Sir Stanley's 56, the challenger ultimately fell short of the two thirds majority required to avoid a second ballot. They would have to go again.

The contrast between the candidates, as they waited for the next round of voting, was marked. Havelange was in his element. A polyglot who could converse with diplomats and officials with ease, he worked the room again, seeking out those still wavering who could push his bid over the line. Meanwhile Rous, as reclusive as ever, kept his distance, standing at the back of the hall nursing a glass of orange juice with an air of defeat. He was not a politician and this new style of campaigning had left him exposed and relying on his record in office.

As it transpired, that was not enough. As predicted by Zaire's flamboyant coach, Havelange duly won the second round and the presidency outright by 68-52. Rous was initially phlegmatic in defeat, congratulating his victorious opponent before proceeding with the remaining business of the assembly. In return, Havelange offered a kiss and a bouquet of flowers while FIFA awarded Rous the title of honorary president in recognition of his contributions to the game over the previous dozen years as compensation. He would later confess to waiting British journalists that it had been 'the most political congress in my experience.'

'For them they are a bouquet, while mine is more in the nature of a wreath,' he continued. 'It will be difficult to realise I'm no longer president.'

Once the dust had settled, Rous, who became the first and so far only incumbent FIFA president to be voted out of office, grew increasingly bitter, accusing Havelange of stabbing him in the back. He would later learn that Greece had joined France in supporting his opponent but it was the Third World that truly swung the vote. The many visits Havelange had made to the African continent had paid off, with 21 of the 37 continent's associations backing him, having been won over by his persona and promises.

'The election was purely a matter of personalities and ideals,' explained Benin official Joseph Houndokinnou to *The Guardian*. 'We like Sir Stanley very much, but he is an old man and we wanted someone who is more dynamic.'

In the coming years Havelange would honour the many pledges he made on his extensive campaign trail. Together with Horst Dassler, he would transform the World Cup into a financially lucrative proposition that in turn would fund a number of projects in developing countries across the globe. He would also enlarge the number of teams contesting the finals to twenty-four by the 1982 edition but the whiff of corruption and bribery that was evident in Frankfurt would stay with him throughout his tenure.

The staging of the tenth World Cup would therefore be Sir Stanley Rous' last meaningful act as FIFA president. It was not the only change ahead of the finals. It was a case of 'out with the old, in with the new' with regards to the trophy the sixteen finalists were competing to win too. Holders Brazil had been allowed to retain the

Jules Rimet Trophy in perpetuity having won the competition for a record third time in Mexico so a replacement was required. Fifty-three submissions were received from sculptors in seven countries before the commission was awarded to Italian artist Silvio Gazzaniga. Standing 36.5 centimetres tall, the 18-carat gold statue, simply called the FIFA World Cup, would be awarded for the first time on July 7th.

The bookmakers made the hosts and European champions West Germany favourites to lift the new trophy, closely followed by Italy then Brazil. At 250-1, Zaire were rank outsiders but as the first sub-Saharan Africa team to reach the finals, they were already assured their place in the history books. Anything else would be a bonus.

10. Highland Fling

THE DAY HAD FINALLY ARRIVED. After months of speculation and questions around whether the African Champions deserved their place on the greatest stage of all was about to be answered, the world was about to get their first look at Zaire in action and playing the role of pantomime villains, on this occasion at least, was Willy Ormond's Scotland. Nonetheless, despite being overwhelming favourites to win, nerves were evident within the Scottish camp.

It had been sixteen long years since Scotland had last graced the World Cup and their record in the competition was patchy at best. They had missed the first four tournaments through self-imposed exile. A row over broken payments had seen all four British teams withdraw from FIFA en bloc in 1928 and play no part in the pre-War finals yet when they were welcomed back to the fold in 1950 the Scottish Football Association impudently turned down the chance to travel to Brazil alongside England. Having declared they would only send a team if their players won the British Home Championship, which served as a qualifying group, they stubbornly refused to back down when Scotland finished second.

They finally made their debut in 1954 but suffered a calamitous campaign as a result of mismanagement and poor organisation, culminating in a 7-0 humiliation at the hands of Uruguay. The SFA's decision to travel with just thirteen players rather than the permitted eighteen, leaving plenty of room on the aeroplane for the wives of committee members, exposed their attitude towards the competition. Their choice of kit - thick cotton jerseys and shorts to combat the supposedly freezing mountain temperatures - exposed their naivety. Undermined and in an impossible position, manager Andy Beattie resigned after their opening game against Austria in protest and was replaced by the team physio. 'It was a shambles', recalled future Scotland boss Tommy Docherty, who played in both games, 'that is the only way to describe it.'

Although they fared little better four years later in terms of qualification, the Scottish team of 1958 were more competitive than their predecessors. Drawn in a tough group against France, who would go on to impress while reaching the semi-finals, Yugoslavia and Paraguay, they picked up their first World Cup point in their opening match before suffering two narrow defeats. The next three editions of the competition ended at the qualification stage for the Scots (they narrowly missed out in 1962 after losing to eventual runners-up Czechoslovakia in a play-off match in extra time, having been 2-1 up with six minutes left). To make matters worse, their exile in the wilderness was compounded by England's victory in 1966 but Sir Alf Ramsey's men were absent in West Germany and the Scots had something to prove.

It was a strong side too. In goalkeeper David Harvey, midfielder Billy Bremner and strikers Joe Jordan and Peter Lorimer they had the nucleus of the Leeds United side that had just won the English league title. Celtic's 'Quality Street Gang' were ably represented by Kenny Dalglish, Danny McGrain and David Hay while in Denis Law they had a *bona fide* legend of the game, a former European Footballer of the Year who had won the lot with Manchester United. Yet regardless of the talent on show, none of them had ever played in the World Cup before and nagging doubts persisted over the suitability of Ormond as manager, who had replaced Tommy Docherty the year before after "The Doc" accepted a lucrative contract to manage Manchester United rather than stick with the national team.

Ormond, who had also been a member of Scotland's squad in Switzerland, had been a surprise choice for the job. With only five years in the hot-seat at St. Johnstone under his belt, he was relatively inexperienced compared to his competitors for the role. However, his performance with the Saints, which included leading them to their highest ever league placing and European qualification, had impressed the selection panel. In turn, the manager had repaid their faith by getting his country to the finals but was not enjoying the best of relations with the nation's press in the run up to the competition, having won just five of his fifteen games in charge.

He had also made the mistake of predicting an easy victory for his side, a foolhardy move for any Scotland manager at the best of times, and had promised to 'walk barefoot back to Glasgow' if his side didn't beat Zaire. Having travelled to Egypt in March to scout the Leopards during their African Cup of Nations triumph, Ormond reportedly closed his notebook after ten minutes and concluded that 'they cannot play'. Then, after watching the Leopards lose 2-1 to Congo in their second group game, his bravado got the better of him and he confidently predicted victory. 'I just want the people back home to know that we have nothing to worry about', he declared. 'We will beat this team - and beat them well. Zaire are not in the same class - any of our First Division teams would beat them'. However, having attended the Africans' warm-up game against VfB Oldenburg, the Scotland manager began to backtrack on his earlier comments and admitted he was surprised by the apparent improvement in their performance.

'No one is treating this match as an easy matter,' Ormond told *The Guardian* newspaper on the eve of the game. 'When I watched them in Cairo earlier this year I felt then that we would beat them easily. Since that time, however, they have improved beyond recognition, and we will have to play to our full potential if we are to get the result we want.'

The cautious tone was echoed by his captain, Billy Bremner, who was only too aware of his nation's tendency to slip up against supposedly weaker teams. 'Our record against poor sides is so bad that we cannot afford to take anything for granted against Zaire,' he warned, yet he was also conscious of the dangers of being over-cautious. 'We need to score goals in what should be our easiest match,' he continued. 'Not only to build up confidence in the team but because goal difference could be so important.'

The Oldenburg game may have altered Ormond's thinking but it did not lead to a revision of his tactics. There were no real surprises in his starting line-up when the team sheet was circulated to reporters, with the manager opting for a 4-3-3 formation that may have lacked width but was full of attacking intent. With winger Jimmy Johnstone omitted in favour of the veteran striker Law, goals were clearly the order of the day. Moreover, the formation suggested his team would play the robust, direct approach that was popular in the British game at the time, something that had worried Ormond's opposite number in the build up to the match.

'Of course Brazil and Yugoslavia will be hard,' observed Blagoje Vidinić wrily, 'but Scotland will be the hardest game for us because the British style is exactly contrary to ours. They are a very good team with very big players.' The Yugoslav was clearly concerned about the physicality of the Scottish squad and allusions to their size had been a recurring theme in the coach's press conferences. Having watched them labour to victory over Norway during a warm-up game in Oslo, Vidinić quickly identified the aerial threat posed by the Scots to his defence and aptly described Joe Jordan as 'a powerful spearhead'. Offensively, he had doubts his strikers could compete with the likes of central defender Jim Holton, who he likened to an elephant albeit 'a very good one, especially in the air.'

Zaire did have one weapon in their armoury that Vidinić could exploit - pace. The team were not called the Leopards without good reason and the country's Minister of Publicity and chief football advisor, Lucien Tshimpumpu wa Tshimpumpu, had described the team as 'eleven high-speed motorboats, who are artists of football'. The coach therefore opted to counter Scotland's lack of width by playing two wingers in an attack-minded 4-2-4 formation that included ten of the starting line-up that had contested the Cup of Nations Final back in March, with Kilasu Massamba replacing Mavuba Mafuila in midfield. Kazadi continued in goal as expected behind the now established first-choice back four of Mwepu, Mukombo, Bwanga and Lobilo. Captain Kidumu and the aforementioned Kilasu would operate in the centre of the pitch supporting a forward line blessed with speed consisting of Mana, Ndaye, Mayanga and Kakoko. It was arguably the strongest possible side at Vidinić's disposal yet his selection was challenged by members of Zaire's delegation the night before the game.

Drunk on the power they mistakenly believed their relationship with Mobutu entitled them to, officials from the Ministry of Sports had insisted that the coach change his line-up to make room for SC Imana forward Mbungu Ekofa. The fact that Mbungu was injured and not match fit did not dampen their resolve. They claimed his injury had been healed by the party's witch doctors but Vidinić refused to back down. After three hours of badgering, his patience finally snapped and he called Zaire's Minister of Sport Sampassa Kaweta Milombe to remind him that there was only one coach on the team, not twenty. Sampassa agreed to intervene and the team sheet remained unaltered but the incident did not bode well for the future.

One thing beyond Vidinić's control was the weather. Zaire had struggled in cooler European climes during their warm-up games and the forecast predicted a wet and windy evening. Regardless, he wanted his team to go out and impress the watching millions around the world and prove Ormond wrong in his initial assessment of Zaire. 'Although we do not like the weather and the rains have made the ground too soft for us, I believe we can show Scotland that we are not the weak nation they think we are,' asserted Vidinić in his last round of interviews before the game. 'I think we have improved out of all recognition since Ormond saw us win the Africa Cup. Nobody believes in us and that's okay because we can surprise them. Millions of Africans will be watching the World Cup on television and we must not disappoint them. Africa is awakening to football, and we are the leaders.'

As the sides lined up for their respective national anthems, it was Zaire that looked the more relaxed. Shortly before they emerged from the tunnel, Vidinić had read aloud a telegram from President Mobutu to the team: "Go out onto the field and move with the speed and stealth of the leopard. Go out and bring glory to your country. Become heroes. Become legends." The words had fired up the dressing room and left the players in little doubt about who they were representing. 'It was overflowing with nationalistic zeal. That's the only way you could describe it,' recalled Mwepu Ilunga. 'We felt we were doing it for Africa, for ourselves, and for Mobutu.'

As the teams broke, Zaire spaced themselves out around their half of the centre circle then turned and waved to the crowd in a choreographed move that brought the first cheer of the night from the crowd at the Westfalenstadion. The venue had been purpose-built to stage four games in the competition and had a capacity of 54,000 yet was only half-full, leaving large pockets of empty terracing that exposed drab, prefabricated concrete as the television cameras panned across the ground. It was a far cry from the slick, corporate experience of today, emphasised by the eclectic mix of billboards advertising the *Daily Mirror*, British Caledonian Airways and Skol lager alongside one urging viewers to 'Go to Zaire', which was paid for by Mobutu and would be seen at all three group games along with a second hoarding that simply read 'Zaire - Peace'.

Having promised to deliver a bit of colour to the tournament, Zaire lived up to expectations before the game even started as they removed their tracksuit tops to reveal one of the most vivid and exciting kits in World Cup history, giving at least one journalist the impression of tropical hummingbirds at play. Yellow in colour with a green and red trim, it featured the Leopard insignia that had allegedly been designed by the president himself. The effect was slightly ruined by the vests the players wore underneath to combat the temperatures of the German "summer" but Scotland's strip looked a little dour and dated in contrast. As the game got underway, the same could be said of their style of play.

Scotland's stars would later admit to succumbing to nerves before kick-off but in a scrappy opening period, it was the Africans who looked the more composed on the ball. The Scots did have an opportunity to settle any jitters in the second minute but failed to capitalise when Jordan headed the ball wide from a Peter Lorimer cross. Zaire, meanwhile, began to play themselves into the game and were frightening the Scottish defence with bursts of pace, particularly Mayanga Maku down the right wing. And when the winger let a shot fly from twenty yards after a neat interchange of passes, Willie Ormond's men knew they had a game on their hands. Although the effort was wide of the post by some margin, it was greeted with a huge cheer from the crowd. By contrast, when David Hay tried something similar minutes later with the same result, it was greeted with howls of derision. The Scots had been left in little doubt of where the loyalty of any neutrals in the stadium lay when a back-pass from the centre circle by Holton to his goalkeeper David Harvey in the opening minute was met with a chorus of boos and whistles. They antagonised the crowd further with some ferocious tackles and cynical gamesmanship as they looked to soften-up Zaire. Defender John Blackley somehow avoided a booking for clattering Mana early on and then clumsily pulled back Ndaye Mulumba when the striker looked set to break free into the Scottish half. Joe Jordan, meanwhile, was making his presence felt up front and after he barged the acrobatic Kazadi to the floor when the keeper had cleanly collected a Lorimer through ball, it was clear that Scotland were happy to play the bad guys.

As if to underline their new-found role, Jordan wasted no time clattering into the Zaire goalkeeper for a second time after he bravely pounced onto a scuffed shot from Denis Law. While Sir Alf Ramsey saw nothing wrong with the challenge from the commentary box, the *Daily Mirror's* Frank McGhee felt the Scottish striker could easily have pulled up. Replays supported McGhee's view yet referee Gerhard Schulenburg was happy to let play continue. He was later criticised in a Football Association report on the match, who felt the West German official was too slack in his handling of the game, allowing Scotland to intimidate their opponents with their wild tackling in the early stages.

Zaire, bruised but not intimidated, carved out their first real chance of the game shortly afterwards. In truth, they should probably have taken the lead and it certainly was a passage of play that deserved better. Kidumu, more than holding his own in midfield, controlled a diagonal ball from Mwepu on the edge of the box then, before Sandy Jardine could react, skilfully flicked it through to Kakoko. The winger teed himself up perfectly but missed his kick as Holton attempted to close him down. Recovering his composure, Kakoko chased the ball down and hit a hard, low shot under the body of Harvey but the angle proved too tight and he could only watch as the side netting bulged, much to Scotland's relief.

Stung into action, the Scots immediately went on the attack and had a half-chance when Bremner floated yet another high ball into the box for Jordan, who had little trouble winning the header. The ball fell kindly to the on-rushing Law on the edge of the six-yard-box but he was robbed of possession by the outstretched leg of Lobilo Boba, who then audaciously dribbled past Kenny Dalglish and carried the ball out of danger, leaving the two Scottish legends in his wake. Law and Jordan then got in each other's way trying to connect with a Danny McGrain cross before Kazadi comfortably saved a long range free-kick from Lorimer.

Scotland were enjoying a prolonged spell of dominance but creating very little in the way of clear chances. In the twenty-third minute they were handed a gilt-edged opportunity to open the scoring when they were inexplicably awarded an indirect free-kick thirteen-yards out from goal. It was a questionable decision to say the least. As Lobilo dived to head away a low Dalglish cross, Jordan, who seemed to be at the centre of every Scottish attack, was sent tumbling after he crashed into the Zaire centre half. The German referee immediately blew his whistle and walked over to Jordan, who was already pleading his innocence, having seemingly penalised the striker for dangerous play. However, while Lobilo lay prostrate in the penalty area holding his face, Schulenburg stood over the defender and pompously pointed in the opposite direction. Tempers flared as Bremner tried to take the kick quickly from the wrong place and a small scuffle broke out as the official momentarily lost control. As if to reassert his authority, the referee ordered the Zaire wall back further than the obligatory ten yards to the point that they were almost upon their own goal-line. Yet chaos still reigned and in a portent of what was to come later in the tournament, several Zaire players broke from the wall anticipating the lay off, until Ndaye was finally threatened with a caution. When the free-kick was eventually taken, it was something of an anticlimax with Kazadi blocking Lorimer's drive with a little help from his teammates.

Less than a minute later David Hay came even closer to opening the scoring. Again Joe Jordan was involved, this time rising to meet Dalglish's deep cross from the right before cushioning a header back to Hay on the edge of the Zaire box. The midfielder controlled the ball perfectly before unleashing a curling, left-footed volley that beat Kazadi's acrobatic dive but with Dalglish already celebrating a goal, the ball rebounded off the goalpost and fell kindly for Mwanza Mukombo, who put it behind for a corner.

After a brief interlude that saw Kidumu almost thread a pass through to Ndaye in the opposition penalty box, Zaire's resistance finally broke. A patient Scottish build up saw the ball eventually played out to McGrain on the left flank, who rolled it back to Hay. Jordan (who else?) rose highest to meet Hay's centre and headed the ball down for Peter Lorimer, who rocketed home an unstoppable volley past Kazadi, who was left rooted to the spot. It was a goal well worth the wait for those watching on television around the world and was greeted with delight by the 7,000 Scottish fans, whose ranks had been bolstered for the day by the crew of the *HMS Hampshire*.

Vidinić, who had spent most of the game so far chain smoking, looked anxious on the bench, concerned how his players would react to going behind. Rather than crumble, Zaire went looking for an equaliser and, having endured a barrage of high balls at the other end, it was their turn to put the Scotland defence under pressure. Mwepu, supporting the attack down the right, whipped in a dangerous cross to Kakoko at the back post, who surprisingly beat Holton in the air, but the winger was unable to get above the ball and direct his header. Kakoko then had another chance to draw Zaire level. Having skilfully controlled Kidumu's cross field ball on the edge of the Scottish penalty area, he skipped past Jardine with a turn of speed into the box and, having spotted Harvey out of position, attempted a curling shot but was unlucky to see the ball ricochet off Bremner. Replays suggested it struck the arm of the Scotland captain as he turned his back but it would have been a harsh call had the penalty been awarded.

Minutes later Zaire found themselves 2-0 down. Kidumu, snapping at the heels of Lorimer, caught the Leeds player. Bremner's free-kick, aimed at the penalty spot, was weighted perfectly for Jordan, who had escaped his marker and timed his run perfectly to find himself in acres of space as the Zaire defence stood motionless on the 18-yard line. His powerful downward header was on target but directed straight at Kazadi. The Zairean goalkeeper, expecting the referee's whistle to blow for offside, seemed to lose concentration momentarily and fluffed his save, allowing the ball to escape his grasp and trickle over the line. It was a bad mistake and Denis Law may well have been in an offside position when the kick was taken but Scotland did not care. They smelt blood and believed Zaire were now there for the taking.

Billy Bremner certainly felt the game was over and began show-boating as early as the 35th minute, showing off his party tricks when passing the ball to Lorimer, who whipped in yet another cross for their Leeds teammate Jordan, who this time headed the ball harmlessly over the bar. The Scotland captain's antics almost landed his team in trouble shortly afterwards when he miscontrolled the ball and was caught in possession by Ndaye, who only had Blackley to beat for a clear run on goal. Demonstrating his years of experience, Bremner went to ground and the referee gave the midfielder the benefit of the doubt, to the obvious dissatisfaction of the many neutrals and the small pocket of Zaire supporters in the stands. From the resulting free-kick Scotland moved the ball forwards and won a corner, which was taken short to Lorimer who tried to catch Kazadi napping at his near post. However the Zaire goalkeeper, having clearly put his earlier error to one side, made a fine save. The rebound was cleared but fell kindly to Bremner who was caught by Kidumu. The Zaire skipper picked up a booking for his trouble and, as Clive Leatherdale recalls in his book *Scotland's Quest for the World Cup*, "became the latest in a growing list of players cautioned for their dislike of the Scottish captain".

Having been out-muscled for much of the game, Zaire were beginning to bite back - they were now winning tackles and, more importantly, headers. This new found aggression saw the combative reputation of Jim Holton, Scotland's towering centre half, take a dent when he was sent crashing to the floor when going shoulder-to-shoulder with the diminutive Ndaye Mulamba, who was only 5ft 7in. Perhaps this incident was fresh in the mind of referee Schulenburg when he penalised Lobilo seconds later at the other end of the field, who was adjudged to have fouled Joe Jordan while coming away with the ball. Once again the decision was met by jeers as the official indicated the Zaire player had nudged Jordan, completely ignoring the Scottish striker's ugly attempt to barge his opponent off of the ball.

Undeterred, the Leopards continued to try and find a way back into the game and out of nowhere almost pulled a goal back via an uncharacteristic "route one" attack. Having been awarded a free-kick for offside, Kazadi launched the ball into the Scotland half and Mayanga rose highest to beat McGrain to the ball. Blackley seemed to have the flick-on header covered but the defender misjudged the bounce, allowing the sprightly Ndaye to take advantage of the error. As the striker raced into the box, Holton moved across to cover and with the Scottish defence all at sea, Kidumu burst into the box unmarked. Ndaye played an inch perfect pass to his captain but the midfielder's first touch was heavy and Harvey was able to smother Kidumu's attempt to poke the ball under him.

As Zaire rued the missed opportunity at one end of the pitch, Law almost punished them at the other. The striker peeled away from his marker and should have made it 3-0 but with only Kazadi to beat headed the ball over the bar. Scotland attacked again, Dalglish playing a first time pass through to Jordan following a mistake by the otherwise impressive Lobilo but the alert Kazadi raced from his line and slid in to deny the striker, who took exception to the goalkeeper's challenge. Kazidi remonstrated with Jordan in return, lifting his shorts to complain about the stud marks left by the player, and the situation threatened to boil over when the Scottish forward got into an altercation with the keeper's brother, Bwanga. Denis Law, acting as peacemaker, quickly restored order before the referee had words with Jordan, who escaped a booking for deliberate handball a minute later after punching a Lorimer cross towards goal.

Both sides enjoyed glimpses of goal as the half-time whistle approached. Kakoko and Mana linked up nicely to put the Scottish defenders under pressure only for Mana to misread the final pass. Ndaye tried to pick out Kakoko but Harvey, sensing the danger, came off his line quickly to intercept the deep cross. At the other end, Law was unable to direct his header as he stretched to connect with a Lorimer cross then snapped at his shot when played in by Jordan and fired the ball into the arms of Kazadi, who had no trouble dealing with the striker's effort.

It was the last piece of drama of an eventful and open half. Despite the scoreline, the Leopards had made a favourable first impression with their approach to the game yet general opinion was that Scotland would launch an all-out assault in the second period. Jock Stein, who had enjoyed a good view of the first forty-five minutes from the commentator's gantry where he was working as a pundit with the BBC, was certainly optimistic . 'The team have run the legs off the Zaire team,' he argued. 'All they can do is add to their own goal tally.' However, the future Scotland boss caveated his comments by offering a cautious 'if they're careful' at the end of his interview with David Coleman.

As the players emerged from the tunnel, to the accompaniment of traditional German oompah music, Zaire looked the more lively of the two sides. After the teams traded a couple of high balls into the box, it was Scotland that had the first chance of the half; Dalglish, capitalising on a mistake by Mana, threaded a through ball to Law, who raced into the Zaire penalty area as Kazadi rushed from his goal. The striker tried to play a return pass through to Dalglish, who would have had a simple tap-in, but the goalkeeper blocked Law's attempt and safely gathered the ball before the whistle went for a belated offside. Again the Scots attacked and again Kazadi denied them, beating Jordan to the ball as Lorimer got to the byline and whipped in a cross. Bremner tried a long range shot but could only watch as his effort flew wide of the Zaire goal before Lorimer saw one of his thunderbolts bravely charged down by Lobilo. When Law attempted a spectacular overhead kick, however, it appeared to be an attempt borne out of desperation rather than conviction.

For all their possession, Scotland were failing to create anything meaningful. The tactic of peppering the penalty area with high balls that had served them so handsomely in the first half was faltering, with Law unable to feed off Jordan when they did manage to find the head of the big centre forward. The latter was growing increasingly frustrated, not only by the poor service he was receiving but also by the presence of Lobilo, who, under instruction from Vidinić, was sticking to the centre forward like glue. Jordan's patience finally snapped after he was upended by the Zairean centre-half in the fifty-fourth minute. Clearly unhappy with the attention he was receiving from his opponents, the striker made his feelings known as he walked away, first clashing with Mwepu before petulantly lashing out at the innocent Kilasu on the edge of the penalty area, catching him as he ran past the midfielder. Yet despite having a perfectly good view of the incident, referee Schulenburg decided to keep his cards in his pocket, ignoring the pointed protests of Kidumu, and merely awarded a free-kick.

Feathers suitably ruffled, Zaire went on the offensive. Mana had a shot charged down following a slick, twelve-pass move involving nine different players that cut open the Scottish formation with ease. Kidumu gave Harvey a taste of the kind of treatment Kazadi had suffered in the first half when he went in hard on the Scottish goalkeeper, challenging for a superbly flighted cross from Mayanga following another quick break. Picking up the ball on the edge of the centre circle, the winger then showed the world why he was nicknamed *The Brazilian* as he ran at the Scottish defence and unleashed a fierce left-footed drive from twenty-yards out that stung the palms of Harvey.

Scotland were struggling to cope with the lithe movement and fluidity of Zaire's one-touch football but were granted a respite and the chance to regroup when the floodlights failed after the resulting corner kick was taken, plunging the stadium into darkness. It was a remarkable moment in the history of the competition, leaving both the players and the officials dumbfounded as a swarm of photographers invaded the pitch and buzzed around them, taking full advantage of the break in play to try and get the perfect snap for the morning papers. As the referee sought clarification on how to proceed, the Scottish fans sang 'We cannae see Zaire' while the track-suited Vidinić, cigarette in hand, gesticulated wildly on the touchline, optimistically trying to get the game abandoned. Up in the commentators' box, ITV's Hugh Johns asked Sir Alf Ramsey what he thought the problem may be. 'I am not an electrician' came the clipped reply from the former England manager.

After four minutes, with the lights still not on full power, the game resumed. The unscheduled stoppage had failed to dampen Zaire's attacking intent as Bwanga raced into the Scotland penalty area from deep and unleashed a speculative effort that was always rising. The Scots, for their part, were struggling to regain a foothold in the game and when Bremner passed the ball back to his goalkeeper from all of thirty-five yards, it prompted yet another chorus of boos and whistles. The African champions were enjoying their first prolonged period of possession in the match but their intricate one-touch passing movements repeatedly broke down in the final third of the pitch, usually due to the weight of numbers in the Scottish defence.

Almost against the run of play Lorimer let fly with another powerful shot as he latched onto a Hay cross at the far post. Kazadi, having put his glaring error of the first half behind him, pulled off a breathtaking save, racing across his goal then quickly diving to his right to block the ball but another late whistle, this time adjudging Law offside when the cross came in, sadly ruined the aesthetic of the moment.

Back came Zaire. Kakoko, driving down the left, played a one-two with Mayanga but the return pass was over-hit allowing Harvey to beat the winger to the ball as he raced towards goal. Kakoko and Ndaye linked up, again on the left, to create space for Mayanga who took a touch and tried his luck once more from 20-yards only for Holton to get his body in the way. It proved to be the player's final contribution, with Vidinić opting to replace him with the fresh legs of centre forward Kembo Uba Kembo.

The substitution seemed to unsettle Zaire, allowing Scotland the opportunity to assert themselves once more. Holton headed a corner straight into the arms of a grateful Kazadi before Jordan spurned a golden opportunity to increase his side's lead. Lorimer, in full flight down the right flank, beat Mukombo, who had earlier felt the full force of Denis Law's boot when the striker had attempted his second bicycle kick of the game, and whipped in a low cross. Kazadi could only parry the ball, which fell invitingly to the Scottish forward eight yards out. To the goalkeeper's relief, Jordan smashed his shot past the upright.

Zaire responded through the unlikely figure of Mwepu. A burst of pace saw the defender cut in from the right flank, skip past Danny McGrain then hurdle the sliding lunge of Blackley before trying to beat Harvey from outside the box. His shot lacked power and failed to trouble the goalkeeper but it served as a reminder to Ormond's team that the game was far from over. Jolted out of any complacency, it was now Scotland's turn to threaten the scoreboard, this time through Dalglish on the left. His cross was cleared by Bwanga but it fell to Lorimer who hit a powerful volley from the edge of the area only to see his shot superbly tipped onto the bar by Kazadi. As Mwepu booted the ball into touch, the Scottish winger held his head in his hands in disbelief.

As the game became stretched in the humid heat of the Dortmund night, both sides made a substitution. The industrious Kidumu was replaced in midfield by Kibonge Mafu for Zaire while Scotland boss Willy Ormond opted to take off Dalglish in favour of winger Tommy Hutchison. It was Hutchison who made the first telling contribution of the two newcomers, chipping the ball through to Law, who initially miscontrolled the pass before recovering sufficiently to dig the ball out from under his feet and get a shot away, only to see Kazadi dive across his goalmouth to turn the ball behind for a corner. Law was to be denied one final time by the Zaire goalkeeper in the next Scottish attack. As the ball broke free from a Bremner free-kick, Bwanga hesitated and the alert Kazadi leapt at the feet of the on-rushing striker to remove the threat, receiving a pat on the back from the former Ballon D'Or winner for his efforts.

Declining to rest on his laurels, Kazadi immediately initiated a counterattack, finding the fresh-legged Kibonge with a long throw. The midfielder trapped the ball, turned and charged through the ragged Scottish midfield with ease, towards Harvey's goal. As McGrain's attempt to stay with the pace withered, Kibonge found Kembo on the right flank, who hit a first-time cross into the area. Jardine hacked clear under pressure from Kibonge, who had continued his run into the box, but merely returned the ball to Kembo on the wing. This time the forward attacked the byline, beating Blackley in the process, and floated the ball to the far post. Kakoko, stretching with all his might, rose to meet it but the cross was a fraction too high.

Kibonge's introduction had provided Zaire with an outlet in the middle of the park and he was the catalyst once more when Ndaye came close to pulling a goal back a minute later. Picking the ball up in his own half, he was allowed to advance unchallenged before spraying the ball wide to Kilasu. He attempted a one-two with Kakoko but although the winger lost control it ran kindly for Kibonge, who burst into the Scotland box and cut the ball back to Ndaye. With Harvey's goal at his mercy, the striker, who had scored nine goals in the African Cup of Nations earlier in the year, scuffed his shot wide of the goalkeeper's right post.

Alarm bells were now ringing for Scotland, who were rapidly tiring as the match wore on. Their defence was struggling with the speed and movement of Zaire as they used their intricate close control to attack from deep. Billy Bremner in particular was acutely aware of the threat posed and under the direction of their captain, the Scots slowed the game down, preferring to concentrate on preserving their lead rather than extending it. Not that they looked like adding to their goal tally. Law had run out of steam and Lobilo now had the measure of Jordan, having grown in stature as the game progressed. The only real threat Scotland possessed was the ferocious shooting of Lorimer but even he was struggling to find the space afforded to him in the first half.

Spurred on by the crowd, Zaire were now in the ascendancy. Bwanga, momentarily unshackled from his defensive duties, powered down the left wing and hit a low cross into the box. Holton's scrappy clearance looped up into the air and Ndaye beat the static Lorimer to head the ball back into the danger area. It fell for Kibonge but as the midfielder went to play the ball, he was halted in his tracks by the flying boot of Blackley, his studs leaving their mark on the chest of the Zairean. It was a clear penalty but as Kibonge writhed on the floor in agony, Schulenburg awarded a free-kick for dangerous play, uninterested in the protests of Zaire. 'The referee closed his eyes' was the forthright view of Mayanga after the match while the BBC's David Coleman described it as 'an interesting decision'.

While Kilasu helped the wounded Kibonge to his feet, the German official pushed the Scottish wall back the obligatory ten yards until the entire team was encamped in David Harvey's six-yard box. Somehow Ndaye found a way through the wall, forcing the Scotland goalkeeper, who saw the shot late, to tip the ball over the bar. The cameras cut to the forlorn face of Vidinić in the dugout, who was left thinking of what might have been.

As the game entered stoppage time Bwanga charged through the Scottish ranks for a second time from deep within his own half. Effortlessly skipping past a half-hearted challenge from Bremner, the defender raised a cheer from the crowd when he sold Holton a dummy, leaving his opposite number flat on his backside, before Blackley brought his run to an unceremonious end. Suitably chastened, the Scotland captain opted to kill the game dead once his side had reclaimed possession. Arrogantly juggling the ball as he brought it out of defence, he incurred the wrath of all but the Scottish fans inside the stadium, as derision poured from the stands with each negative pass as his side looked for the final whistle. Such was the animosity towards Bremner that when Kembo robbed him, the crowd erupted in delight. 'Scotland have not won themselves many friends in the second half,' observed Coleman dryly in his commentary.

The earlier delay due to floodlight failure meant Scotland would have to huff and puff for a bit longer. Jordan had a brief sight of goal before it was extinguished by Bwanga. Jardine was forced to head the ball behind for a corner to deny Kakoko after an excellent ball from Kibonge, who had impressed since his introduction. With the chant of "Zaire! Zaire!" accompanying their every move, Vidinić's men pressed for one final attack. Kakoko, breaking in from the left, rode the challenges of the Scottish defence before finding Kilasu, who took a touch and let fly from twenty yards before Hutchison could close him down only to see the ball fly over the bar and into the crowd.

As the full time whistle blew, Scotland's celebrations were muted, despite recording their first ever World Cup win, and there was a marked difference in the reaction of the two coaches. As Vidinić stood and applauded his side's efforts, Ormond, who had so readily dismissed the opposition, slipped away down the tunnel. Having expected Zaire to tire, maybe even collapse under the pressure of the aerial threat, they had done neither and it was Ormond's side that were the more grateful to hear the referee's whistle. Now the autopsies would begin in a very public manner in front of the assembled press waiting for him to arrive.

To his credit, the Scotland manager conceded he had been wrong about the African opposition. 'I must admit it was something different to what I expected,' he told journalists at the post-match press conference. 'I am surprised that Zaire were able to finish the game so strongly, whereas my players were tired and played possession football for the last fifteen minutes but,' he added, 'I don't think you can disagree with our victory.' Jim Holton was slightly more honest in his appraisal of the game. 'Let's face it, we underestimated them,'

Zaire goalkeeper Kazadi Mwamba goes through the pain barrier to deny Scotland's Denis Law a World Cup goal.

he admitted. 'For fifteen minutes I wondered what the hell was going on, where had this lot come from, playing stuff like that'. Meanwhile Vidinić was magnanimous in defeat. 'Scotland were very good and I have no objections to their victory,' he declared, singling out Peter Lorimer as the man of the match. 'But don't they play rough, hard football?'

Zaire may have been unable to conjure up the giant killing they had been hoping for but they had not disgraced themselves. They had, for the time being at least, silenced those that had expressed doubts about their right to play in the finals with their buccaneering performance, a view shared by none other than Pelé, who paid a morale-boosting visit to the Leopards after the game to congratulate the team on their efforts. 'The mood in the dressing room was fairly upbeat', remembered Mwepu fondly. 'We felt we'd acquitted ourselves quite well'. The world's press agreed. 'Zaire were an eye-opener' wrote Geoffrey Green in *The Times*. 'Gay, gallant and mischievous, they were defiant to the end.' *The Guardian's* David Lacey admired the brisk one-touch movement of Mayanga, Kakoko and the 'sharp-eyed' Ndaye up front, concluding that the Leopards had 'showed the potential that lies in the football of black Africa' while *France Football* succinctly described Zaire as 'a pure breath of fresh air'.

The differing styles of the teams brought additional comment, with Scotland criticised for their over-reliance on high balls into the box. 'While Scotland played it in the air,' observed Green in his match report, 'Zaire were always stroking the ball along the ground. In ball control and speed they lacked nothing.' Authors Allen Wade and Colin Murphy concurred with *The Times* journalist but were more forthright in their analysis of the match, which formed part of their report on the 1974 World Cup for the Football Association. They praised the technique displayed as 'far superior in both range and quality' than that of Scotland's and compared Zaire's passing style favourably to Brazil. 'Their techniques were entirely natural and extremely effective,' the report declared. 'They had players who could produce instant, very high quality passing with surprise and over an impressive range. In the air, however, Scotland were superior.'

It was a tactic that had clearly formed the basis of Ormond's game plan and perhaps led to an over-reliance on pumping balls up to Joe Jordan in the second half. 'Zaire surprised us,' admitted Bremner, who had deliberately restrained the Scottish attack in response to the opposition threat. 'They played better than we ever believed possible but the manager told us the way to beat them, with those high balls'. Reflecting on the game in later years, winger Mayanga Maku was in agreement. 'We were weak in aerial duels' he conceded, 'and that, basically, was the difference.' One of Scotland's reserves, defender Willie Donachie, who watched the game with the rest of the non-playing squad members from the stands, offered a different perspective and felt their real weakness lay elsewhere: 'Zaire were very athletic and skilful but lacked composure in the final third of the pitch.' It was a perceptive appraisal of the match as a whole. Although Vidinić's team were initially all at sea trying to deal with Joe Jordan, the Scottish striker had little joy in the second period as the Zaire defence adapted to Scotland's style of play, with Lobilo and Bwanga in particular rising to the challenge as the game matured. Going forwards, however, Zaire were guilty of wasting several opportunities, with promising attacks breaking down due to balls being played too early or the wrong decisions being taken whenever they got sight of goal. With a little more experience and level-headedness, they may have scored the goal they were desperate for.

Amid all the positivity, there was one sour note to the occasion. Complaints of racial abuse were made against Bremner after the game. The midfielder, who had long been a divisive figure within

Zaire skipper Kidumu tussles with Billy Bremner during the team's opening group game in Dortmund. The Scotland captain came in for criticism after the match for racially abusing his opponents.

British football, had angered several of the Zaire team with his behaviour both on and off the ball, targeting Ndaye Mulamba in particular. 'The captain shouted "Nigger, hey nigger" at me a couple of times during the match' recalled the striker. 'He spat at me too, and he spat in Mana's face. Scotland's number four was a wild animal.'

'He was shouting "Go back to Africa, darkie",' confirmed Mwepu. 'It was terrible, and the referee did nothing to stop it.' Vidinić would later take umbrage with the standard of refereeing during the game but Bremner's actions, coupled with Jordan's heavy-handed treatment of Kazadi, would not be forgotten by Zaire and the repercussions would be felt later in the tournament.

As the Leopards boarded the team bus for the journey back to Ascheberg morale was high. They had passed their first test, not quite with flying colours but they had shown the world they could at least compete. Despite the defeat, the coach remained optimistic, believing the best was yet to come. 'We will learn from each game,' Vidinić told reporters before dangerously tempting fate. 'I expect us to fare better against Yugoslavia.'

11. All the President's Men

THE WORLD CUP has a habit of pairing football managers against the country of their birth. In 1954 Switzerland's Karl Rappen saw his team knocked out by his native Austria in the quarter-finals while compatriot Ernst Happel engineered a crushing 5-1 victory over *Das Team* as Netherlands head coach on their way to the final in 1978. World Cup winner Jack Charlton, who had unsuccessfully applied for the England job earlier in his career, earned a draw against Bobby Robson's side at Italia '90 with the Republic of Ireland, yet got off lightly compared to Sven Goran Eriksson in terms of the reaction back home. The British tabloids had a field day when England were drawn in the same group as Sweden for the 2002 tournament, going to great lengths speculating on whether the team's Swedish coach would sing both national anthems. Yugoslav Blagoje Vidinić had no such issues with the Zaire press when his Leopards were drawn against the country of his birth but there was no denying there was an element of romance about the fixture. Could the Olympic Gold medal winner pull off an upset and effectively end the hopes of the country with whom he had won eight caps?

Despite their previous World Cup pedigree there was no real reason for Zaire to fear Yugoslavia. Although their playing style was more refined and less physical than their British counterparts, they were roughly on par with Scotland in terms of strength, with many observers unable to separate the teams prior to the competition. The Yugoslavs were a team very much in transition, however, and the squad contained just four survivors from the side that had shocked World Cup holders England to reach the final of the 1968 European Championship. They had ridden their luck during qualification too. Grouped together with Spain and Greece, Miljan Miljanić's men were on the verge of being eliminated on goal difference before striker Stanislav Karasi fired home from 12-yards in the 90th minute of their final qualifying game against the Greeks in Athens. A 1-0 win in a play-off match against Spain secured their place in West Germany but their performances ahead of the tournament had been far from impressive.

Their hopes appeared to rest on their captain and star of the side Dragan Džajić, a player once described by Pelé as the most natural footballer he had ever seen. Predictably dubbed "The Magic Dragan" by the British press after he scored the winner against England, great things were expected from the winger but he had been struggling to recapture his form in time for the World Cup, having spent a year out of the game following his conscription into the Yugoslav army. Head coach Miljanić was not short of talent, however, and his side were far from a one-man team. They had an exceptional goalkeeper in Enver Marić while play-maker Branko Oblak looked impressive pulling the strings in midfield alongside the talented Jovan Aćimović. Indeed, all three had played their part in the goalless draw against Brazil in the opening game of the tournament. Marić produced saves to deny Valdomiro and Marinho Chagas and the legs of Brazilian keeper Émerson Leão stopped Aćimović from opening the scoring before Oblak almost won the game at the death with a header that hit the post. Odd flurries of attack aside, the match ultimately proved to be another disappointing World Cup curtain-raiser but the result left Group 2 delicately poised ahead of the second round of games.

Theoretically any of the four teams could qualify for the next phase, even if the odds on Zaire doing so were extremely long. Going into the finals, Vidinić believed his side had the potential to spring a surprise but he knew that they were never going to return home with the trophy. His ultimate aim was to win respect for African football rather than the competition. Encouraged by their display against the Scots, he felt his side had taken a big step towards achieving this goal despite the 2-0 defeat. Yet in order to prove once and for all that the Leopards, and in turn the continent as a whole, deserved their place in the tournament, his side would have to match, if not better that performance in their remaining two fixtures. In order to do so, Vidinić needed the players to be at the top of their game, both physically and mentally, but instead of rising to the occasion, Zaire imploded.

Money, or more accurately the lack of it, had been an increasingly disruptive issue within the Leopards' camp but now, on the eve of the match against Yugoslavia, it had reached a tipping point. The financial rewards promised to the team prior to their departure for Europe were so great that Mwepu Ilunga admitted that he and the rest of the squad had 'the erroneous belief that we would be returning from the World Cup as millionaires.' Yet to date, each player had received just 1000 Zairean zaires (approximately £600) for their efforts and the gap between the team's expectations and reality was only growing wider.

Before the Scotland game, Zaire's players found themselves in the unique situation of proudly owning a villa and a car but with no income to maintain either. President Mobutu had delivered on his commitment in that respect, even if the cars were supplied free of charge by Volkswagen, and provided a generous expense account as he had vowed to do when the team visited his luxurious Nsele residence.

However, the players were still technically amateurs who had been denied the opportunity to earn lucrative contracts abroad and relied on payments from the country's football federation to support their families. The prospect of additional financial bonuses was therefore not something to be taken lightly. Unfortunately for Vidinić's men, their continued success - and the adulation that accompanied it - had led to a certain amount of jealousy among a number of high ranking government officials and civil servants, who were only too keen to divert these funds into their own bank accounts.

There had been warning signs after their Nations Cup triumph in Egypt. The overseas holidays that had been promised by Mobutu failed to materialise. 'The money for that disappeared. Or I should say, disappeared as usual,' recalled Mayanga Maku wistfully, along with the expected bonuses that had been raised in celebration of the team's victory. Midfielder Mana Mambwene remembers the public collections, dubbed a 'Soccer Tax' by the state, which would have totalled a significant amount, but despite the seeming transparency of the effort, not a penny had found its way to the players. 'The state collected ten zaires from all over the country,' he explained. 'Unemployed or salaried worker, everybody contributed. Where was that money? Nobody knew.'

The collections continued in the run up to the World Cup for what was now known as the 'Leopards Fund' but it soon transpired that some of those involved were taking advantage of the situation. In Katanga, Ndaye Mulamba witnessed government officials knocking on doors in his local neighbourhood demanding donations for the national side. If no money was forthcoming, they helped themselves to any livestock, including hens, cows and goats, a situation that led to a feeling of ill-will towards the team, forcing the striker to speak out against the racketeering.

Against this backdrop of corruption and greed, Zaire sent one of the biggest delegations in World Cup history to West Germany. Aware that few, if any, of his subjects would be in attendance at the team's matches, Mobutu decided a demonstration of collective strength in front of the world's media was required and assembled a specially selected group of government aides, presidential bodyguards, military personnel and association officials in addition to the phalanx of witch doctors to accompany the squad. However, despite the flag waving and show of support on display inside the Westfalenstadion, watching football was not the prime objective for everyone who travelled, as aptly demonstrated by Sampassa Kaweta Milombe, Zaire's Minister of Sport, who had not even bothered to attend the match against the Scots. Qualifying for the finals had been a profitable exercise thus far. The prize money alone was worth $500,000 and the team were due to receive an additional 125,000DM (approximately £58,000) in travel and living expenses from FIFA for the duration of their stay. With sponsorship deals, appearance fees and other sundries further contributing to the pot, not to mention the aforementioned expense account, there seemed to be plenty of money to go around for everyone.

With the World Cup offering a once-in-a-lifetime opportunity to secure their futures, the players were understandably keen to receive their share, even if it meant continually pestering those in authority for an answer. After several promised deadlines were missed, it appeared as if their persistence had finally paid off when assurances were made that the long overdue bonuses for their African Cup of Nations victory together with their World Cup money would be paid ahead of the team's opening match. Yet the Fédération Zaïroise de Football Association, who were of the opinion that footballers were supposed to represent their country as a matter of pride rather than for money, seemed reluctant to make any sort of payment on the morning of the game but promised the players that the money was en route.

'We had been given this mentality that we should play for the love of the country,' confirmed Mayanga. 'It was Mobutu who put that mentality into us but we knew that money had been paid. Before the Scotland game, the authorities told us, "Go out and play and, even if you lose, and lose honourably, we'll give you your bonuses." We were disappointed with the score but everybody was saying we gave a good account of ourselves but we got nothing.'

As the team bus trundled along the autobahn back to Ascheberg with their police escort in tow, the topic of conversation quickly turned to the whereabouts of Zaire's esteemed Minister of Sports, who had not been seen by the squad since their arrival in Switzerland the month before and was believed to be in possession of their money. On learning that he had chosen to watch West Germany's opening game against Chile in Berlin rather than the Leopards, the players were beside themselves with anger. This led to a frank exchange of views with FEZAFA officials and despite being within earshot of several of Mobutu's advisors, many were vocal in their criticism of the minister and openly candid in their castigation. Vidinić, sympathetic to their frustrations and withholding his own doubts about the integrity of the politician, promised to speak to Sampassa Kaweta. Yet before the Yugoslav had the chance to call the minister, the squad were dealt a further blow; the expense account set up by Mobutu and from which the electrical shops of the town had profited so richly, was empty.

The first inkling something was awry came shortly after their arrival back at the Hotel Jagdschlösschen. Keen to celebrate their World Cup debut in the town's bars and clubs, a few of the players approached their coach to ask for permission to leave the premises. To their surprise, they received a curt reply from an increasingly haggard Vidinić. 'A few of us wanted to go out and sample the night life', recalled Mwepu. 'We asked if we could have some of our money but the answer was to forget it. "Stay in your rooms and behave like professionals," he told us. I couldn't believe what I was hearing, because I liked Vidinić. I thought he was a good coach and a good person. It was only when I saw Mobutu's people hovering around that I realised what was going on. His security service had pocketed the money. They sent us to our rooms and told us that we weren't in Germany to socialise.'

As it transpired, it was not only the president's security men that had acted dishonourably. The various suited hangers-on, flown in to reinforce Zaire's World Cup delegation, had also been buzzing around the players' expense fund like proverbial bees around a honey pot. The sizeable kitty provided by Mobutu, funded through the aforementioned Soccer Tax rather than his own bank account, had been bled dry. Clearly distracted and unsettled by this sudden turn of events, the players struggled to retain their focus and Vidinić knew he was fighting a losing battle. They wanted answers but no one in authority was prepared to provide them. The coach's revelation that he had been unable to locate Sampassa Kaweta, let alone speak to him, only riled his squad further.

Two days before the match against Yugoslavia an unlikely figure walked into the team hotel to pay a social visit, 'a Congolese expat who had been living in West Germany for 25 years,' remembers Kilasu Masamba. The visitor was keen to take advantage of the fortuitous opportunity afforded by the World Cup to converse with his compatriots and the players happily welcomed the distraction. Fluent in German, the team's new-found friend inadvertently set the cat among the pigeons when he began translating reports in the daily papers to entertain them, with one article in particular proving to be of great interest. 'He showed us a German newspaper where it said each player would get $25,000 for the first round,' revealed Kilasu. 'Compared with what we were promised, the players got angry and demanded to be paid.'

Just how truthful the piece was is a matter of conjecture. The international press had been obsessed with stories of the gifts bestowed upon the team after qualifying and had a habit of exaggerating when it came to what the Leopards were earning. The figure reported is certainly in line with what Mobutu had allegedly promised the team back in Zaire but then the president had a habit of telling people what they wanted to hear, only to renege at a later date. In comparison with other teams in the competition, it was extremely generous to say the least. Group rivals Scotland stood to earn a mere £7,500 as a team if they qualified from the group and would share £100,000 if they won the entire competition, although this was to be paid by a sponsor rather than the Scottish Football Association. The Italian and Dutch squads meanwhile could expect around £55,000 per head but only if they too lifted the trophy.

The article may have been prompted by the host nation's own monetary problems. The West German team almost curtailed their World Cup ambitions just days ahead of the tournament in a row over bonus payments that saw manager Helmut Schön at one point threaten to send all 22 of his players home (indeed, FIFA were informed that there may be some changes to the provisional squad that had already been submitted). True or not, the Zaire players certainly believed what they were told, to the point that Kilasu even picked out the $12,000 Mercedes he was going to buy with his share of the money from a car dealership in the town. He was not alone. 'We had already done our window shopping,' laughed Mana. 'Kabasu (Babo) had already put some things on hold!'

At the very least the story confirmed the rumours the players had heard about the size of the dividends on offer from FIFA, strengthening their resolve to seek the truth from delegation officials. For captain Kidumu Mantantu, an explanation was long overdue. 'We knew that every team received a big premium for qualifying - Half a million dollars. That was our money. We had been asking for it for days but our Minister of Sport was too busy walking around with his briefcase, arranging financial affairs with FIFA.'

As the players congregated in the hotel common room tempers flared amid an atmosphere of mistrust. "They are lying to us!" declared Kakoko Etepé. "It has been like this since our return from the African Cup of Nations. They take us for nothing. They have no respect for what we have done." Surprisingly, Sampassa Kaweta became the focal point for their anger rather than Mobutu. The squad knew the absent minister had watched Italy beat Haiti the night before in Munich, and the room erupted with applause when winger Kibonge Mafu, who would have political aspirations of his own in later life, asserted that he was using their bonus money to enjoy a European holiday. By contrast, Mobutu was perceived as an innocent party in the entire affair. "We have to notify the president," argued Ndaye Mulamba. "I am sure he is not aware of what is going on. He promised that we would receive this money as soon as we arrived in Germany and Mobutu does not lie."

In the corner of the room, observing from a large leather armchair, sat Blagoje Vidinić. He too was now convinced that Sampassa Kaweta had absconded with the team's bonuses, which also included payments due to the coaching staff, and surmised that the money had either already been spent or was sitting in a Swiss bank account, earning interest. He had been trying to reach the minister for three days in a conciliatory attempt to mollify his players ahead of their game against Yugoslavia but having failed to do so, now bore the appearance of a defeated man.

Midfielder Mavuba Mafuila was almost as downhearted as his

coach. Renowned for his good natured and humorous approach to life, he had become sullen and withdrawn since the Leopards arrival in Europe. He did not seem to share his teammates' appetite for the fight and cut a lone figure as the debate raged. Kidumu was equally unenthusiastic about the idea of contacting Mobutu but his concerns were of a more personal nature; as captain, he had been chosen to act as the squad's representative in any negotiations with the president. "He will agree to speak to you," asserted Kakoko in his new-found role of chief agitator. "Go to see his advisers. They are up there, in their room, smoking cigars in front of the television. Tell them we have a problem and we want to speak with the president. Because otherwise we will not play against Yugoslavia."

It was the first time the threat of a strike had been mentioned but it was a topic that would dominate conversations among the players over the coming 48 hours. In the meantime, Kidumu duly informed the president's advisors of the team's wish to talk to Mobutu. They did not have to wait long for a response. 'About half an hour later, a minister came to get the players,' remembers the captain, who, along with the rest of the squad, was told that the president would call them in five minutes. All twenty-two members of the squad gathered around the telephone expectantly, waiting for it to ring. When the call finally came through, the trembling hands of Kidumu picked up the receiver. 'As captain, I had to answer the telephone. "Hello Mr. President. I present to you all my respects. Thank you for being so kind as to call…" But the president was angry. Pissed off! A strike? He would sit in front of the television, he told me, to see whether or not we were on the pitch.'

Although the call lasted several minutes, it was very much a one-sided conversation. With no speaker on the phone, the tense silence in the room was only punctuated by the respectful replies offered by Kidumu. When the captain finally replaced the receiver, his teammates could contain themselves no longer and a cacophony of voices erupted, with everyone wanting to know what was said. It appeared to be good news.

Despite his initial anger at the players' threat, Mobutu assured Kidumu that he had spoken to Sampassa Kaweta, confirming that the minister was in Munich, where he had been attending a number of meetings on behalf of Zaire. State business would prevent him from attending the match against Yugoslavia so the president had instructed one of his advisers to leave the hotel that evening and fly to the Bavarian capital to collect the team's promised bonuses, not only for the World Cup but also for the African Cup of Nations victory. As if to underline his promise, Mobutu concluded the conversation by explaining that his advisor would travel to Gelsenkirchen on Tuesday morning to personally hand over the money on his behalf before kick-off. But before Kidumu could finish reciting his telephone call, the bubble of optimism was pricked by Mavuba. "I do not believe it," he told his teammates, who were still digesting the news. "These are lies. He said that to calm us down. We will never see the colour of his money. If we do not have these bonuses on Tuesday morning, I will not play."

"If Mobutu was lying," countered Ndaye, "He wouldn't have bothered to call. You have to trust the president."

"You are naive" retorted Mavuba as the atmosphere threatened to boil over. "Here in Europe, people believe in Santa Claus and you are like them. You believe in Papa Mobutu but Santa never brought a gift to anyone and neither will Mobutu."

Mavuba's cynicism was as powerful as it was unexpected but his forthright view on the situation resonated with other members of the squad.

Could they really trust the president?

With Kazadi Mwamba and Kembo Uba Kembo acting as shop stewards, the players retreated to the goalkeeper's room after dinner to discuss their next move. The meeting did not go smoothly. 'It was total chaos,' remembers Mayanga. 'Certain players were upset and we started arguing. It was almost midnight, we should have been in bed but we were awake, discussing it all.' The main topic of conversation was Kakoko's suggestion of boycotting the game but although many of the senior players were in favour of such a move, the majority were against it, leading to an impasse. 'I think that eight of the players, including Kazadi, voted against playing,' explained Mwepu Ilunga. 'But the rest felt they'd be betraying their country if they decided not to turn out. The atmosphere was very tense.'

With the division threatening to create irreparable fissures within the squad, they collectively agreed that nothing constructive could be done that evening. Despite Mavuba's reservations, they would give their President and the county's Minister of Sport the benefit of any doubt, for the time being at least. With Mobutu's advisor due to leave for the airport as promised the following morning, all talk of a boycott was put to one side but it had been a tiring evening. 'We went to bed around 2 or 3 in the morning,' admitted Bwanga Tshimen. 'It was not the best way to prepare for this game'.

On the morning of the match, the cloud that had hung over the team since the final whistle blew against Scotland had seemingly lifted. There was a positive vibe in the air as the players assembled in the hotel lobby ready for their departure to the Parkstadion in Gelsenkirchen. Even Mavuba Mafuila's jocular disposition had returned. Complimentary reports in the international newspapers supplied to them by a Zairean journalist, praising their performance in the opening game, heightened their mood further. *France Football* had even gone so far as to make them favourites for the game against Yugoslavia but there was one person whose mood was at odds with the rest of the delegation.

Blagoje Vidinić was not a happy man. The relationship between the coach and his employers had slowly deteriorated since the team's arrival in Europe, with the Yugoslav becoming increasingly frustrated by the continued interference from delegation officials and even the president himself. Having upset Mobutu by refusing to have anything to do with the various witch doctors that had travelled with the team, Vidinić further alienated himself by banning Sampassa and his associates from the players' dressing room. In retaliation, the Minister of Sport made it abundantly clear who he felt was to blame for the Scotland defeat, insisting that the Leopards would have won the game if Vidinić had not instructed his team to play a more European style of football. It was a view shared by the President of AS Vita Club and parliamentarian Simon Opango Ibombo Malamu Ma Tongo, who vented his frustrations to Swiss newspaper *L'Express* in the aftermath of the opening game.

'We don't understand why Vidinić had advocated such a defensive tactic against Scotland,' he moaned. 'Usually, the Zaireans shoot fifty times on goal, but in Dortmund, the shots were rare. I came to encourage my players. I don't get involved in tactics. Vidinić has full powers, he takes responsibility. But, believe me, I'm sure that my club, which won the African Cup of Champions, would have done better in front of the Scots.'

The Zairean press, still possessing unrealistic expectations about their team's chances in the competition, adopted the same narrative,

very likely at the behest of Mobutu himself, and accused the coach
of conspiring with his countrymen to plot the Leopards' downfall at
the World Cup.

Considering Vidinić's contribution to Zaire football, such claims
would appear farcical, more so after allegations of treachery were
levelled at the coach in the Yugoslav media, but the campaign
against him was gathering momentum within the delegation.
Attempts by Mavuba to humour him as the team bus made its way to
Gelsenkirchen were met with a look of contempt and stony silence.
The players surmised that his disposition could be attributed to pre-
match stress but when the party finally arrived at the stadium, Vidinić
was unceremoniously whisked away by government officials as the
team made their way to the dressing room.

A short while later a representative from the Ministry of Sport
entered the changing room and called for the players' attention. To
their astonishment, the official began reading out a revised starting
line-up for the game and informed them of a number of tactical
changes that contradicted the instructions they had received from
their coach the previous day on the training ground at Seppenrade.
To his dismay, Mayanga Maku was dropped to the bench, despite
his impressive performance for the Leopards in the opening game,
along with Kibonge Mafu, who had been due to start following his
cameo against the Scots. The winger's replacement was Kembo Uba
Kembo, one of the players government officials had lobbied for on
the eve of the Scotland match. Still not match fit, Kembo would start
the game with a heavily strapped knee to support his injury in a now
otherwise unchanged team from the one that kicked off in Dortmund.

The ad-hoc team-talk was met with stunned silence by the
bemused audience of players and coaching staff. Having been
denied a place in the starting line-up, Kibonge was the first to speak,
questioning not only the official's authority to make such widespread
changes but also the absence of the team's manager. The response
would leave the room shell-shocked.

'The official looked a little embarrassed as he cleared his throat,'
Ndaye Mulamba noted. 'Then he spoke to us: "We have good reason
to believe that Blagoje Vidinić was approached by the Yugoslav
authorities and that he gave them information about our playing
tactics. Therefore, we decided to isolate him until the start of the
game and make some changes."'

The players looked at each other in disbelief. The man who had engineered their progression to the finals and was the architect of their success in Africa would play no meaningful part in the match. Any instructions from the coach were to be ignored and all tactical advice dismissed. Mobutu's advisors were now in charge of all team matters. But for the serious nature of the situation, the team could be forgiven for thinking that they were the butt of a very poor joke.

'Vidinić loved the Congo, he called it his second homeland,' asserted Kilasu in defence of his coach. 'There was no reason why he should betray the country.'

Mavuba, visibly shaken by the news, lambasted the official and questioned the reasoning behind the decision. Any hopes he had of support from his teammates were quickly dashed when he argued that Vidinić, like the rest of the squad, had been performing despite not being paid. Thoughts immediately turned to the missing bonuses with Kibonge quick to address the elephant in the room and reminded the ministry representative that the president had promised payment prior to the game. The official shuffled uncomfortably, looked at his shoes then confessed the money was not at the stadium. Although the bonuses had been recovered, Mobutu's advisor had been recalled to Zaire on urgent business by the president and had left that morning with the FIFA bounty. Payment would now be made when the squad returned home, with the added incentive of an increase should they beat Yugoslavia.

Instructing his incredulous audience to get changed and warm up, the official slipped out of the door before anyone could respond. In his wake, the room filled with animosity and indignation. Sitting in a Brussels bar some 40 years later, team captain Kidumu Mantantu painted a vivid picture of the scene. 'The players were angry. All of them. Me too. Furious. If the money went to Zaire, we would never see it again. If it had, we wouldn't be playing against Yugoslavia. Never before had a team forfeited a World Cup match. Well then, we would be the first.'

Goalkeeper Kazadi Mwamba was adamant that he did not want to take part in the match and, climbing on one of the dressing room benches, urged his teammates to take a stand, delivering a speech that was met with thunderous applause on its conclusion: "This time I think we really have to react. Since we are not getting paid, we are not going to play. I do not keep the goals of Zaire for zero dollars.

They will just have to fend for themselves and put Sampassa Kaweta in goal, the witch doctors in defence, the officials of the Ministry of Sports in midfield and the advisors of the president in attack. Because all these guys, they are the ones who have filled their pockets during this World Cup while we have nothing at all."

The Leopards were now unanimous in their decision. They would not take to the field to face Yugoslavia and duly informed their de facto management team of their decision. Concerned by the unfolding events within the Zaire camp, FIFA officials were hastily dispatched to resolve the crisis but on arrival found a sparsely populated changing room. What followed was a farcical game of hide and seek, with some of the players taking refuge in various corners of the stadium, refusing to talk. Reserve goalkeeper Tubilandu Ndimbi, who would go on to play a major role in the forthcoming match, remembers the ensuing chaos prior to kick-off and the increasing desperation of the emissaries as they tried to get the players to reverse their decision. 'At first, there were only nine players. We had to make radio calls to get the others to come back. The World Cup organisers wouldn't let a team refuse to play because of the money problems. They begged us to play because they feared the image of the Cup would be tarnished. To calm us down, the organisers paid us each 3000 Deutschmarks, which I think was about five or six hundred dollars.'

Yet it was not the last minute payment that convinced the players to take to the pitch. With kick-off looming, Blagoje Vidinić entered the dressing room. As he slowly closed the door behind him, the Leopards fell silent, confused by the sudden return of their coach and shocked by his appearance. He looked haggard and browbeaten as he stood before his team. The enthusiasm he typically demonstrated had been replaced by something altogether more serious, which was confirmed by the tone of his voice as he began to address them. 'I have just spoken to Mobutu on the telephone. He is mad with rage. If you do not play this game, you are going to face serious problems. Mobutu was clear. If you do not take to the field, it is not worth returning to Kinshasa because neither you nor I will find our wives, children or families there.'

They knew their coach was not bluffing. It was a clear threat from a dictator who thought nothing of hanging his political opponents if such action was warranted. Worried by the potential presidential repercussions and with a little money finally in their pockets, the team reluctantly agreed to play. 'The president was angry and we were afraid of the sanctions,' Kidumu admitted. 'Not for ourselves but for our families in Zaire.' The strike was over but an element of defiance still existed among some of the team, including Kibonge, Kakoko and Kazadi. The bitterness and ill-feeling would remain, long after the final whistle blew. They had been robbed not only of their bonuses, but also of the opportunities that came with such a windfall.

'Our coach told us whoever's name was on the roster for the World Cup, their life was assured,' recalled Bwanga ruefully. 'We went with our heads full of plans. We were banking on that money.'

The 1974 Zaire World Cup squad pose for the cameras on their arrival in West Germany.

Tshinabu Wa Munda poses for a photograph with a couple of autograph hunters outside the team's hotel in Ascheberg. Third choice goalkeeper Kalambay Otepa is the player loitering in the background.

Friend or Foe: Sir Stanley Rous and João Havelange indulge in small talk FIFA's annual congress where the Englishman found himself outflanked by Brazilian's election campaign.

Mayanga Maku on the ball during the team's final warm-up game against German amateurs VfB Oldenburg, which saw the Leopards stroll to a comfortable 5-2 victory.

Leopard in flight: Ndaye Mulamba runs at the Scottish defensive line during Zaire's opening game at the World Cup.

Midfielder Mana Mamuwene receives a thumbs up from Scotland's Denis Law after the final whistle.

Yugoslavia's Dragan Džajić and Zaire's Kidumu Mantantu perform the traditional pre-match rituals under the watchful gaze of referee Omar Delgado Gómez.

The Leopards' trauma summed up in a single picture. Goalkeeper Tubilandi Ndimbi punches the floor after conceding another goal against Yugoslavia.

The game of their lives: the Leopards line-up for the national anthems ahead of their final game against the reigning world champions knowing a heavy defeat would have serious consequences.

Rivelino manages to get his shot away despite the best efforts of defender Lobilo Boba.

Like it or not, the free-kick incident against Brazil was the moment that made Zaire famous. As Mwpeu Ilunga charged from the wall before launching the ball downfield there was an audible gasp and then amusement from the crowd and consternation from opposition players. John Motson on BBC commentary called the action 'ignorant' while the player himself has claimed it was a protest against Mobutu. Whichever is true, that moment has lingered longer in the public imagination than everything else at the 1974 tournament.

Defenders Mwepu Ilunga and Lobilo Boba team up to deny Brazil's Edu in their final group game clash.

Busman's holiday: Each competing nation was provided with transport by Mercedes-Benz. There is no truth in the rumour that the Zaire team attempted to drive their coach back home to Kinshasa.

...rn of the Leopards: Bwanga Tshimen, Mayganga Maku and Kibonge Mafu ...ose for photos alongside Mayor of Gelsenkirchen Karin Welge, Schalke 04 ...rts Director Peter Knäbel and Schalke's record scorer Klaus Fischer during a visit to the Parkstadion in February, 2022

The Leopards'
very own
Mr Football,
Nicodème
Kabamba,
captain of
the victorious
1968 AFCON
winning side
and assistant
coach when they
reclaimed their
title in 1974.

Members of the class of 1968 and 1974 line-up at a reunion in 201(
Left to Right: Nicodème Kabamba, Philippe Mvukani, Mana Mamuwe
Lobilo Boba, Mwape Mialo, Augustin Ebengo, Léon Mungamuni
and Baudouin Bayungasa Mbimba

12. Nine Below Zero

THERE WAS LITTLE EMOTION on the faces of the Zaire players when the teams finally emerged from the tunnel. The carefree attitude that had been so evident before the Scotland game had been replaced by grimaced scowls. The official team photo, taken just after the national anthems had boomed out across the stadium, is a telling portrait of eleven unhappy faces. Most of the players cannot bring themselves to look at the camera. Some peer into the distance. Others glance sheepishly to the side. Kilasu Massamba has his head bowed, refusing to make eye contact with anyone while an animated Kidumu Mantantu appears to be having a conversation with someone off-camera. Kazadi Mwamba and Mwepu Ilunga stand at either end of the back row, both staring resolutely into the photographer's lens as if trying to lay a sense of guilt on someone. None of the team are smiling.

To the millions of television viewers around the world, who had little inkling of the drama that had unfolded over the course of the day, the situation did not appear out of the ordinary. Nor to the many commentators and journalists covering the game. Even the Yugoslav players were oblivious to the problems faced by their opponents in the build-up to the game. They were focused on securing the win and progressing to the next round. Most of the watching neutrals and those back home in Zaire were hoping for a cup upset. The Leopards just wanted to get the game over and done with.

The pre-match rituals had the usual air of mundanity about them but like all good dramas, in the middle of the tragedy there was an element of comedy. An hour before kick-off, the Zaire delegation realised that they had forgotten to pack the pennant that is traditionally exchanged between the two captains. Manfred Krebber, the local Bundesliga linesman from Seppenrade, was tasked with retrieving the item from the team's hotel, to the amusement of his wife Walburga, who has fond memories of the incident. 'My husband had to call Ascheberg to see if the police could help,' she explained. 'They had a helicopter already waiting so flew the pennant to Gelsenkirchen. My husband handed it over with minutes to spare!'

Yugoslavia coach Miljan Miljanić had made one change to the team that had held Brazil to a draw, signalling his intent to attack Zaire by replacing midfield Dražen Mužinić with striker Dušan Bajević, who had missed the tournament's curtain raiser due to suspension. His side looked supremely relaxed prior to kick-off, none more so than midfielder Branko Oblak who casually played keepy-uppy in the centre circle with the match ball. By contrast, ITV's Gerald Sinstadt noted the apprehensive features of the Zaire bench as the camera panned across it, casually catching Blagoje Vidinić lighting up a cigarette as it did so.

With pleasantries and pennants happily exchanged, Colombian referee Omar Delgado Gómez, officiating just his fourth international fixture, signalled he was ready to get the game underway and Zaire, wearing an all green strip for the occasion, kicked off in front of a crowd of just over 30,000 spectators, roughly half the stadium's capacity. The opening five minutes of the game were scrappy to say the least. The Leopards, displaying none of the eagerness or enthusiasm they had shown against Scotland, seemed incapable of retaining possession. Yugoslavia, meanwhile, probed the opposition defence, patiently looking for weaknesses to exploit only to find their attacks wanting. The first meaningful effort fell to Vladislav Bogićević, who broke free of his marker after being played through by Oblak, but his cross-shot was comfortably saved by Kazadi. Ivica Šurjak tested the opposite flank, only to see his low effort across the box again cut out by the goalkeeper, but the Yugoslavs were learning quickly. It was time to try a different tactic.

Building patiently from the back, there seemed to be little danger when Yugoslavia goalkeeper Enver Marić collected the ball from Jovan Aćimović in the seventh minute of the match, yet within thirty seconds they had opened the scoring. It was a quick, fluid move that began with Marić finding Ilija Petković out wide on the right with a long throw. The midfielder cut inside and moved the ball forward, angling a pass to Oblak in the centre circle, who turned and picked out Dragan Džajić on the left flank. The winger attacked Mwepu and, having beaten the defender for pace, put in a deep cross for Dušan Bajević at the far post. With left back Mwanza Mukombo guilty of ball watching, Bajević made the most of Zaire's frailty in the air and rose unmarked to head home past the stranded Kazadi to the delight of the partisan crowd.

Seemingly riled by the goal, Mana Mambwene decided to take on the entire Yugoslavian team single-handedly from the restart, beating four players with ease as he forged headlong into the opposition half. The attack was eventually thwarted by the sheer weight of numbers in front of him but it was the first glimpse of the skilful flair that the Leopards had so ably demonstrated in their opening game against Scotland. It also woke his teammates from their slumber. Zaire began to see more of the ball and a clear cut chance to equalise presented itself when Mana, who was enjoying a productive spell in the middle of the park, intercepted a lazy misplaced pass from Petković. The midfielder quickly played the ball forward to Kembo Uba Kembo who, though surrounded by four defenders, was able to slip a perfectly weighted pass into the path of the unmarked Kakoko Etepé bursting through on goal at high speed. With only the goalkeeper to beat, the winger was denied by Marić, who sprinted from his line to narrow the angle.

Just when it looked like Zaire were beginning to find their way into the game, Yugoslavia scored their second from a free-kick, awarded after Šurjak was sent crashing to the ground by Lobilo. The African champions had started to look comfortable on the ball but with confidence growing, Kidumu was guilty of being over-ambitious with his passing. Having received the ball on the edge of the centre circle, well inside the opposition half, he attempted to play a cross-field pass but failed to beat the first defender with an effort that was reminiscent of a previous attempt just seconds before. Regaining possession, Yugoslavia broke quickly, Bogićević playing a defence splitting pass to Šurjak. Through on goal, the big number nine was quickly closed down by the covering Lobilo, who brought the striker's run to an ignominious end after losing his footing. It was a clumsy challenge, one that would have earned the defender a red card in the modern game, but Šurjak made the most of the contact, with accusations of diving from some observers. Džajić made no mistake from the resulting free-kick, however, bending his shot up and over the wall and into the top far corner of Kazadi's net from the edge of the box.

The immediate response from the Leopards was almost identical to that of the first goal. Collecting the ball on the right wing, Mana again cut through the Yugoslavian midfield with a surging run that seemed to frighten the life out of his opponents. This time he found his captain with an exquisite pass executed with the outside of his right boot that cut open the Yugoslav defence. But with Kembo and Kakoko waiting expectantly in the box, both unmarked, Kidumu lost his footing at the vital moment and his cross failed to beat the first man yet again. With that went Zaire's best opportunity to get back into the game.

Yugoslavia were soon 3-0 up, a scoreline that arguably flattered them. Miljan Miljanić's men had not looked particularly threatening after scoring their second but they punished the Leopards for being profligate in possession when Jovan Aćimović intercepted a loose ball. Before the Zairean defence could recover, a quick interchange of passes worked the ball to Šurjak inside the box, who turned smartly and fired a low, left foot drive beyond the reach of the goalkeeper diving at full stretch. Up in the commentary boxes, Gerald Sinstadt, full of admiration for Yugoslavia's clinical finishing, correctly predicted that it 'could be a heavy night for Zaire'.

Bogićević almost increased his side's lead straight from the kick-off after the Leopards allowed the midfielder too much time and space on the ball but his volley was comfortably saved by Kazadi. It proved to be his final contribution to the game. On the sidelines, Zaire's backup goalkeeper, Tubilandu Ndimbi, was being readied for action, his World Cup debut seemingly imminent. And so it proved when the diminutive custodian, sporting a pair of white gloves, entered the field of play and sprinted over to his penalty area with obvious enthusiasm, making a small piece of history as he did so. It was the first occasion a goalkeeper had been substituted during the final stages of the competition for reasons other than injury, and it was a baffling move by the Zaire coach. Standing at just 5'4", the AS Vita Club keeper had only made one previous appearance for the national team, when he made his debut in the 4-1 victory over Mauritius in the African Cup of Nations group game back in March. By contrast, Kazadi was the most experienced player in the squad with 53 caps to his name and had not been at fault for any of the three Yugoslav goals. Indeed, he had looked sharp in the opening stages and along with Manu, had been one of the few positives for Zaire. Yet it was clear to the players at least that the decision to haul Kazadi off was not taken by Vidinić. As the bemused goalkeeper trudged back to the bench via the corner flag, Ndaye Mulamba observed him raising his middle finger in defiance to a tracksuited presidential advisor seated among the substitutes as he passed. By the time he had taken his place on the bench, his replacement was picking the ball out of the back of the net and the Leopards were down to ten men.

In hindsight, Kazadi's substitution was arguably the catalyst for the events that immediately followed his departure, which appeared to have unsettled the entire team. Contemporary reports were less favourable, however, accusing the Leopards of ball-watching and naivety as they stood by and let an unmarked Josip Katalinski fire home from close range. Yet Zaire had justifiable grounds for complaint. Not only was there a hint of offside in the build-up to the goal, but their newly installed goalkeeper was not afforded the opportunity to organise his defence before the free-kick was taken. While the Yugoslavia defender celebrated his strike, the Leopards surrounded the Colombian referee, who appeared unmoved by their protests. As he walked back to the halfway line, frustration got the better of one of the Zairean players and Mr. Delgado Gómez felt a sharp pain in his backside, courtesy of Mwepu Ilunga's boot. In the ensuing chaos the indignant referee mistakenly identified Ndaye Mulamba as the culprit and promptly sent him off.

Ndaye's pleas of innocence fell on deaf ears, despite the supportive attempts of two Yugoslav players who pointed out the real offender, who by now was sheepishly hugging the far touchline. 'I cried terribly when I was sent off', recalled the striker in later years. 'I told the referee that it wasn't me but he wasn't interested. You could tell that he couldn't tell us apart.'

With no reprieve forthcoming, Ndaye, tears streaming down his cheeks, reluctantly headed straight to the locker room, bringing to an end arguably the craziest three minutes in World Cup history, but further repercussions awaited the player after the match. West Germany's television broadcaster had somehow missed the incident altogether and although press reports correctly identified Mwepu as the guilty party, FIFA's disciplinary committee upheld the decision. Ndaye, who had been warned by a marabout back home that he would be the victim of a great injustice prior to the tournament, was banned from international football for one year as punishment for his red card.

Back on the pitch, Tubilandu was already looking shaky between the Zairean goalposts. A fine header from Šurjak, who easily out jumped his marker to meet a teasing cross from Džajić, had the goalkeeper scrambling across his goalmouth straight from the restart and he was fortunate to see the ball bounce past the wrong side of the upright. A fifth goal looked inevitable as Yugoslavia asserted further pressure on the newly installed keeper, yet out of nowhere Zaire won a corner.

A lazy, overplayed pass from Hadžiabdić was seized upon by the impressive Mana, who broke free and carried the ball deep into the Yugoslav half. His delicate chip found Kakoko, bursting through into the penalty box, but although the winger was driven wide by two defenders, he did enough to earn the Leopards their first corner of the game and a small moral victory of sorts. Taking the kick himself, Kakoko delivered a deep, high ball to the back post, where both Kembo and the on-rushing Kidumu, who had skilfully lost his marker, were waiting but it was claimed by Marić in the Yugoslav goal. As if to prove it was no fluke, Kakoko won a second corner a minute later following another pacey run but on this occasion the referee blew for a foul after the goalkeeper clattered into Kidumu, who was simply standing his ground on the edge of the six-yard box.

On the terraces, the Yugoslavian fans, who had greeted every attack with a roar of approval in the early stages of the match, were growing weary and whistles began to echo around the stadium as they aired their frustrations with the apparent lull in their team's performance. The reaction from their team's players was immediate and clinical. Pouncing on a weak pass from Bwanga Tshimen, Šurjak laid the ball off to Ivan Buljan, who advanced a couple of strides before playing it out wide to Petković. The Troyes midfielder broke into the box unchallenged and delivered the perfect cross for Bajević to head home his second and Yugoslavia's fifth goal of the game past the outstretched arm of Tubilandu. Worryingly for Zaire, there was still an hour left to play and their substitute goalkeeper had yet to make a save.

Remarkably, the Leopards almost reduced the arrears when Mana (who else?) was allowed time and space on the right flank following some good link up play with Kilasu. The midfielder's high ball into the box saw Kidumu challenge Enver Marić for a third time but on this occasion the Leopards captain got the better of the goalie, who dropped the ball into the path of Kakoko. With two Yugoslavian players scrambling to cover their keeper, the Zairean winger hastily swung his boot at the ball, leaning back as he did so, and ballooned it over the bar. It was a golden opportunity and Kakoko knew it, throwing his arms in the air in despair.

Bajević's goal aside, the African champions were enjoying their best spell of the match. The shock withdrawal of Kazadi had stoked the dormant fires in the bellies of a team that had appeared disinterested when the game kicked off. The injustice of Ndaye's red card fuelled the players further, as if personal pride had overcome monetary ideals. Even Tubilandu rose to the occasion, albeit temporarily, turning Petković's twenty-yard drive past the post for a corner but just as it looked like the Leopards might reach half-time without conceding further, Yugoslavia netted their sixth to put an end to Zaire's spirited resistance. Had the goalkeeper stayed on his line things may have played out differently. Instead Tubilandu charged out to meet a cross from the left boot of Džajić that he had no hope of claiming and was sent crashing to the floor after colliding with teammate Bwanga Tshimen and Ivica Šurjak, who at 6'3" was nearly a foot taller than the Leopards' keeper. The ball looped up off of the head of the striker and fell kindly for Vladislav Bogićević, who nodded home despite a valiant acrobatic attempt from Mwepu to clear it from underneath the crossbar.

An injury to Šurjak afforded Zaire the opportunity to come together on the penalty spot, seemingly to dissect what had just happened. As Tubilandu pleaded his case, the circle of players broke away and began to move back to their positions in readiness for the restart. Kidumu and Kilasu looked unimpressed with their goalkeeper's excuses, Mana and Bwanga appeared intent on remonstrating with him further. Sympathy and forgiveness were in short supply. On the bench, their coach looked on, puffing away on a cigarette. 'The face of a resigned man,' quipped Gerald Sinstadt. 'Possibly the face of a man about to resign.'

Yugoslavia continued to press in search of yet another goal before half-time. They were almost handed a seventh when Mwepu, having done well to cut out a pass in the first instance, failed to notice the run of Branko Oblak and played his goalkeeper into trouble. Fortunately for the defender, Tubilandu was alert to the danger and blocked the effort on goal. Another quick passing move from the Yugoslavs saw Bajević break free into the box and get his shot away but the substitute keeper was in the right place to beat the ball away. Such was their thirst for goals, however, that they appeared to completely disregard any notions of defending their healthy lead.

At the other end of the pitch, Zaire were at least trying to make a game of it, creating a threat of sorts with a series of deep crosses from the right flank. First Kilasu launched a high ball to the far edge of the penalty area to an unmarked Kakoko, who cushioned a header back into the box for Kembo, but his first touch let him down and the chance was lost. The striker was then denied by Marić in the Yugoslav goal, who was forced to come off his line and punch the ball clear following another cross from the right, this time from Mwepu. Zaire continued to expose Yugoslavia's own defensive frailties when Kembo turned provider following a sweeping move that saw the Leopards swiftly move the ball from one end of the field to the other. His cross, again from the right, was aimed at Kakoko, who had pulled away from his marker, but the winger was always stretching to meet the ball and he was unable to direct it back across goal. Zaire were afforded one last opportunity before the end of the first half but Kakoko's neat turn on the edge of the box was not equalled by the shot, that lacked pace, power and direction and drifted harmlessly by the post.

The first forty-five minutes had been littered with mistakes by both sides but one that had proved costly for Zaire in so many ways. As the players made their way towards the tunnel, the cameras zoomed in on the villain of the piece, Mwepu Ilunga, in an animated discussion with Bwanga, fortunate to still be involved in proceedings.

Blagoje Vidinić emerged for the second half with a stone-faced expression that strongly suggested harsh words had been exchanged in the dressing room. As he made his way back to his seat in the soulless concrete dugout of the Parkstadion, the television director switched to another Yugoslavian playing keepy-uppy with the match ball. This time it was Dragan Džajić showing off his party tricks, who ended his routine by flicking it up for his teammate Dušan Bajević to continue the show. But Bajević was miles away, deep in thought in his own little dream world, and had a rude awakening when the ball smacked him in the face.

Despite enjoying a comfortable lead, Miljan Miljanić chose not to alter his team. Zaire meanwhile made one further change to their line-up during the break. Perhaps as punishment for his profligacy in front of goal, Kakoko Etepé would play no further part and was replaced by Mayanga Maku, who had lost his place as a result of the machinations behind the scenes in the build up to the game.

Again it was a strange decision. Kakoko had been at the heart of every Leopards attack in the first half and could consider himself unlucky not to get his name on the scoresheet. Having originally replaced Mayanga in the starting eleven, his strike partner, Kembo Uba Kembo, was arguably a more worthy candidate for substitution. Clearly lacking match practice, he had struggled with the pace of the game and been ineffective in the Leopards' attack but would now see out the game.

The opening ten minutes of the second half was another scrappy affair, with both sides guilty of squandering possession all too easily. Bajević had a chance to increase his side's lead but fluffed his chance after Tubilandu failed to claim a deep cross from Ivan Buljan. At the other end, Mwepu had a sniff of goal after a neat one-two with Kembo that forced Katalinski to put the ball behind for a corner but despite some slick passing and one touch movement from both teams, neither side had posed any real threat in the final third of the field. The only other incident of note saw Hadžiabdić booked for deliberate handball in the 54th minute, having denied Zaire a clear opportunity on goal but as the floodlights began to take effect against the darkening Gelsenkirchen skies, the match burst into life once again. First Oblak fired a fierce drive from twenty-yards out that Tubilandu did well to tip over his bar then Šurjak went close from the resulting corner, heading over when he really should have done better. Not to be outdone, the Leopards exposed Yugoslav defensive frailties yet again with a blistering break from their own half when Mana seized on a loose ball from Bogićević and set Mayanga free. The substitute motored magnificently deep into the opposition half, successfully evading a crude challenge from Katalinski, only to be met by the onrushing Marić, who dived at the winger's feet and palmed the ball away, despite being well outside his area. With the referee seemingly playing an advantage, Mayanga found his goal-bound shot blocked by Aćimović's desperate lunge before Mana, following up, attempted to lob the ball into the empty net. As the midfielder's effort sailed harmlessly over the bar, Mr. Delgado decided no advantage was forthcoming and blew his whistle to bring play back for the initial handball by Yugoslavia's goalkeeper, who miraculously escaped a caution for his actions.

It quickly became a tale of two free-kicks and a lesson on how to organise a defensive wall. Zaire were unable to make the most of the opportunity afforded them by the referee, with Lobilo shooting high and wide after the ball broke to him. Swift distribution from Yugoslavia saw play shift immediately to the other end of the pitch, where Bajević's run on goal was brought to a premature end by Bwanga's untidy challenge just outside the penalty area. It was in a dangerous position, just to the right of the centre of goal but the severity of the situation was clearly lost on the Leopards, who were slow in organising a three-man wall to protect their goalkeeper's near post and by the time Branko Oblak had struck the free-kick it had disintegrated completely, leaving huge inviting gaps for the Hajduk Split player to exploit. As it transpired, the defensive lapse was immaterial. Aiming for the far corner, the midfielder had opted to try his luck by bending his shot around the Zairean defenders and although he saw it all the way, Tubilandu allowed the ball to slip through his hands and into the back of the net for 7-0. As the Yugoslavian players celebrated, the goalkeeper punched the ground in frustration, watched by his teammates, who made little attempt to disguise their exasperation.

Six different names were now listed among the goalscorers and Yugoslavia showed no signs of easing up. Aćimović fired over from the edge of the box then Bajević had a golden opportunity to complete his hat-trick when he found himself in acres of space with only the goalkeeper to beat but Tubilandu atoned for his earlier error by making an excellent save. 'The Yugoslavs just shrug their shoulders, walk away and know they'll be back for more,' opined Gerald Sinstadt from behind his microphone and so it proved. Less than thirty seconds later it was 8-0. Petković added his name to the scoresheet in some style, slotting the ball past the Zairean goalkeeper after running onto a loose ball, but there was an element of good fortune about his strike. Bajević had looked favourite to score once again but his run was brought to an end by Bwanga's excellent and perfectly-timed sliding tackle. The defender certainly deserved a better slice of good fortune but he could only watch as the ball fell invitingly into the path of the onrushing Petković.

Buoyed by the fillip of two quick goals, Yugoslavia had a spring in their step and were in no mood to see the game out by passing the ball between themselves as their Scottish counterparts had done. Intent on adding to their tally, they continued to exert pressure on their increasingly jaded opponents and Tubilandu had to be alert to first deny Šurjak then Aćimović, tipping the midfielder's long-range drive over the bar. Dušan Bajević would not be denied his hat-trick, however, and completed it in style, meeting a Džajić cross to volley home his third and Yugoslavia's ninth goal of the evening, despite the best efforts of Mwepu on the goal-line.

Battered and bruised, the ten men of Zaire were running on empty and in danger of making history for all the wrong reasons. Hungary had beaten South Korea 9-0 in a group game back in 1954 and that record was seriously under threat. With their spirited second-half resistance finally broken, they appeared to be at the mercy of the Yugoslavs, who were in no mood to offer any sort of reprieve. Had it been a boxing bout, the referee would have already stopped the contest but there were still twenty minutes of the match remaining (the timings of the three second half goals have been incorrectly listed in modern reports of the game, with Bajević's goal erroneously recorded as being scored in the 81st minute). Yet try as they might, Yugoslavia somehow failed to take any of the chances afforded to them.

Double figures proved elusive thanks to a combination of poor finishing, complacency and some dogged defending from the Leopards, who to their credit continued to press forward in search of a consolation goal of their own. Šurjak was the first to try his luck for Yugoslavia, latching onto a through ball from Bajević only to see his left foot strike charged down by the unpredictable Tubilandu, who was making saves and errors in equal measure. The keeper would deny Šurjak again when he cut out a low cross from Džajić after the winger had successfully sprung Zaire's offside trap and charged through on goal but Yugoslavia really should have scored in their next attack. With the goal at his mercy, Bajević appeared to have too much time to pick his spot after Oblak pulled the back to him and somehow managed to skew his shot wide with the outside of his boot, much to the relief of Tubilandu.

Nonetheless, it was not all one way traffic. Zaire were enjoying their own forays, displaying some tidy one-touch passes in the process. A quick interchange between Mana, Kidumu and Kembo almost released Mayanga, but the forward was denied by the outstretched boot of Katalinski. Kembo then had a shot from the edge of the box blocked but as the ball looped up in the air, Bogićević played a lazy back-pass to his goalkeeper unaware of the lurking presence of Kidumu, forcing Enver Marić to race from his line to beat the Leopards' captain to the ball. Despite the clever build up play, the Leopards' attacks were breaking down whenever they got within sight of goal, with players typically picking the wrong option at the vital moment. Had he chosen the right ball, Kembo Uba Kembo may have been credited with an assist and Zaire potentially could have reduced the arrears. Instead, the striker opted to cross the ball to the tightly-marked Kidumu, who was easily beaten in the air, rather than the stealth-like Lobilo Boba, who had somehow taken up a position at the far post without anyone noticing.

In his elevated commentary position, Gerald Sinstadt became increasingly vocal in his criticism of both sides as the game wore on. Bwanga Tshimen, who had earlier waltzed past four Yugoslavian players with ease with a run from deep, was singled out by the commentator for failing to live up to his reputation as the *Black Beckenbauer*, with the cutting suggestion that he 'now a very grey Beckenbauer'. And although he had a hat-trick to his name, Bajević's miss irritated Sinstadt immensely, who scarcely hid his contempt when telling viewers that the striker 'couldn't be bothered to take his time to shoot' and complained that the edge had disappeared from Yugoslavia's game. In truth the match was beginning to resemble a friendly rather than a World Cup game and large gaps began appearing all over the pitch, with each team abandoning any resemblance of a midfield to reinforce their forward lines.

As the game slowed, the shrill whistles of a dissatisfied crowd increased in volume. Having been spoiled thus far, more goals were expected. As if to satisfying the baying mob, Mwanza Mukombo played his goalkeeper into trouble unnecessarily with an under hit back pass that Ivica Šurjak seized upon, looking to take advantage, but despite his height advantage, the Yugoslav came off worse when the two collided in the box and was sent sprawling to the ground. As he clambered to his feet, still feeling the after effects of the challenge, he was clearly in an offside position but the referee allowed play to continue as Bajević collected a return pass and sprinted through on goal. Remarkably, with only the goalkeeper to beat, Bajević fluffed his chance for a fourth, blasting the ball straight at Tubilandu.

Zaire responded with arguably their best attack of the second half. Salvaging the ball on the near touchline, the hard working Kembo, who was now a different player to the one that had been so pedestrian in the first half, slipped a pass through to Mayanga who in turn played it back to Mana. The Zaire midfielder split the Yugoslavian defence with a through ball back to Mayanga who, having continued his run, cut into the box and fired a hard, low left-footed shot that forced Marić into a smart save. It was a flash of brilliance from the Leopards that deserved a goal.

As the game entered the final stages, the attacks continued, albeit not as frequently as before. Petković should have done better when the ball broke to him in the penalty area but his attempt to curve a shot into the top corner misfired and he could only stand and watch as it floated harmlessly into the arms of the grateful Tubilandu. Mayanga, growing in confidence after his earlier effort, turned on the party tricks down Zaire's left flank, pulling off a cheeky dummy to confound Katalinski before racing to the byline then beating the defender again. Once more his clever play merited a more successful conclusion but his pull back to Mukombo resulted in the left back spooning his shot over the bar. Two minutes from time it was Yugoslavia's turn to rue a missed opportunity after Oblak had been hacked down on the edge of the box. Džajić's deft free-kick caught the Zaire defence flat-footed but Šurjak somehow managed to head the ball wide when left unmarked at the far post and with that went his side's chance to hit double figures.

It was the last meaningful action of the match. As Mr. Delgado blew for full time, the camera cut not to the victorious Yugoslav bench but to a sombre Blagoje Vidinić, who slowly rose from his seat and made his way to the touchline. As Gerald Sinstadt gave a damning verdict on the quality of African football, Zaire's coach stood and waited for his players, offering each a fatherly sympathetic pat on the back as they passed. He knew there would be repercussions and as he turned to follow his team down the tunnel, he had the mannerisms and look of a condemned man.

13. Losing Their Way

TIME IS SUPPOSEDLY a great healer yet for Zaire's players the crushing defeat by Yugoslavia remains a painful and embarrassing memory. The humiliation was so great that the squad wanted to leave West Germany straight after the final whistle, only to be cajoled into staying by frantic FIFA officials, determined to keep the image of their tournament intact. The European press revelled in their defeat, using the result to justify the argument that the developing nations had 'the tactical grasp of savages', as Simon Kuper put it in his book *Football Against the Enemy*, and by turn no right to be competing in the World Cup finals.

Unaware of the ongoing drama behind the scenes in the build-up to the game, the journalists who had witnessed the carnage did not mince their words in the following day's newspapers. The British press in particular seemed to take great delight in the Leopards' sobering defeat. 'The immaturity of Zaire was embarrassing,' wrote Harry Miller in the *Daily Mirror*. 'It was impossible not to feel sorry for these World Cup upstarts as Yugoslavia exposed and exploited every weakness.' *The Guardian* took a similar churlish tone in a report headlined "No mercy shown to hapless Zaire", while *The Times* back pages lead with "Yugoslavia emphasise abyss in standards". Beneath the headlines, however, there was very little analysis of the game, aside from the basic facts, and Ndaye's red card barely registered in some write-ups. Nonetheless, the common opinion was that the side that had earned such glowing reviews against Scotland were now considered to be naive, unprofessional and not worthy of their place. One newspaper even went so far as to suggest the performance had 'set back the cause of African football by 10 years,' a somewhat hyperbolic statement that was proved woefully inaccurate following Tunisia's victory over Mexico at the finals in 1978.

Applying a patriotic filter to their reporting, the magnitude of Yugoslavia's victory was seen as a damning indictment of the state of football in Britain. The fact that Willie Ormond's side had laboured to a less than impressive triumph only days before served to highlight these perceived inadequacies further. Inquests were held in the editorial rooms of the nation's tabloids, with pundits invited to air their views and offer their solutions with regards to the apparent crisis at hand. Just how far British football had fallen in comparison with their continental neighbours if they could only beat these clueless African minnows 2-0? Yet the criticism Zaire received in the foreign press was mild compared to the vitriol dished out by their own national newspaper back home, *Salongo*, who stuck firmly to the rhetoric fed to them by Mobutu's aides.

Taking no prisoners, the publication launched a scathing attack on the man they regarded as responsible for the entire fiasco - Blagoje Vidinić. Happy to fuel the conspiracy theories that were already taking hold in the country, *Salongo* claimed to have spoken to Mwepu Ilunga at the team's hotel in Ascheberg and reported that the Yugoslav had 'treated the players with an arrogance that upset everyone'. The newspaper went on to accuse the coach of betraying Zaire and intentionally weakening the team to hand the win - not to mention a healthy goal difference - to his native Yugoslavia to further their cause at the expense of the Leopards. The inclusion of Kembo Uba Kembo in preference to Mayanga Maku and the substitution of Kazadi Mwamba were both cited as evidence of his guilt in an editorial headlined "Night of the Long Knives" that also sought to exonerate the Mobutu's acolytes that had travelled with the squad from any wrongdoing. The bombastic nature of the article resonated with the patrons of the bars and social clubs in Kinshasa and Lubumbashi and its tone was so extreme that Vidinić immediately evacuated his family from the country's capital city.

The supposition of collusion was rife within the Scottish camp too, where the result was greeted with astonishment. Although no official complaint was ever lodged, Hibernian defender John Blackley was convinced something underhanded had occurred. 'I don't think any of us could believe Zaire had been beaten nine-nothing,' he admitted. 'I'll give Yugoslavia their due, they were technically really good players but they were never a nine-nothing team. Zaire weren't that bad. I still think there was a conspiracy and for me I always believed that nine-nothing was a ploy.'

More colourful rumours involved witchdoctors from Lubumbashi, envious of the World Cup involvement of their Kinshasa counterparts, allegedly placing a curse on the Leopards. Similarly, an American periodical recounted a tale of workers in Zaire raising the necessary funds to hire their own medicine men to smite the team in retaliation for enforced contributions to the Government's Soccer Tax. There was even a suggestion that the official team witchdoctors had punished the players in response to Vidinić banning them from the dressing room and training ground in West Germany, further reinforcing the belief that the Yugoslav was ultimately responsible for Zaire's sudden reversal of fortunes on the football pitches of Europe.

The coach had not helped his own cause by failing to quell any conjecture in the immediate aftermath of the match, preferring instead to focus on Ndaye Mulamba's red card. When asked why he had replaced Kazadi, he refused to be drawn into a discussion on the reasons behind the decision, declaring the incident a 'state secret' to the amusement of the assembled audience of journalists and television reporters. Yet a couple of days later, in an interview that took place outside of the confines of the team hotel, he gave a more frank explanation to the Dutch magazine *Vrij Nederland*: 'Mr. Lokwa (Lokwa Bobandjola, President of Zaire's football federation) said after the third Yugoslav goal "Take that keeper off", so I did.'

Vidinić's account of the substitution was corroborated in part by Ndaye, who noted that it was Mobutu's track-suited advisor who motioned for goalkeeper Tubliandu Ndimbi to prepare rather than the coach. Nonetheless, the reasons behind Tubliandu's introduction remain a mystery and open to speculation. Rumours, if they are to be believed, suggest that the AS Vita Club keeper was a favourite of a high-ranking official - some say Mobutu himself - who had been lobbying for his inclusion in the side and forced Vidinić's hand in front of the watching television audience, much to the dissatisfaction of his teammates. There is a suspicion that Kazadi was replaced because the authorities believed he was executing his threat of strike action, even though he was powerless to prevent any of the goals conceded, and the whispers of a bribe have not been totally silenced ('That story did the round for years,' confirmed Mwepu Ilunga). Regardless of how he ended up on the pitch, Tubliandu appears to be the victim of circumstance and has unfairly shouldered much of the blame for the events that unfolded. His performance may have been a tad erratic, but the damage had already been done by the time he took his place between the sticks.

Vidinić wisely chose to keep his counsel while Mobutu's aides were within earshot but free of their attention, he revealed the extent of their meddling in team matters to *The Guardian's* Paul Wilcox a week later, having stayed on in West Germany to watch the rest of the tournament.

'Not too much notice should have been taken of the nine goals they scored against us', he explained. 'The Yugoslavs were able to run up that score only because of interference from my technical delegation. At half time, I ran to my players and asked them what they thought they were doing. They told me that the delegation had asked that they forget my plans and to play African football! The players could see what was happening and the delegates made sure that they kept out of my way afterwards.'

With a delicious sense of irony, Vidinić's claims were unwittingly confirmed by the editors of *Salongo* who, in their rush to pin the blame of the defeat squarely on the Yugoslav, reported that Minister of Sport Sampassa Kaweta Milombe had indeed interfered with the team selection on the eve of the game. The reports of disharmony between the players and their coach were also dismissed by members of the squad, including the misquoted Mwepu, who absolved his coach of any blame for the defeat. 'They were accusing him of taking a bribe from his countrymen,' remembers the defender. 'But we lost because we played dreadfully, though. I don't think our coach could have done anything about it. We were angry over money matters.'

Ndaye Mulamba is in agreement. 'Looking back on it, I can say Vidinić had nothing to do with the débâcle. It was said that he'd betrayed the team's secrets to the opposition but I don't think so. Vidinić was very professional in his attitude to everyone. He was simply misunderstood by our leaders and the national press. It was a great shame the leadership called him all sorts of names but that's all history now.'

'Frankly, we'd lost our morale,' he continued. 'We could easily have let in 20 goals.'

The off-field tribulations had broken the players' spirit. The limited training time afforded to the squad by Mobutu's officials, not to mention the interference in team selection, only compounded matters. Disorganised, disinterested and ill-prepared, the Leopards were a shadow of the side that had given Scotland a fright or two in their opening game and cruelly exposed by the skill and physicality of arguably the best team they had played up to that point. For their coach, it was a missed opportunity, not only for his team but also for him personally. 'Contrary to what people have said, Vidinić's wish was that we win the game against his country of origin,' explained his assistant Nicodème Kabamba. 'This victory would have raised his rating. After the first match, Vidinić asked them, "Did you receive your money?" They responded they had not and this is when the players started to become demoralised.'

The margin of Yugoslavia's victory still rankles with winger Mayanga Maku, as it does with many of those that played in the game. Having been dropped from the starting line-up, he witnessed the carnage unfold from the relative comfort - and safety - of the substitutes' bench before coming on at half-time. Despite the result, he is in little doubt that the Leopards possessed the ability and potential to compete with the very best on their day but was pragmatic and honest in his appraisal of the game and his side's approach to it.

'I'm not saying we would have won but I don't think we would have lost 9-0,' the winger argues. 'We didn't want to play this game. We were static on the field, the defenders were nervous, our marking wasn't up to standard and our clearances were poor. We had really shown our amateurism but you also have to remember that Yugoslavia were one of the best teams of the era.'

However, Zaire's captain, Kidumu Mantantu, is more bullish in his assessment of the match and takes umbrage at the suggestion that they would have lost the game regardless of the financial problems that hampered his side's performance. 'I maintain that Yugoslavia were no stronger than us. They weren't stronger. It was only down to one thing: money.'

As much as they would prefer to bury the past and their own actions of that day, the players are not allowed to, thanks in part to the humbling reminders served up every four years. Clearly embarrassed by the infamy that still haunts them, their recollections, although still defiant, are tinged with regret and a degree of sadness. Their pride is hurt, primarily by the aspersions cast upon their abilities and skills, aspersions that helped establish the narrative surrounding Zairean football and fuelled lazy football-related entertainment shows for many a year. Yet although attitudes towards the team have softened with the passage of time, some would argue the Leopards have only themselves to blame. Author David Goldblatt certainly has little sympathy with the Zairean players and pulled no punches in his book *The Ball Is Round* when questioning the proclaimed lack of

The Zaire players surround the referee after his controversial dismissal of striker Ndaye Mulamba in the 22nd minute of the match against Yugoslavia. The real villain of the piece Mwepu Ilunga (2) is lurking in the foreground.

effort from those that started the game. 'Do you throw a World Cup game just because the boss has made off with the cash? Like that had never happened in Zaire before' he wrote. 'It is better not to read between the lines. There's no mystery here, just the cruel and relentless contrast of poverty and wealth.'

Goldblatt's theory is an oversimplification of the game and the events that took place before the team left the dressing room of the Parkstadion and entered the field of play. The inexplicable substitution of Kazadi and the comments of Vidinić following the match have a strong whiff of mystery about them and to suggest otherwise could be considered churlish. Observed in isolation and without context, it is easy to criticise the performance of Zaire and extol the virtues of Yugoslavia. Yes, the Europeans were bigger, fitter, and technically superior, but they also played the majority of the game with a full complement of players and exploited their man advantage to good effect. They were also guilty of lapses in concentration and defensively suspect at times. Despite ultimately qualifying for the Second Round, they would not win another game at the tournament and such was

The stark reality of Zaire's unwanted World Cup record, since beaten only by El Salvador's 10-1 tonking by Hungary in 1982. Interestingly neither Yugoslavia nor Hungary did nothing else of note in either tournament.

the unconvincing nature of their performances after their sole victory that *The Guardian* openly questioned whether the side had flattered to deceive as result of their 9-0 victory. The Leopards meanwhile were sluggish, error prone and lacked fluidity as a team, particularly in the opening stages. Individually, they still showed flashes of brilliance and could easily have reduced the arrears had Kakoko not been so wasteful in front of goal. It was a far cry from their spirited performance against the Scots and perhaps Melbourne newspaper *The Age* got it right when they called the result a 'freak'.

The hapless Tubliandu is only too happy to correct any assumptions about the scoreline. 'People talk about our 9-0 defeat to Yugoslavia, but you have to put it in context,' explained the goalkeeper. 'We were swindled. We didn't get our World Cup money.' Goldblatt is correct when he speaks of the disparity between rich and poor as the underlying cause of the defeat but not between the relative wealth of the two footballing nations. Rather it was the distinction back home in Zaire that was at the heart of the matter and what ultimately broke the spirit of the Leopards.

'We went onto the pitch when our morale was at its lowest and that was fatal,' sighed midfielder Kilasu Massamba. 'We knew we could lose, but not in such a catastrophic way.'

14. The Boys from Brazil

A DARK CLOUD hung over the Leopards as they quietly assembled in the dining room at the Hotel Jagdschlösschen. The laughter and merriment that had filled the chamber on so many occasions since their arrival in West Germany had been replaced by an uneasy silence, broken only by the occasional sound of a chair being scraped along the floor as someone shuffled in their seat. As senior officials cleared the lobby of any lingering journalists, the tension grew. The players knew they would be feeling the full force of Mobutu's wrath before long and this was simply the calm before the storm.

'We knew it was going to be bad,' remembers Mwepu Ilunga, 'and we were absolutely terrified. After a few minutes, in walked three serious-looking officials with faces like death. They'd come with a message from Mobutu. "You have all brought shame on the country of Zaire. You are scum, and sons of whores. The great leader says that if you concede more than three goals against Brazil in the final match, you will never see Zaire or your families again. Your leader is disgusted in all of you." They ranted on at us for around 30 minutes, before leaving the room. There wasn't anyone inside that room who doubted that those men meant every last word of what they said.'

The first act of retribution was quickly followed by the second. Such was the president's ire that he telephoned the hotel to berate them directly for the defeat, a long-distance call that consisted of nothing but screaming, shouting and more threats. 'The Marshal was very clear,' recalled Ndaye Mulamba. 'He would not tolerate a second snub or we would expose ourselves to the worst possible reprisals.'

Contrary to popular belief, Mobutu did not send an army of henchmen to Ascheberg to intimidate the players further. He didn't have to. Aside from the fact that he already had enough of his own men present within the camp, his word was enough to instil fear into the team and it did not take long for the repercussions of his actions to surface. A day before the Leopards' final game, Blagoje Vidinić announced to the squad that he would not be returning to

Zaire with them, no matter what happened against Brazil. His family had already fled to Yugoslavia following the president's thinly-veiled threats, he told them, and following the match he would be leaving his post as coach.

The news came as a hammer blow to the players, who fondly looked upon the Yugoslav as a father figure having adopted him as one of their own. Before he arrived, the World Cup had been nothing more than a pipe dream for an international side that lacked cohesion and organisation. Regardless of the result against Yugoslavia and the missing bonuses, he had transformed them into Africa's most powerful football team and those that followed him to the finals recognised the contribution he had made, even if some of their countrymen had long since forgotten. 'He made me the player I was and we looked up to him,' admitted winger Mayanga Maku. 'I made my international debut at 18 and played under eight different coaches. Vidinić was by far the most influential. He worked on my weaknesses to make me a better player.'

Mobutu's threats and Vidinić's impending departure changed the dynamics of the Brazil game and gave it a new dimension. Sensing that the adventure was coming to an end in more ways than one, the quarrels over bonuses and monies owed ceased and a common goal to restore some of the pride they had lost over the past week began to permeate the camp. In truth, the performance against Yugoslavia was such that their bargaining position was now very weak ('when you've lost by nine goals, how are you going to argue about money that you're owed?' confessed Bwanga Tshimen) but the players knew their president was not bluffing and the stakes had been raised considerably.

'The Brazil match was about honour,' confirmed Mayanga. 'We had to come out with honour: three goals or less. Vidinić told us to go and enjoy it, that it would be his last game with us, and that Brazil played the same style as we did so we had a chance to show something.'

Outside of the team's hotel the world's media had been patiently awaiting confirmation on whether the Leopards would actually take to the field to fulfil their last fixture. News of the players' reluctance to carry on had filtered out and speculation had been rife about what would happen next. Certain newspapers got wind of Mobutu's warnings and reported that the team had been given an ultimatum to "play or die", others upped the ante by informing their readers that Zaire had to "win or die". One publication erroneously reported that the president had even offered a prize of 15 days as a guest in his official house to any player that scored as an added incentive to do well. Finally, at 6pm on the eve of the match, an official spokesman finally put the speculation to bed and informed the gathered throng of journalists and TV crews: 'We will play against Brazil and hope to get away leniently.'

Surprisingly, considering all that happened to Zaire over the previous seven days, the reigning champions were far from confident going into the fixture. Despite boasting a line-up that included such talents as Jairzinho and Rivellino, the *Seleção* had mislaid their football heritage. Somewhere in the intervening period between winning the Jules Rimet Trophy in Mexico and the start of their campaign in West Germany, they had replaced the flair and grace that was so evident in 1970 with a more European brand of soccer that involved kicking the opposition almost as much as the ball. Coach Mário Zagallo had made history by becoming the first person to win the World Cup as both a player and manager but was now under pressure to deliver. An over-cautious approach in their first two games had left them without a win and still to score at the finals. Yet he continued to remain apprehensive and unlike Scotland boss Willie Ormond, he had refused to write Zaire off ahead of the competition. 'They have their share of world class players and we're not going to underestimate our task,' he told the *Sunday People*. 'Beating them will not be easy.'

Pride was very much at stake for both sides as they lined up for the national anthems prior to kick-off at the Parkstadion in Gelsenkirchen, albeit for wildly different reasons. Brazil needed to win by three clear goals to progress to the Second Round, the Leopards needed to avoid defeat by four goals to avoid further recriminations at the hands of their president. It would make for an intriguing encounter and the African champions were certainly fired up for the task ahead.

'We started that game with firm conviction to show the world that we could play football,' admitted midfielder Kidumu Mantantu and Mwepu echoed his captain's sentiments. 'We knew we'd lose,' he said, 'but we could make sure that we went down fighting.'

The suspension to Ndaye had forced Vidinić to shuffle his pack but pressure from above also led to a number of changes elsewhere in the team. There was a touch of sentimentality about the coach's selections, evident by the inclusion of Jean Kalala N'Tumba, despite not being fully fit. The striker, who was commonly known by his nickname *Tumba Pouce*, had been forced to watch his teammates lift the African Cup of Nations from a hospital bed in Yugoslavia, having picked up a serious knee injury before Christmas, and likely would have started ahead of Ndaye in Egypt but for his misfortune. He was due to be partnered upfront by Mbungu Ekofo, only for the forward to be injured in the last training session prior to the match so there was a recall for Mayanga, who was preferred to Kembo Uba Kembo, and midfielder Kibonge Mafu, the man who had given Scotland a fright late on in their opening match. Kilasu Massamba dropped to the bench, despite having started the first two matches, as did Kakoko Etepé, who had arguably been Zaire's best player so far. In a surprise move, Vidinić opted to play TP Mazembe winger Tshinabu Wa Munda, a fringe player who had helped unlock a number of defences when the going got tough during the qualification rounds, instead. There was no room on the substitutes bench for Mavuba Mafuila, however. An outspoken critic of Mobutu, he was forced to watch from the stands alongside Ndaye for his unpatriotic comments in front of party officials.

There was one further postscript to Vidinić's lineup. With emotions running high after the Yugoslavia match, team captain Kidumu had been temporarily ostracised from the group after a training ground spat, having been accused of deliberately over-hitting passes to make his teammates look bad during a practice match. After being forced to eat his meals alone and train by himself, there was a question mark over whether he'd play any part in the match, let alone retain the captaincy. But having apologised for his behaviour, the coach opted for consistency rather than rock the boat any more than was necessary and Kidumu was restored at the head of the team when they emerged from the tunnel.

The game kicked off in glorious sunshine with Brazil straight away looking to attack their opponents, who were suitably dressed for the occasion in their now iconic strip of green shirts with a yellow leopard on the front, yellow shorts and green socks, the team's third strip of the tournament. Unsurprisingly, Vidinić had set his side up to defend and when the ball was passed back to Kazadi in the Zaire goal for the second time in quick succession just ninety seconds into the game, the move was met with boos and whistles from the

36,000-strong crowd, who were clearly expecting another bloodbath.

As the sides settled into the game, it was the African champions who looked the more composed and relaxed during the early exchanges. Their South American counterparts meanwhile were anything but and when Rivellino played a pass with the outside of his boot to no one in particular, the lack of confidence running through the *Seleção* was there for all to see as the ball trickled out of play. 'They were tense, you could tell,' remembers Mwepu, who took the resulting throw-in.

Conversely, there was a new-found assurance flowing through Zaire that was ably demonstrated by Lobilo Boba in the fourth minute of the match. Having initially been beaten for pace by Marinho Chagas, the central defender recovered and timed his tackle to perfection as his opponent ran dangerously through on goal. Rising to his feet, he proceeded to calmly dribble the ball across his own six-yard box before handing possession over to his defensive partner Bwanga Tshimen, who in turn coolly picked out Kibonge in midfield despite the attentions of the on rushing Jairzinho. This triggered a slick passing move involving six members of the Leopards team that only ended when Tshinabu was beaten to N'Tumba's knock down in the Brazilian box by none other than Chagas, who had sprinted the length of the field to get back into position.

A minute later Kazadi's palms were stung by a twenty-yard effort from Rivellino, the goalkeeper diving full stretch to turn the ball around his right post. From the corner, the Zaire stopper came racing out of his goal to try and cut out the cross but ended up clattering into Leivinha, who bore the full brunt of the collision. Despite being in obvious agony, the Brazilian midfielder received little sympathy from Romanian referee Nicolae Rainea, who insisted that he leave the field of play. Unable to stand, he was hauled up over the trainer's shoulder in what can only be described as a failed attempt at a fireman's lift and unceremoniously carried off the pitch in what would prove to be the final act of his international career.

He was eventually replaced by Valdomiro in the twelfth minute yet despite being a man down, Brazil pressed forward, probing the Zairean defences looking for weaknesses. Chagas had a snapshot well-saved by Kazadi and Lobilo was again called into action, sliding in on Edu after the striker displayed an unexpected burst of pace to drive into the area from the left, but there was a lack of invention in and around the box. When they did manage to penetrate the penalty area the Leopards were able to hack the ball to safety.

It was shortly after Valdomiro's introduction that Brazil finally made the breakthrough they desperately needed. The goal stemmed from a free-kick conceded by Kidumu just inside the opposition half and when Rivellino picked up the ball still in the centre circle there seemed to be little threat to the scoreline. Even after his delicately flighted pass was nodded down to Jairzinho, Zaire didn't look to be in too much trouble and appeared to have the situation in control when the winger attempted to chip the ball into the path of the onrushing Luís Pereira. But Brazil had a slice of good fortune as the defender's header ricocheted off his shoulder and fell invitingly into Jairzinho's path, who showed his class by volleying the ball low and hard into the back of the net. It was an excellent finish and one that was at odds with the scruffy play that preceded it but the celebrations that followed were more of relief than obvious delight, on both the pitch and terraces, where a group of fans played up to the cameras.

The quality of Jairzinho's goal was matched by a world-class double save from the much-maligned Kazadi minutes later. As the ball pin-balled around the Zaire penalty area, the Leopards' goalkeeper raced across his six-yard box to first deny Valdomiro before springing to his feet and diving to his right to block Carpegiani's ferocious drive on the follow-up. It was a brave piece of goalkeeping that left Kazadi with a couple of battle scars that needed treatment from the team doctor, Mambu Moura. The break in play afforded Rivellino the opportunity to change his boots, a mundane activity at the best of times but something the West German television director found fascinating, offering viewers a close up, as if he expected something magical to happen once the midfielder had finished tying the laces on his new pair.

Midway through the first half Zaire finally had a shot on target, which brought the second loudest cheer of the game so far as the neutrals in the crowd began to get behind the underdogs. The Leopards had begun to frustrate their more illustrious opponents and having repeatedly tried to exploit the space behind Brazil's defence with over-the-top passes, they suddenly changed tack. Collecting the ball in midfield, Mayanga made a beeline for goal, riding the challenge of Wilson Piazza, who crudely tried to trip him up, and skipping past Pereira's half-hearted attempt to stop him. Yet having done the hard work, *Goodyear* scuffed his shot, which lacked the power to really trouble Émerson Leão. Nonetheless the party mood continued inside the Parkstadion, with the fans roaring their approval when Bwanga turned Jairzinho with ease less than thirty seconds later and with the momentum building, Tshinabu decided to have another crack at goal from distance but he too failed to test the Brazilian goalkeeper.

The camaraderie running through Vidinić's side was clearly evident and a far cry from the dispirited performance against Yugoslavia. Hugs, high fives, and words of encouragement followed every positive move or last ditch tackle. Defensive walls stood firm at free-kicks, players wanted to receive the ball and their offside trap snared many an unsuspecting attacker. Brazil, on the other hand, were a disjointed collection of individuals who seemed to be on different wavelengths to one another, their forays into the Zaire half were becoming increasingly pedestrian in nature and lacked the panache and verve one normally associates with the Brazilian national side.

That said, the Leopards rode their luck as the half progressed and Brazil should probably have had a penalty when Mwepu Ilunga brought down Marinho Peres with a clumsy challenge. Whether Mwepu actually touched the ball is open to question but the referee was probably dissuaded by the theatrical dive of Peres, who played up to the crowd when his protests were waved away by pretending to play dead inside the area.

He wasn't the only Brazilian to fluff his lines. Jairzinho had a great opportunity to extend his side's lead after bludgeoning his way through Zaire's defence but with just the keeper to beat, the winger contrived to put the ball wide of the post, which could have proved costly after Peres was caught in possession at the other end of the field. Fortunately for the defender, Nelinho came to his rescue, frantically putting the ball behind for a corner after Mayanga had tried to pull it back for N'Tumba.

Devoid of ideas and unable to break down Zaire's stout defence, Brazil resorted to trying their luck from range. Yet such was their ineptitude in front of goal that a frustrated shrill of whistles echoed around the terraces as an effort from Nelinho drifted harmlessly wide into the massed rank of photographers at the side of Kazadi's goal. Carpegiani didn't even manage to hit the crouching cameramen, firing high and wide with the outside of his left boot to send the ball bouncing onto the athletics track that circled the pitch in what was arguably the nadir of the South Americans' attempts on target.

As the match headed towards the half-time interval, they finally beat the Leopards goalkeeper for a second time but still failed to score. Although Kazadi had got a firm hand to Luís Pereira's close-range shot, the defender having been put clean through by Rivellino, it wasn't enough to divert the ball away from goal. But just when it looked like Brazil had doubled their lead, Mwanza Mukombo appeared from nowhere to boot the ball off the line and ended up getting entangled in the netting for his troubles.

As Zagallo and his coaching team watched on from the bench, not quite believing what they were seeing, Edu tested Kazadi again from the edge of the area. The keeper blocked the shot and although the ball ran kindly for Jairzinho, he was surrounded by a swarm of green shirts who had sprinted to their goalie's rescue. The Leopards had managed to restrict the reigning world champions to just a single goal and as the teams made their way to the dressing rooms at half-time, Brazil were jeered by supporters.

What happened next is open to conjecture but several Zaire players have since claimed that there were discussions between the teams during the break to ensure Brazil scored at least three goals to guarantee second spot in Group 2. Speaking in 2010, suspended striker Ndaye Mulamba recounted a conversation he had with fellow outcast Mavuba Mafuila during the course of the second half to journalist Claire Raynaud where the midfielder informed his teammate of the alleged collusion between the two sides. 'The Brazilians came into the locker room during half-time and begged our guys to let them score a third goal, because with this goal they would overtake Scotland and qualify for the second round,' Mavuba explained before accusing Kazadi of taking a bribe and bemoaning the situation the players found themselves in. 'We are truly the shame of Africa,' he continued. 'Everything is rotten with us, everyone is corrupt.'

The story was repeated by Kibonge Mafu in the Congolese documentary *Entre la coupe et l'élection (Between the Cup and the Election)*, who confirmed that they had been asked to concede the necessary third goal during the interval but not for monetary reasons. According to some sources, the Zaire team still held a grudge against Scotland captain Billy Bremner for his behaviour towards some of the Leopards during their opening clash, something the Zaire number 15 was only too happy to confirm. 'We got nothing for it, we did it for pleasure,' he revealed, as if confessing to the murder of an unpopular historical figure. 'Firstly, because the Scots treated us badly. Secondly, they won because the referee cheated. We had to make them pay, so we did.'

Suspicions had been rife within the Scottish camp that something was amiss. While many of Willie Ormond's squad pointed fingers at Yugoslavia, at least one player believed it was the result against the South Americans that ultimately knocked his team out of the World Cup. 'There were rumours at the time,' remembers winger Peter Lorimer, 'rumours that Brazil had agreed to go there and play friendly matches, which I could well believe because in those days football was a little bit corrupt, to a degree. Brazil just beat them in the end, by the amount of goals they needed but the game was a bit like that at that particular time.'

'The coach did cheat,' asserted captain Kidumu Mantantu in 2020. 'He fixed that match together with the goalkeeper. Kazadi, our goalie, later told us this. Brazil had to win at least 3-0 to qualify and they arranged that. Watch those last two goals. A blind woman would have stopped those balls!'

Taken at face value, it is very easy to accept that there was some collusion between the two sides. Except for one small detail. The last two fixtures in Group 2 were played concurrently and the score in the game between the Scots and Yugoslavia was still goalless at half-time and would remain so until late in the match. As such, Kibonge's claims appear to be little more than a flight of fancy because had Scotland won, they would have topped the group and Yugoslavia would have been packing their bags instead.

Regardless, if there were some shady shenanigans taking place in the tunnel at half-time, no one bothered to inform Mwepu Ilunga, whose memories of the interval were at odds with those of his teammates and decidedly more positive. 'At half-time the mood in the dressing room was positive, we were only 1–0 down,' recalled the defender. 'We thought that at least we could possibly deny the great Brazil a place in the last stages. That would have been something.'

There were no indications the game had been manipulated in Brazil's favour when play resumed. Contrary to Kibonge's claims that Vidinić had instructed them not to attack, Zaire went on the offensive and put the South Americans' defence under pressure immediately from the kick off, with Leão getting an early touch of the ball when he had to come and claim a deep cross from Mwepu to deny the charging N'Tumba. Mayanga then waltzed through the Brazilian midfield with ease before lifting a perfectly weighted ball over the defence and into the path of Kidumu, forcing the goalkeeper, who had been pretty much a spectator in the first half, to rush from his line to intercept him.

At the other end, Nelinho, having found space on the right flank, attempted an ambitious curling cross-shot, similar to the one that would famously beat Dino Zoff in the Italian goal during the Third Place Play-off game in Argentina four years later, but on this occasion his effort did not have enough bend to trouble Kazadi's goal. The ball was played out wide to the defender again a minute later, who whipped in a dangerous cross that had the goalkeeper stretching for all his worth to palm it away before Edu had the chance to head home. Frustratingly for Kazadi, the ball dropped into the path of Chagas but he recovered quickly to cut out the low cross that followed, pouring scorn on the suggestion that he was willing to give up his goal to the opposition.

Chagas had been a thorn in Zaire's side for most of the game. With his tanned skin and flowing blond locks, the defender would not have looked out of place on the surfing beaches of California but he had a deceptive turn of pace and now showed Tshinabu a clean pair of heels after beating the Leopards number 7 with ease and racing to the byline. His pull back was blocked but once again the ball ran kindly for Brazil and although Edu's shot was going wide, Mukombo decided to swing a boot at it. Failing to make a clean contact, he could only watch in horror as his sliced shot just cleared the crossbar. It was the closest the Brazilians came to a goal in the opening period of the second half as they again struggled to find a way past the twin pillars of Bwanga and Lobilo in the heart of the Zairean defence.

In the 54th minute Zaire very nearly equalised from a free-kick, awarded after Tshinabu and Mayanga had panicked Luís Pereira into slapping the ball away in an amateurish fashion following an attempted one-two over the top of the Brazilian defence. N'Tumba's shot from all of 25-yards had pace, power and direction but not enough curve and skimmed the woodwork at the point where the crossbar meets the goalpost with Leão well-beaten. It was a warning that Brazil failed to heed and their languid approach to defending saw Marinho Peres come unstuck as he casually waited for a high ball to come down. He looked to be in no danger but as he dallied, Tshinabu's pace saw him win possession, to the delight of the crowd, and the defender was forced to use all his guile and skill to recover the situation. The neutrals at the Parkstadion were now firmly in favour of the African champions and every tackle, back-pass and move that thwarted their opponents was greeted with a roar of approval.

Brazil finally had another glimpse of goal on the hour mark. Jairzinho got the better of Bwanga for once and fired a low, inviting drive across the face of the Zaire goal but the pace of the ball beat both Pereira, darting in at the near post, and Edu, who came crashing in at the far. As Zaire looked to play their way out of trouble, frustration got the better of Jairzinho and he left his foot in on Lobilo as he cleared the ball, leaving the centre half in a crumpled mess on the edge of his own area clasping his ankle. Zagallo had seen enough and used the break in play to make a change, hauling off his captain Wilson Piazza in favour of the more attack-minded Mirandinha. The forward wasted no time getting involved in the action, appealing for a penalty after Kazadi sprinted out of his goal and clattered into him as they raced for the ball. Yet just like Peres in the first half, the Brazilian over-dramatised his fall and the referee gave the benefit of the doubt to the goalkeeper, who raised his hands in time-honoured fashion to protest his innocence.

Kidumu's involvement in the game came to a premature end after he landed awkwardly attempting to charge down a clearance and was replaced by Kilasu Massamba. Kazadi, meanwhile, was on the receiving end of some rough treatment from Pereira, who gave Joe Jordan a run for his money by charging into the goalkeeper from a corner. To his credit, Kazadi held onto the ball, leaving Pereira looking a tad sheepish in the midst of some angry Leopards, but the goalkeeper was left dazed by the incident. A minute later, he appeared to lose his bearings altogether and went walkabout, leaving the goal gaping for Nelinho who, having spotted Kazadi off his line, attempted another curving shot that skimmed the top of the crossbar.

N'Tumba won Zaire's first corner of the half after they had again caught Brazil on the break. Not wishing to push men forward, Tshinabu only had three of his teammates to aim for amid a sea of yellow but still managed to find the head of Kibonge. His effort lacked power to truly worry Leão but Pereira panicked and booted the ball out of his keeper's hands. Zaire kept the ball in the final third of the pitch and Brazil struggled to clear their lines as Mukombo, Mana and Mwepu took turns delivering a trio of crosses in quick succession. This spell of possession merely served to anger their opponents, who promptly went down the other end of the field and scored their second.

It was a well worked goal that involved no fewer than eight members of the team and began with Pereira picking up the ball near his own corner flag on the right. It ended with Chagas cutting in from the left touchline and finding Jarzinho on the edge of the Leopards' area, who laid a perfectly weighted pass into the path of Rivellino who fired a full-blooded volley past Kazadi. Despite Kidumu's claims, the keeper had no chance of stopping it, let alone a blind woman, but the relief on Zagallo's face was evident for all to see.

With their tails up, Brazil went in search of the goal that would see them through to the next round. A succession of corners did little more than add a few more bruises to Kazadi's body however, with Jairzinho twice penalised by the referee for roughing up the goalkeeper with some heavy challenges as they competed for the ball in mid-flight.

The match settled into a dull rhythm that was more toing and froing than end-to-end excitement. Brazil would attack only to see their path to goal blocked by the flailing limb of a Leopard then Zaire would launch their own ill-fated offensive that typically ended when a high ball was launched towards the solitary figure of N'Tumba, who would invariably be marked by three defenders. For the television viewers watching from the comfort of their homes, it wasn't much of a spectacle but the crowd inside the stadium were certainly enjoying the defiance being offered by the African side and roared with delight when Lobilo coolly waltzed his way through the Brazilian midfield and Mukombo produced a cheeky Rabona to escape the attentions of Nelinho.

The monotony of this repetitive period of play was finally broken in the 76th minute. Carpegiani's defence splitting pass found Mirandinha who unleashed a powerful, angled shot that Kazadi was unable to hold. Displaying that certain brand of courage pertaining to goalkeepers, he bravely dived head first to recover the rebound but as he did so the striker swung his boot for a second time and caught Kazadi full in the face. Mirandinha protested his innocence but his pleas held little weight with either the goalkeeper's teammates, who ploughed into the attacker, nor the referee, who promptly booked him.

As the melee broke out around him, Kazadi lay motionless on the grass, as if he had been knocked unconscious by the blow, and a concerned Kibonge summoned the trainer and team doctor onto the field, who rushed to the keeper's aid. Mirandinha no doubt argued that the ball was there to be won, but he was fortunate not to have been given a red card for dangerous play. While viewers were entertained with slow motion replays of the incident, the goalkeeper slowly got back to his feet and was given the all clear to continue but when play finally resumed, the cameras zoomed in on a groggy-looking Kazadi still wiping blood away from his nose with a handkerchief.

Less than 90 seconds later, Brazil scored their third. There appeared to be little danger when the ball was played to Valdomiro down the right, more so when he miscontrolled it, but his harmless-looking cross-shot pitched up just in front of the Zaire goalkeeper and bounced under his body. It was a goal that was described in equal measure as a 'freak' by the *Sunday Mirror* and 'unworthy of the Watney Cup, let alone the World Cup' by Peter Corrigan in *The Observer* and would later fuel conspiracy theories surrounding the game. Yet Kazadi could be forgiven for having double vision or a similar ailment, such was the ferociousness of Mirandinha's kick, and his anger at conceding such a soft goal belied the accusations that would later be hurled at him.

The scale of the celebrations that followed were embarrassingly at odds with the quality of the goal but demonstrated the immense relief amongst the Brazilians, who were shameless in their euphoria. While the world champions were busy congratulating one another pitchside, Vidinić shuffled his pack, replacing the hard working Tshinabu with Kembo Uba Kembo, who was given ten minutes to help the Leopards try and find a goal. His impact on the game was immediate, finishing a move that had started in Zaire's own half after Mukombo had robbed a none too impressed Jairzinho of the ball. His cross on the overlap, having beaten Chagas with ease, found N'Tumba seven yards out but inexplicably the striker chose to head the ball back across goal in an attempt to pick out Mana rather than test Leão.

If a deal had been struck at half-time, Brazil showed no intent of honouring it and continued to press for a fourth goal. Chagas was sent tumbling in the box, having clearly been tripped by Mwepu but Mr. Rainea was once again unimpressed. Clearly annoyed by the decision, yellow shirts surrounded the referee to point out the error of his ways while Zagallo angrily prowled the touchline looking for someone to remonstrate with as the Zaire players helped Chagas to his feet.

The referee was far more willing to give the South Americans the benefit of the doubt outside of the penalty area and when the combined force of Kilasu and Bwanga sent Mirandinha tumbling to the floor five minutes from time, he had little hesitation in halting play for a free-kick. Twenty yards out and just left of centre, it was the ideal position for another crack at goal but while no less than five Brazilians were enjoying a conflab over the ball, the referee was having trouble getting the Zaire wall to retreat the required distance. The constant shrill of the official's whistle was heard high above the noise of drums and horns coming from the terraces as chaos reigned for a full minute. The Brazilians were not happy with the position of the wall while the Leopards took umbrage at Nelinho's decision to join them, unceremoniously pushing him away. After what seemed like an age, the ref finally blew for the free-kick to be taken, only for Mwepu to break from the wall and launch the ball downfield to the delight of the crowd and the bemusement of the South Americans.

The moment has long since become part of World Cup folklore and a popular choice for football blooper reels. In 2002 it was voted the fourth most memorable moment in the tournament's history in a poll conducted by Channel Four in the UK and four years later it came sixth in a similar poll held by Brazil's leading sports channel. Mwepu even had the good grace to recreate the incident for ITV's *Fantasy World Cup* with Frank Skinner and David Baddiel, displaying a surprisingly good sense of comic timing in the process. At the time there was very little to laugh about and the incident came to epitomise the perceived immaturity of football in Africa, strengthening the arguments of those opposed to increased involvement of the continent's teams at the expense of some of the more traditional powerhouses of the international game.

Yet the reasons for Mwepu's behaviour remained something of a mystery for nearly thirty years. It wasn't until after Mobutu was deposed that rumours began to emerge about what really happened behind the scenes during the team's stay in West Germany but

Mwepu's own recollections of events have changed over the years. In an interview with the BBC, also in 2002, the player shone a light on the team's missing bonuses and the president's threats towards the team if they conceded more than four goals but failed to explain why he booted the ball away. By 2010 he had added further colour to the story, telling author Jon Spurling that he had panicked and opted to kick the ball away to waste some valuable time, admitting that he felt a bit foolish almost immediately ('It was hard to deny that I looked like an idiot,' he conceded). Yet later that year Mwepu told *World Football* magazine that it was a deliberate act of protest against the Mobutu regime, the aim of which was to get sent off. 'I did not have a reason to continue getting injured while those who will benefit financially were sitting on the terraces watching,' he explained. 'I know the rules very well, but the referee was quite lenient and only gave me a yellow card.'

Whatever his reasons, Mwepu's teammates were oblivious to them. 'I have no idea why he did that,' confessed a flummoxed Kakoko Etepé. 'Possibly he thought that the ball was in play, but he did not explain it to us and it remains a mystery'. Ndaye Mulamba and Mayanga Maku were also puzzled by the incident while Mavuba Mafuila, who was in no doubt that his colleague had done it on purpose, expressed his anger towards Mwepu for making the team 'look like monkeys'. 'It was later said that this was his way of protesting,' asserted the Leopards captain Kidumu Mantanu, 'but I don't think so. It was stupid. *Une absurdité.* He must have simply lost the plot.'

For years, many observers opted to reinforce the myth that Zaire didn't know the laws of the game, following the misguided example set by BBC commentator John Motson who infamously described the incident as a 'bizarre moment of African ignorance.' Some even alluded to a long-forgotten rule that was prevalent in the Belgian Congo when football was first introduced that allowed all free-kicks to become a 'free ball' if not taken within three seconds of the referee's whistle. Such accusations are patently absurd, bordering on offensive. Not only had the Leopards already successfully defended two Brazilian set plays from similar positions but Mwepu was a seasoned international, winning his 23rd cap in his second major tournament.

Perhaps a more rational explanation for the fullback's actions can be found in Zaire's defence of a free-kick awarded against them just minutes after Brazil had made it 2-0. Taken twenty yards out from Kazidi's goal, albeit from the goalkeeper's left on this occasion, the ball had been neatly teed up for Nelinho by Rivellino, but before he could unleash his shot he was charged down by none other than Mwepu, who had raced from the wall the moment the kick was taken in an effort to block any attempt on goal. Just as before, the defender had been positioned at the end of the wall, covering the post nearest the ball, strongly suggesting that the defender had been instructed to close down the attacker in such situations as part of Vidinić's tactics to deal with the known threat from Brazilian set pieces. Mwepu may have innocently jumped the gun the second time around and, having found himself in no man's land, simply panicked.

According to Mwepu's son Dominic, the Leopard had always proudly maintained that he was protesting against Mobutu. He wanted Zaire's failure to be associated with the president, just as their many victories had been. Whether that was an afterthought or not, Mwepu certainly succeeded in his aim and probably deserves the benefit of the doubt.

One person who was not so willing to tolerate such behaviour was the Romanian referee, who wasted no time in getting his book out. Still cast in his role of pantomime villain, Mwepu accepted his punishment by bowing before returning to his place in the wall, where a heated argument was raging between his fellow countrymen and Jairzinho, who had clearly angered the Zaire players. Whatever was said, Brazil's winger lost his composure and was caught by the cameras slapping Mukombo in the mouth. After all the drama, the actual free-kick was something of an anticlimax and with the crowd anticipating something special, Marinho Peres could do little more than smash the ball straight into the wall.

The last five minutes saw the game slowly fizzle out of life, save for one final effort on target from a Chagas freekick that forced Kazadi to palm the ball away for a corner. Zaire were running on empty, Brazil had done enough to win the game and both seemed content to see the game out without any further threat to the scoreboard.

The final whistle brought a sense of relief for both teams, for vastly different reasons. The Leopards had successfully completed their damage limitation exercise but were in no mood to celebrate, opting to quietly leave the field with their heads bowed. Their opponents soaked up undeserved adulation from the 8,000 or so supporters who had shown great patience with their team as they served up a disjointed display peppered by bickering among themselves. Zagallo meanwhile was hugged by his backroom staff and surrounded by journalists seeking a reaction and post-match interview. The weary frown that he had worn for much of the game had been replaced by a broad smile but the following day's newspapers would have made unpleasant reading. The world champions' performance was universally panned, described in equal measure as 'totally shoddy', 'disorganised' and 'unconvincing' and *The Observer* did not hold back on their criticism. 'Brazil qualified at the end of their third unsatisfactory performance of the tournament,' wrote Peter Corrigan, 'and any harsh words reserved to criticise the presence of a team like Zaire in this most elevated of all football tournaments must now be turned on that team we regard as the supreme.'

By contrast, the same newspaper praised the Leopards' robust defence, offering the backhanded compliment that Zaire were 'able to play to their peak, as low as that is'. Kazadi was the pick of the bunch and labelled a 'brave little imp of a goalkeeper' while the *Sunday Independent* of Ireland colourfully described the back four as a 'forest of legs…defending like wizards.' Free-kick misdemeanours and goalkeeping mistakes aside, it had been a much improved performance.

'We didn't play badly actually,' agreed Mayanga, 'Better, I think, than we had against Scotland.'

Admittedly they could not have sunk any lower after the débâcle against Yugoslavia but a certain amount of pride had been restored. Lobilo performed admirably in the heart of the defence while N'Tumba had provided an outlet that had been missing from the Leopards two previous games, despite playing with a heavily-strapped knee. It had been a resilient performance but one that has long since been forgotten. The damage had already been done and an uncertain future now awaited the team when they returned to Zaire.

'The thing we hadn't considered was what would happen if the team didn't play very well in Germany,' recalled Mwepu.

They were about to find out.

15. Fallen Idols

ON THE EVENING of their defeat to Brazil, the players were
allowed to overeat and drown their sorrows with alcohol for
the first time since their arrival. They had been in Europe
for two long months and together as a team for a lot longer but this
would be the last time they sat down as one. They would be leaving
without their coach and mentor Blagoje Vidinić, the man they had
referred to as "His Excellency", who had already informed them that
he would be staying in West Germany with his wife to watch the
rest of the tournament before moving on to pastures new. Presents
were exchanged and gifts presented, with Walburga Krebber, the
local resident whose husband Manfred had been enlisted to act as
an intermediary for the African team, receiving a couple of signed
jerseys and a plate from Tubilandu Ndimbi as thanks for her help
during their stay, their official duties having also ended that evening.
The team were due to fly back to Kinshasa three days later but the
coach wasn't the only member of the squad who planned to miss the
flight.

While assorted members of the official delegation and other
government lackeys mounted one final raid on Ascheberg's electrical
shops, some of the players received offers to extend their stay in Europe
from clubs in France and Germany. Impressed by their individual
performances during the tournament, Saint-Étienne renewed their
interest in Mayanga and Kakoko and Schalke 04 enquired into the
availability of Lobilo Boba. Marseilles meanwhile were in contact
with Kidumu Mantantu and striker Ndaye Mulamba was later
approached by Paris Saint-Germain. Alerted to the possibility of a
mass exodus by Sampassa Kaweta Milombe, his faithful Minister of
Sport, Mobutu acted swiftly to thwart the proposed moves. A decree
was issued, similar to the one that saw the enforced repatriation
of Congolese players plying their trade in Belgium in the 1960s,
prohibiting any Zairean footballer from playing abroad, one that was
accompanied by a thinly disguised ultimatum.

'President Mobutu threatened us,' revealed Kilasu Masamba,
who had also sparked interest from Schalke. 'It was clear. He said

"any player who stays in Europe, I will exterminate his family". In hindsight, you can say he might not have done it. We'll never know. But in 1974, Mobutu was at the height of his power. Who could doubt the execution of such a threat?'

Not willing to risk the wrath of their president, the players reluctantly rejected the opportunity to stay and returned home with the rest of the squad where the national press, following the official line handed down to them, reported that they had done so with the honour of Zaire in their hearts.

Of course, this being Zaire, they weren't allowed to leave quietly. Even as the team were flying over the Mediterranean, stories emerged in the press that the Leopards had stolen the bus provided to them by the organising committee for the duration of the tournament and had attempted to drive it back to Kinshasa. According to Simon Shirley in his book *The World Cup - A Definitive History*, a representative of the company who had supplied the vehicles called at the squad's hotel to collect it only to learn that they had 'already departed, speeding down the autobahn towards Africa with their newly acquired means of transport.' Even as late as 2006, *The Independent* newspaper repeated the tale of the BMW coach being stopped by guards at the German border, further adding to the mythical appeal of the Leopards. Yet as much as part of you would like it to be true, the story was a complete fallacy, made up by someone to fill a few column inches.

Aside from the fact that all the team coaches were made by Mercedes-Benz, the logistics of driving from the northern reaches of West Germany to Kinshasa would arguably have seen the bus break down at some point south of the Algerian city of Tamanrasset. Today, such a journey would take roughly five days non-stop by car, if you exclude the lengthy queues at the nine border crossings, two ferry terminals and numerous petrol stations along the way. In 1974 such a trip would have been far more hazardous, considering the lack of infrastructure at the time, and a tad pointless, as the president had already arranged a flight to bring the team home. In truth, the final journey in their distinctive mode of transport consisted of nothing more than a mundane trip to the airport terminal that passed without incident.

In retrospect, the Leopards may have probably preferred the longer journey by road, such was the greeting that awaited them in Kinshasa. Landing in the dead of night, there was no welcoming committee at the arrival lounge aside from a few journalists and assorted ground staff, both of whom demanded answers from the weary team. It was a far cry from the welcome they had received after their African Cup of Nations victory only months earlier.

'There certainly wasn't a big crowd,' remembers Mayanga. 'People had believed that as the best team in Africa we would be one of the best in the world. People just looked at us sadly. They asked: "How did it happen? How come we lost?" We had to give answers to reporters and their questions were severe. We had to explain that up against high-level professionals, we couldn't unfortunately match them.'

Following the ad hoc press conference, the players filtered out into the night only to discover no transport had been laid on for them to get home. Left stranded, they had to rely on the goodwill of the drivers assembled on the taxi rank outside.

'We found no one at the airport,' recalled Kabasu Babo, one of the reserves in Vidinić's twenty-two man squad. 'We were picked up by the taxi drivers and fans that recognised us, who found us wandering around the terminal in the early hours of the morning.'

The following day the entire team was summoned to appear before President Mobutu via an official announcement broadcast across various media channels at regular intervals, ensuring that the entire country knew that the Leopards were going to have to answer for their failings on the football pitches of West Germany in person. It was a short, sharp directive with a chillingly sinister undertone. 'All the players heard about it on the radio, or via television,' said Mayanga. 'Every hour they repeated this. It kind of scared us.'

One player was so terrified by what potentially awaited the squad that he fled the city and went into hiding. The rest dutifully gathered at the predetermined location on time, where they were taken by bus to the President's Residence at Mont Ngaliema. There, Mobutu was waiting to receive them in the Ministers' Hall, seated with a sceptre-like cane in hand, while his bodyguards slyly positioned themselves between the Leopards and the exit. As they stared at the floor like naughty schoolboys, Mobutu addressed them, looking over his glasses in the same way a headmaster would when about to address a school assembly. His opening gambit sent fearful shivers through the team: "So, you wanted to rebel? Even though I gave you a house and a car?"

Tapping his cane on the hard floor in rhythm with his words to emphasise his displeasure, he admonished them for their performances before menacingly turning his attention to those that had received lucrative offers to play overseas, instantly crushing any dreams they may have still harboured.

'He was a bit vexed,' recalled Mayanga, who was one of those targeted. 'He didn't shout, but he was absolutely firm. He said "Listen, I called you here because certain players want to be mercenaries. Certain players want to act as mercenaries here in my house. But not in my house. No one will leave to go play abroad. No one. You will play here and you will finish your careers here. No one can go and play abroad as long as I am alive." He was really furious. We were frightened and personally, I felt threatened. '

A tense atmosphere filled the room at the conclusion of Mobutu's speech, accompanied by an awkward silence as the president waited for a response, which ultimately came from the team's captain, Kidumu Mantantu, in the absence of their manager. 'No player dared to say anything, you could hear a pin drop,' he said, thinking back to the day in question. 'In the end I silently asked to speak and apologised for what had happened. What else could I do?'

The skipper's apology proved futile. With Mobutu in an unforgiving mood, the entire squad spent an uncomfortable four days under house arrest at Mont Ngaliema, a venue that reputedly housed a number of well-equipped torture chambers, while he mulled over their fate. On the fourth day, the president called the team before him and, after an hour-long dressing down, issued one final threat: "Next time I'll throw you all in prison". They were allowed to return home to their families but the entire squad was banned from leaving the country with immediate effect.

'I couldn't even take the boat to Congo-Brazzaville on the other side of the river,' continued Kidumu. 'In the harbour, lists with the names of the players were displayed under a description that read *Forbidden to leave the country*, just like at the airport. My name hung out at Kinshasa airport for years.'

Contrary to some contemporary reports, those that had been presented with cars and houses prior to the World Cup were allowed to keep the gifts and according to Ndaye, Mobutu promised they would receive their bonuses once his anger had subsided, but even the most optimistic members of the Leopards remained doubtful of them ever materialising. As they left the Presidential Residence they were quietly advised in no uncertain terms by Sampase Kaweta to stay away from the limelight and avoid all public appearances as Mobutu's PR machine went into overdrive in order to deliver the right message to the Zairean people.

At the beginning of July, the government's mouthpiece, *Salongo*, publicly condemned the team, publishing a photograph of the players, lined up in red tracksuits, on their front page accompanied by a headline underlined in red that screamed "The Leopards on trial". Mobutu then issued a spiky press release in response to the continued transfer speculation surrounding the squad, insisting there was 'no question that Zaire will become the cradle of sporting mercenaries'. Finally, on the day hosts West Germany beat the Netherlands 2-1 in the World Cup Final, the state commissioner for youth and sports delivered a report to the national executive council on the team's performance at the tournament. In summing up, Mr. Sakombi Inongo, spokesperson for the council, described the event as 'an extraordinary experience for Zairean football', and as such the national executive considered it its duty, in accordance with the revolutionary demands of the state, to completely rethink the sports policy of Zaire by emphasising 'the political and ideological training of Zairean sportsmen.'

Mobutu played his hand perfectly. By allowing the players to keep their gifts, he could convey the image of a man of honour to his people, a generous benefactor who kept his word despite the team's failings. They would be punished, of course, particularly for their 'unzairean' attitudes, and by focusing on the political shortcomings, rather than inadequacies on the pitch, the president could distance himself from the perceived fiasco. The enforced absence of the Leopards from the public eye removed any possible challenge to this approved narrative. Nevertheless, while the team spent the following weeks holed up in their new homes on the Salongo estate in Lemba, leaving only to train with their clubs, whispers began to filter out of Kinshasa of internments, beatings and worse (one newspaper reported that the players had been fed to Mobutu's pet crocodiles). Keen to understand if Mobutu had carried out his "win or die" ultimatum, foreign journalists began to ask awkward questions surrounding the players' whereabouts.

At the end of July, a European reporter for the *Sydney Morning*

Herald travelled to Brussels to make extensive inquiries into the well-being of the team and met a certain degree of resistance from various representatives of the president's regime. Having first contacted the Zairean Embassy in the city, who rebutted his questions by explaining that they were a 'diplomatic mission not a soccer news agency', he was eventually put in touch with Dielunkunsia wa Luketo, director of the Agence Zaire-Presse, who proved equally evasive. Claiming that he was in Belgium to report about the Common Market and nothing else, Dielunkunsia's patience eventually snapped. 'Nobody has ever threatened them,' he barked. 'Of course they are alive.'

Mobutu could ill-afford any adverse publicity. The much-anticipated title fight for the Heavyweight Championship between George Foreman and Muhammad Ali was on the horizon and the world's press, not to mention a number of A-list celebrities, were due to descend on Kinshasa in great numbers at the beginning of September. The president was already paranoid about the rise in crime in the nation's capital city and the number of attacks on European tourists so could do with one less distraction. As a result, a select number of the Leopards received a temporary reprieve from purgatory and found themselves firmly back in the spotlight ahead of what became known as *The Rumble in the Jungle.*

Having got engaged prior to the World Cup, Ndaye Mulamba married his fiancée in October in a star-studded ceremony that included a reception hosted by popular musician Tabu Ley Rochereau, who played alongside BB King and James Brown at the *Zaire '74* concert held in conjunction with the title fight. The event received widespread press coverage and the following week photos of the happy couple surrounded by the rest of the Leopards team appeared in local magazines and newspapers. Members of the squad, including the newly married couple, were then invited to a star-studded reception held by Mobutu in honour of Muhammad Ali, who had expressed an interest in meeting the players that had triumphed at the African Cup of Nations back in March, a victory that had ensured the boxer's commitment to fight in Zaire. And all seemed to be well and truly forgiven when front-row tickets for Ali's rearranged bout against Foreman, which had to be pushed back a month after the champ received a bad cut while sparring, were hand-delivered by the Ministry of Sport three days before the fight. But it was merely a presidential ruse to assure the visiting media that all was well when it came to the nation's football team.

The irony of the situation was not lost on Ndaye as he sat in the very stadium where the team had secured World Cup qualification. Each boxer had been guaranteed a purse of $5 million by promoter Don King, an amount previously unheard of even in the sport of boxing, and Mobutu was only too happy to stump up the cash to ensure the fight took place in Zaire. There was no direct economic value in staging the bout but he calculated that the publicity generated by such a high-profile event would bring international prestige and expose the world to the beauty and resources of Zaire, not to mention underpin his regime further and enhance his own profile on the world stage. To this end, posters lined the streets of the country advertising the fight with simple propaganda messages that portrayed Mobutu as a generous, father-like figure for the state but one with revolutionary ideals when it came to trumping African imperialism of the past. *"Un cadeau de Président Mobutu au peuple Zairois et un honneur pour l'homme noir"* (A gift of President Mobutu to the Zairois people and an honour for the Black man) read one, another proclaimed "A fight between two Blacks in a Black nation, organised by Blacks and seen by the whole world; that is a victory for Mobutuism". To raise the necessary funds, however, the president raided the country's coffers and diverted the monies raised from the Soccer Tax into the fight's purse. The complimentary tickets were therefore the nearest the Leopards would ever come to receiving their promised bonuses.

The president's gamble ultimately paid off. Mobutu's deeds ensured the country became synonymous with the bout and his face became just as familiar in the build-up as those of Ali and Foreman. The ballyhoo surrounding the event generated an estimated audience of one billion television viewers, all of whom could now pinpoint Zaire on a map and who witnessed Ali pull off one of the greatest sporting upsets of all time when he knocked Foreman out in dramatic fashion in the eighth round.

The result, the positive publicity and the fact the fight grossed an estimated $100 million in revenue worldwide convinced Mobutu to rethink his involvement in football. *The Rumble in the Jungle* had put Zaire on the map with very little risk to the president or the country's reputation.

Football, on the other hand, had proved too capricious for Mobutu's needs and was unlikely to further his cause overseas

Even in Africa, where the Leopards had reigned supreme, there was growing resentment among rival federations towards Zaire, with old adversaries Morocco leading the criticism over their performances at the World Cup. In a forthright interview with *France Football*, Mohamed Benmejdoub, former administrator of the Moroccan National Sports Council, was unequivocal in his belief that the Atlas Lions 'would have done better'. With his enthusiasm and patience having been sorely tested, Mobutu decided he was done with the game and ceased his patronage altogether.

There were early signs of his waning interest when a relative unknown was hired to replace Vidinić. Ștefan Stănculescu had enjoyed a solid if unremarkable playing career as a goalkeeper in the lower leagues of his native Romania before joining the coaching staff of Dinamo Bucharest. He spent sixteen seasons at the club as youth team manager then had a brief spell with Iranian side Aboomoslem prior to his appointment with the Leopards but his achievements, such as they were, hardly made him a worthy successor to the popular Yugoslav.

Considering the average age of the squad that went to West Germany was just twenty-five, a wiser, more experienced coach may have opted for continuity ahead of the next edition of the African Cup of Nations, which was due to be held in Ethiopia in 1976. Stănculescu, possibly acting under the orders of either Mobutu or Sampase Kaweta, decided to ring the changes however and discarded a number of those who had been stalwarts in Vidinić's side for the past two years. Kibonge Mafu and Mavuba Mafuila, both of whom had been vocal critics of Mobutu's regime in the dressing room, would never play for their country again along with midfielder Mana Mambwene and striker Jean Kalala N'Tumba, who had refused to comply with the president's edict requiring Zairean subjects to change their European names. Kazadi Mwamba, another at the forefront of the protests at the World Cup, would spend the next few years in the wilderness before being brought back into the fold, along with Mayanga Maku and Tubilandu Ndimbi, who had equally fallen out of favour. Were they being punished? 'Maybe,' admitted Kidumu, who survived the initial cull, 'but the new coach wanted to build a new team.'

Stănculescu may have felt vindicated when the new-look Leopards won their first three games under his charge but the honeymoon period did not last long. Having beaten Libya in a friendly and recorded back-to-back victories over Upper Volta in their opening qualifier for the 1976 Olympic Games, Zaire won just two of their next ten games. The first signs of trouble came in the Summer of 1975 when they travelled to Tehran to take part in the second edition of the Iran Cup. On paper the challenge offered by Egypt, an Iran 'B' side and Poland's Under-23 team did not appear too taxing but Stănculescu's men contrived to lose all three group games, conceding nine goals. By the end of the year their interest in the Olympics had been ended by Senegal, although the Leopards could have considered themselves unfortunate to go out on penalties, having overcome a two-goal deficit in the first leg to level the tie. With the AFCON fast approaching, it was hardly the ideal preparation for the defence of their title.

The Leopards' campaign in Ethiopia would ultimately prove to be a disappointing experience. Denied the intensive overseas training camps afforded his predecessors, Stănculescu's side were ill-equipped for the challenge and the defensive frailties so evident in Iran were cruelly exposed by a vibrant and emerging Nigeria team in their opening game. Catching the Leopards flat-footed, the Super Eagles raced into a 3-0 lead before the break in front of 4,000 spectators at the Dire Dawa stadium. Babo Kabusu and Ekofa Mbungu managed to reduce the arrears in the second half but their opponents added a fourth in injury time to secure their first ever victory at the tournament and leave Zaire with an uphill task to reach the semi-finals. Under pressure and desperate for a win, the last team they would have wished to face in such circumstances was Morocco but fate had dealt the Leopards with such a hand. Ironically, the reigning champs produced one of their better performances under their Romanian coach but it was not enough to retain their title. Despite dominating the game and putting the Atlas Lions defence under pressure for large periods, they were caught out by a counter attack in the 80th minute that saw Abdellah Zahraoui score the only goal of the game.

Zaire ended their campaign with an uninspiring draw against Sudan, Ndaye scoring one of the last goals of his international career to earn a redundant point and bring the curtain down on the golden age of Congolese football. Having dominated the competition since 1968, the team would not grace the final stages of the tournament for another twelve years.

Unable to inspire his team to the same heights as Vidinić, Stănculescu returned home to see out his career in Romanian football. The Zairean football federation meanwhile would not hire another foreign coach following his departure until appointing German Otto Pfister in the mid-1980s. They couldn't afford to and had to cut their cloth accordingly, turning their attention to local talent instead. The role was first offered to Vidinić's former assistant Nicodème Kabamba, who would have been a popular choice with the players, but the parties could not agree on personal terms ('I had only demanded half of what the Yugoslav was getting!' recalled a light-hearted Kabamba). FEZAFA eventually appointed Célestin Tambwe Leya, a relatively young coach who was forced to retire from playing because of eye problems but had achieved a certain degree of success in his new role, winning the Congolese title with TP Mazembe at the first attempt before repeating the trick with Yanga in Tanzania. A 6-1 victory over Rwanda augured a rosier future of sorts, but off the pitch Zairean football was in turmoil, along with the rest of the country, thanks to a collapse in the copper market.

Qualifying for the 1978 World Cup in Argentina had got off to a fortuitous start when they were awarded a walkover in the opening round after their intended opponents, Central African Republic, withdrew. Pitted against Nigeria in Round Two, the federation opted not to contest the tie however when travel costs proved prohibitive after Mobutu refused a request to fund the away fixture in Lagos. History repeated itself at the start of 1977 when the team were unable to fulfil their opening qualifier for the African Cup of Nations against Gabon (although their leader was quite happy to send a team to China later that year for political reasons). Without the president's money behind them, FEZAFA opted to save face and voluntarily withdraw from all future competitions to avoid any further overseas trips. Devoid of fixtures, Tambwe Leya opted to return to Dar-es Salaam and Zaire went into virtual exile on the international stage, playing just two first class fixtures over the course of thirty-two months. When they returned, they were a shadow of their once great selves.

'We lost momentum (as a nation) after the World Cup because the federation had not considered where the next generation of players would come from,' sighed Jean Kalala N'Tumba. 'The general level of football was too low.'

Mobutu's reign came to an end in the Spring of 1997, having

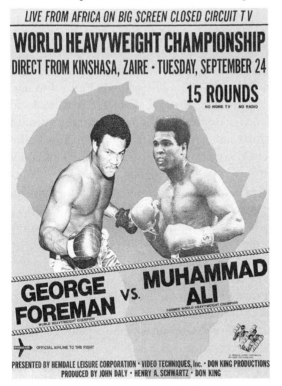

LIVE FROM AFRICA ON BIG SCREEN CLOSED CIRCUIT TV

WORLD HEAVYWEIGHT CHAMPIONSHIP
DIRECT FROM KINSHASA, ZAIRE · TUESDAY, SEPTEMBER 24
15 ROUNDS
NO HOME TV   NO RADIO

GEORGE FOREMAN vs. **MUHAMMAD ALI**
WORLD HEAVYWEIGHT CHAMPION   FORMER WORLD HEAVYWEIGHT CHAMPION

OFFICIAL AIRLINE TO THE FIGHT

PRESENTED BY HEMDALE LEISURE CORPORATION · VIDEO TECHNIQUES, Inc. · DON KING PRODUCTIONS
PRODUCED BY JOHN DALY · HENRY A. SCHWARTZ · DON KING

A poster promoting what would become known as 'The Rumble in the Jungle', funded in part by the Zaire squad's misappropriated World Cup bonuses.

been overthrown from power in what became known as the First Congo War. Zaire was renamed the Democratic Republic of Congo the day after his dethronement and having fled into exile, the former president would die in Morocco from prostate cancer the following September, a month short of his 67th birthday.

The football team experienced an upturn in fortunes the following year when they achieved an unexpected third-place finish at the African Cup of Nations in Burkina Faso, their best performance since they won the title in Egypt and a feat they would repeat in 2015. That elusive second appearance at the World Cup still evades the Leopards however. They came close in 2018, missing out by a single point to Tunisia, and were within touching distance in 2022, having reached the play-offs for Qatar. There they met an old foe, falling at the final hurdle to none other than Morocco, who no doubt saw the result as fitting retribution for the events of 1973.

16. Legacies

MBUNGU EKOFO was the last man standing in the Salongo district of Lemba, still known colloquially as *Leopards' Neighbourhood*, his teammates having long since moved away. As of 2010, he also still owned the green Volkswagen Passat that came with the house, although both had seen better days. After hanging up his boots, the striker made the most of the gifts bestowed on him by Mobutu and became a taxi driver, capitalising on his brief flirtation with fame in the process. 'People were curious to meet me,' he confessed when asked about his new profession, before revealing the secret to his car's longevity. 'She lasted this long because I'm a mechanic. It's hard, but it's my job.'

Yet as the car approached its fortieth birthday, it finally gave up the ghost and he lost his income. Luckily for Mbungu help was at hand. In 2015, a mere 41 years after their appearance at the World Cup, the Leopards finally received financial recompense for their achievements from the Congolese Football Association (FECOFA). It was a far cry from the amounts originally promised but the federation, aware of the financial difficulties experienced by a number of those that had triumphed at the African Cup of Nations not only in 1974 but also 1968, agreed to pay a monthly pension of $200 to those in need still living in the country. The Congolese government had initially promised a similar annuity of $500 four years earlier but, true to form, many had failed to receive any payment, forcing FECOFA to honour the promises of others dating back to 1974. Mbungu was one of the grateful beneficiaries of the allowance but sadly for a number of his teammates, this altruistic act came too late.

Zaire's decline had begun in earnest even before the Leopards had reached West Germany, although very few people were aware of it at the time. Mobutu's Zairianization programme was heading for disaster, as foreign businesses and industries were handed over to the president's cronies and political allies, who had neither the experience nor the acumen to make a success of their new ventures. By the end of the year, the commercial infrastructure was in ruins, leading to a widespread shortage of food and consumer goods. The collapse in the price of the country's key mineral exports only accelerated the inevitable economic crash and as Zaire's trade balance deteriorated further, so did the overall standard of living as the country faced international bankruptcy.

It was not a good time to be in the president's bad books as the Leopards quickly found out. Those that had been discarded by Ștefan Stănculescu felt the pinch first, none more so than Jean Kalala N'Tumba. Shortly after his omission from the national team, the striker underwent surgery to try and fix the problematic knee injury that limited his appearances in Europe. He had first gone under the knife in a Sarajevo hospital in Yugoslavia ahead of the World Cup but, still struggling, he required a second operation in January 1975, which took place in the less refined surroundings of the town of Kisantu. A year later, still with AS Vita Club, he was sent to Brussels for further treatment, where medical staff advised him to retire at the age of 27. On his return to Zaire, unable to secure a suitable position in the game and with a growing family to support, N'Tumba left football for good. He wasn't the only player to face such difficulties.

'We began to find that doors were slammed in our faces because of what happened. Mobutu began to destroy our careers,' explained Mwepu Ilunga, who would make his last appearance for the Leopards during their ill-fated appearance at the Iran Cup. 'Our contracts at our clubs were cut and when some of the more experienced members of the squad tried to get coaching jobs they were turned down. Mobutu's contacts saw to that.'

Mwepu's claims were refuted by Tambwe Musangelu, the Chief of Administration with the Zaire federation at the time, who argued that Leopards had no one but themselves to blame for their situation. 'They received cars, money and the players were all hired by the state as state employees,' he asserted. 'They were scattered throughout the Republic, in the leagues, as trainers. They all gave it up.'

If true, such a career path was not afforded to N'Tumba, who had little option but to rethink his future. He eventually retrained as a teacher and carved out a career in education. He would continue to live in the house he received from Mobutu, with his own green Passat parked outside, until 1988 when he emigrated to France, settling in Clermont-Ferrand with his wife and seven children. His son Zico would play professionally for Metz, De Graafschap and NEC Nijmegen among others and would also win international recognition with the Leopards. He passed away in 2021 in Paris, just days after his 72nd birthday, and was honoured with a minute's silence ahead of the national team's fixture against Libya the following week.

Fellow striker Ndaye Mulamba was also honoured with a minute's silence before a match at the African Cup of Nations in Burkina Faso in 1998. The only problem was that *Volvo* was still very much alive. *Radio La Voix du Congo* had erroneously announced that the tournament's all-time top goalscorer had been killed in a diamond mining accident in Angola, a report that was then relayed to the tournament's organising committee, who acted in haste rather than confirm the validity of the story.

Ndaye read about his demise in a copy of *Le Potentiel*, a daily Congolese newspaper, a week later at home in the South African city of Cape Town, where he was living in exile. He had managed to eke out another fourteen years playing football following the World Cup but saw his match bonuses, his only source of income, fall to such an extent that his family had to rely on the wage his wife received as a secretary at a car dealership to survive. Mobutu's decision to devalue Zaire's currency led to a rise in inflation that swallowed up what little savings he did have and, like N'Tumba, he struggled to find employment following his retirement. Hoping to land a coaching position with either AS Vita Club or CS Imana, Ndaye was instead forced to accept short-term contracts with local amateur teams who could not afford to pay a regular salary and supplemented his income by taking a low-paid job as an admin clerk.

In 1994, on the 20th anniversary of his goalscoring feats in Egypt, the striker was invited by the Confederation of African Football to the latest edition of the continental championship in Tunisia where he received the federation's Order of Merit from President Issa Hayatou wearing a suit paid for by a cigarette company. However, what should have been a celebration of his achievements sparked a series of events that changed his life forever.

Shortly after the ceremony, Ndaye was approached by Zaire's latest Minister for Sport, Charles Bofasa Djema, who offered his congratulations on behalf of Mobutu. To his surprise, the Minister offered to personally deliver the medal to the president as a gift from the player but Ndaye refused to part with it. On his arrival back in Kinshasa, he was met by the Minister's Chief of Staff, who requested the medal for a second time only to receive an equally short shrift.

Later that evening, while Ndaye slept, four armed men broke into his house and held him at gunpoint, demanding not only money but also the medal. In the resulting melee, the striker was beaten and shot twice in the leg. When his 11-year-old son came to investigate the noise, one of the assailants struck him with the butt of a sub-machine gun, inflicting a fatal blow. The ordeal ended when Ndaye was dragged to a car, beaten up and thrown over a bridge onto railway tracks below with a warning to never disrespect the minister again.

Ndaye spent eight months in hospital recuperating; his leg was saved but he was left with a limp. In one of life's cruel twists of fate, in the days leading up to his attack in Kinshasa, Ndaye had been contemplating emigrating to Belgium with his family, having taken advice from Mayanga Maku and seen at first hand the life the winger had built for himself during a fleeting trip to Brussels after receiving his medal from CAF. Fearing for his life and now broke, he fled to South Africa instead, where he lived an anonymous but precarious existence until the day his death was incorrectly announced over the airwaves. Thrust back into the spotlight, he used his plight to remind those in charge of their responsibilities to former players in a valiant attempt to improve their collective lot.

'Former members of the national team are living in very difficult conditions,' he told *African Soccer Magazine*. 'The people who run African football, who should be there to help us, just keep quiet. It's shocking. In Africa, former footballers are not respected. You're adored at the time, but once you're no longer a star, you're finished.'

Pulling no punches, he highlighted the sad end of his friend and teammate Kazadi Mwamba, who had lived two doors down from the striker in the Salongo District. 'Kazadi twice won the Nations Cup and the African Champions' Cup but he lies in a pauper's grave.' The goalkeeper had died just weeks before *La Voix du Congo's* blunder after a long illness. Unable to work, he was forced to sell his home but, in great pain, died penniless in the slums of Kinshasa. 'He was sick, he suffered badly,' revealed midfielder Mana Mambwene, echoing Ndaye's sentiments. 'A great keeper like Kazadi ensured that Zaire won all those cups but we didn't see federation officials or ministers at his funeral. It hurts to think I'll probably suffer the same fate.'

Kazadi remains the only goalie to have been voted Player of the Tournament at the African Cup of Nations and continued to play for his country until 1980, having been recalled to the side following

Stănculescu's disastrous reign. In 2000 he was posthumously named the Democratic Republic of the Congo's Goalkeeper of the Century, placing fifth overall for African keepers, but is still unfairly remembered as the keeper who was substituted for no apparent reason during the game against Yugoslavia.

His replacement that day, Tubilandu Ndimbi, managed to bounce back from his only appearance at the World Cup and was still playing for Zaire in 1985, appearing in an African championship qualifier against Congo in Brazzaville. At club level, he enjoyed a remarkably successful spell with AS Vita Club, winning ten championship titles and the African Cup of Champions Cup, before managing to forge a career as a goalkeeping coach with Vita Club and Racing Club Kinshasa among others. In 2008 he accompanied the national team to the FIFA Under-20s Women's World Cup and would later train the Men's Under-23 team before passing away in June 2021 after contracting COVID.

Ndaye continued to fight for recognition despite his failing health. In 2007 he suffered a stroke and was plagued by heart and kidney problems for the rest of his life, eventually being confined to a wheelchair as a result of the injuries sustained from the shooting. A proud man, he had continued to work as a car park attendant when his knees allowed him but never escaped the poverty that equally crippled him and was forced to rely on the generosity of Cameroon international Samuel Eto'o when his condition worsened. After a long illness, *Volvo* slipped away in a Johannesburg hospital in January, 2019. His remarkable life was captured in a biography published in 2010, the same year he became a focal point for the organising committee for the World Cup in South Africa, and his final years were made slightly more comfortable through discreet payments from CAF, keen to make up for the failings of Mobutu's regime.

His friend and confidant Mayanga Maku made the most of the opportunity afforded to him following his move to Belgium at the tail-end of his career, which seemed to falter in the aftermath of the World Cup. Singled out as a mercenary by the president, the winger became a sporadic member of the Leopards' squad in later years. He made just a handful of appearances after the breakdown of his proposed move to Saint-Étienne and was not even selected for Zaire's defence of their AFCON title in 1976. His final appearance came three years later in an African championship qualifier against Guinea but, despite the 3-2 win, it was not a happy occasion for the player, whose selection and performance was openly criticised by the *Elima* newspaper. Moving overseas, he would finally get his chance to play professionally in Europe, albeit in the lower leagues.

In 1982 Mayanga joined Royal Olympic Club de Charleroi, a third-tier Belgian side where he spent two seasons before dropping down a division to play for Wallonia Namur. After hanging up his boots, he took his coaching badges with the Royal Belgian Football Union, leading to a job training the youth team at his former club in Charleroi. In December 2000 he was named the new boss of the Democratic Republic of Congo's national side, tasked with overseeing the team's World Cup qualifying campaign for Japan & South Korea. He faced a familiar problem, however, when he tried to organise a training camp ahead of his first away game against Tunisia, namely a lack of money which forced him to reduce the number of locally-based players he wished to take from 16 to 10. 'I wanted to camp for 20 days in Morocco, to acclimatise to the conditions in the Maghreb,' he explained, 'but there was no money'.

Lack of funds had been an ongoing issue for the national side ever since Mobutu withdrew his support and the country's football federation remained plagued by corruption and incompetence that continued to undermine a team struggling to compete. In 1996, ahead of the 20th edition of the African Cup of Nations in South Africa, $500,000 earmarked for the squad's wages and bonuses went missing somewhere between Kinshasa and Durban, where it was rumoured that the Minister of Sport, a certain Sampassa Kaweta Milombe, had purchased a new summer house. In an echo of events prior to the game against Yugoslavia, several of the team refused to play until they were paid and their Turkish coach, Muhsin Ertuğral, resigned.

Mayanga's own spell in charge of the Leopards lasted just a few months due to the ongoing financial problems, but he returned for a second stint less than twelve months later. *Goodyear* would return to Belgium, where he continued to work as a coach until retirement. His son, Alba, played professionally in the Belgian Second Division while his grandson Alan was on Anderlecht's books and later also played for Olympic Charleroi. In 2006, he was selected by CAF as one of the best 200 football players in Africa to ever play the game.

Mayanga was one of five former Leopards to leave Zaire

Winger Kakoko Etepé in action for VfB Stuttgart during a UEFA Cup tie against FC Koln in December, 1980.

during Mobutu's reign. Fellow winger Kakoko Etepé, who was also selected in CAF's top 200 list, had Mercedes-Benz to thank for his passage to Europe after they opted to send him to West Germany on a car maintenance scholarship in 1977. Even with the weight of sponsorship from the manufacturing giant behind him, he still had a nervous wait for clearance to leave the country but it proved to be a more fortuitous opportunity than he could have possibly imagined.

'It took a long time for my visa to come through, but when it was finally issued, I went to Germany for the second time,' he recalled. 'I was playing part-time football and working at Mercedes in Stuttgart when VfB Stuttgart heard that there was a player who had played in the 1974 World Cup finals and they asked me to come along to training.'

Kakoko joined *Die Roten's* amateur side, winning the West German amateur championship in 1980 before finally making his professional debut in a 2-2 draw against Werder Bremen later that year. After two seasons in the reserves, he joined FC Saarbrücken, helping the team to promotion to the second tier of German football in his first season. He scored nine times in 27 matches as they consolidated their position in the 2. Bundesliga before winding down his career with

Borussia Neunkirchen in the lower leagues.

Although his time in the spotlight was short, Kakoko remains philosophical about this career. There is no bitterness about the lack of money he made from the game and he considers himself fortunate in comparison to his former teammates. 'Football has given me a lot and I would not have achieved all that I have achieved had I not played at the World Cup. But it makes me sad to think that some of them have nothing to show for their success,' he lamented.

The man who reputedly once ran down a zebra still lives in Germany, although his passing was also misreported at the end of 2021. His son Yannick, who was born in Saarbrücken, was once on the books of Bayern Munich and represented the country of his birth at youth level.

Kidumu Mantantu followed Kakoko to Europe in 1978, having retired the previous year. A divisive figure within the Leopards camp, he was seen as an outsider by many of the team, despite his status as captain. As a consequence it was said that his family had paid for him to fly to the United States and attend university in Michigan while his former teammates struggled to make ends meet. In reality he had flown to Brussels shortly after Mobutu had lifted the ban on the Leopards leaving the country, where he found work with the national airline Air Zaire. After being recognised in the street by a Zairean government advisor, he was offered a role within the Zaire embassy in the Belgian capital. Today he lives in Charleroi, surviving on his Leopards pension, and has not returned home in years, ruefully admitting that 'there is no one there waiting for me'.

Former African Footballer of the Year Bwanga Tshimen departed for Paris in 1981 after a successful career that saw him become one of the most decorated players in the country's history, ending on a high with victory in the African Cup Winners' Cup the previous year. His talents had attracted many suitors early on, including interest from SV Hamburg and Standard Liège, but despite setting his heart on playing in Europe, he was denied a transfer by his club president. On arrival in France, Bwanga spent two years at the National Institute of Sport, Expertise and Performance in Vincennes, becoming a youth coach in the town of Les Ulis just outside the capital, where he still resides. In 2000, he was voted the Democratic Republic of Congo's greatest football player of the 20th Century by the International Federation of Football History and Statistics (IFFHS), completing a family double alongside his brother, Kazadi.

In common with Mayanga and Kakoko, Mavuba Mafuila's son Rio also played professional football but he would sadly not live to see him make his debut. He died aged just 47 in 1997 from amyotrophic lateral sclerosis, more commonly known as Lou Gehrig's Disease, when Rio was just 14. A favourite of Vidinić, if only for his sense of humour and happy disposition, Mavuba's last involvement in international football was watching from the stands as the Leopards lost to Brazil. He would remain with AS Vita Club for the rest of his career, winning three further titles, before the fickle finger of fate intervened. Married to an Angolan, Mavuba, and his heavily pregnant wife, together with their children, fled the civil war that tore Angola apart in 1984 to escape the government death squads that had targeted the former Leopard. Setting sail for France, Rio was born in international waters while at sea but despite arriving at their intended destination with no passports, they were accepted as war refugees and allowed to settle in the country. Further tragedy would befall the family when Mavuba's wife died within months of their arrival, leaving him to bring up their ten children by himself. Orphaned at an early age, Rio would later win international recognition with his adopted homeland and enjoy a successful club career with Bordeaux and Lille.

France would also feature heavily in Kembo Uba Kembo's post playing career, if for slightly differing reasons. Something of a Francophile, Kembo and his wife sent their son Jirès to live with the midfielder's sister in Bondy, a commune in the north-eastern suburbs of Paris, in the hope of providing him with the chance of a better education and quality of life while they remained in Zaire. Jirès, who was named after the French international midfielder Alain Giresse, a player his father had long admired, was spotted by scouts and, in a peculiar turn of events, went to live with his coach at AS Bondy, who became his legal guardian when he was eleven. The coach in question was Wilfred Mbappé and Jirès would become the adopted big brother, role model and first football hero of Wilfred's two sons, World Cup winner Kylian and his brother Ethan. Jirès would himself make the grade with Rennes and follow in his father's footsteps when he was capped by the Leopards.

Kembo Uba Kembo had courted controversy during the early part of his career, allegedly having an affair with the girlfriend of popular guitarist Bavon Marie Marie and for using skin bleaching products, but Bavon's untimely death in a car accident jolted the player onto the straight and narrow. Like many of his teammates, Kembo's international career ended in 1976 but the forward would continue to win domestic trophies with AS Vita Club alongside Mavuba, Tubilandu and others for another four seasons before calling time on his career in 1980. Having sold his house and Passat to support his family and fund his son's passage to France, he died in Kinshasa in March 2007. Nine years later, the new municipal football ground in his hometown of Matete was named in his honour.

Slowly but surely the *Leopards' Neighbourhood* in Salango was shorn of actual Leopards. Once one of the most luxurious and exclusive areas of Kinshasa, many of the buildings have fallen into disrepair and the paved streets have become a distant memory, washed away by devastating rainy seasons over the years. The reasons for the exodus however had more to do with the financial practicalities of maintaining a house and car rather than the district's fall from grace.

'Not everyone could afford to keep their little fortune,' admitted midfielder Kibonge Mafu. 'Most of them sold.'

The majority did so out of necessity rather than to simply cash-in on their windfalls, moving to cheaper properties elsewhere in the city and in some cases into the slums that sprung up outside Kinshasa as Mobutu's failed economic policies began to bite.

Lobilo Boba struggled more than most following the end of his playing days. Despite winning the Silver Ball in *France Football's* annual poll to find the African Player of the Year in 1974, the defender made little money from the game, rarely earning more than $300 in "expenses" from his club. In 1986 he lost his job. Unable to find employment elsewhere, he was forced to sell his home and move his family to a commune on the edge of the city called Kisenso, relying on the good will of others to survive. As a result, Lobilo has long since fallen out of love with the game that seemingly treated him so badly.

'I never thought I would end my life like this,' he ruefully admits. 'I gave up my studies for football. I wanted to reach the top of the world and honour the national flag and I did. Now the country is not grateful. Abroad, people know me, people talk about me to this day, whereas I enjoy no honour even on the avenue where I live. You just have to see where and in what conditions most of us live. It's unworthy of our status. If someone did a job you must give him what he deserves. If you pay me, and I still can't clothe myself, then you insult me. They didn't give me anything, yet called me a beggar. I wasted my time. I regret not completing my studies. If I had, I might be safe from this unfortunate end of life.'

Ashamed by his descent into poverty, Lobilo refused to entertain the great Eusebio, who had requested to meet the defender during a visit to Kinshasa, and later hid from a documentary film crew who had tracked him down in 2008, two years after he was named as one of Africa's greatest players by CAF. With the help of his former teammates, he slowly returned to public life and in 2019 a testimonial was held in Brussels to celebrate the 50th anniversary of his debut.

One of those that had come to Lobilo's aid during that time was Kilasu Massamba, the pair having forged a close friendship in the early days of their career with the national team. Their relationship was so strong that when Kilasu found himself a free agent following a dispute with Bilima (now known as AS Dragons), the president of Vita Club, Franco Lwambo, sent Lobilo to the midfielder's house, accompanied by popular singer Youlou Mabiala, in an effort to capture the player's signature. In demand, Kilasu eventually agreed to join CS Imana instead, having been courted in similar fashion by Kakoko Etepé, who more pertinently brought a contract and a signing-on fee that amounted to two years of his salary at TabaZaire, the country's tobacco giant where he held down a second job.

A precocious youngster, the midfielder was first called up to play in the friendly against Yugoslavian club side FC Zeljeznicar in 1971 and would go on to become a permanent fixture in the Zaire setup alongside Lobilo under Blagoje Vidinić, who once described Kilasu as the only Leopard who could play in any team in the world. After the collapse of the pair's proposed move to Schalke, Kilasu enjoyed a brief spell with FC Babeti ya Kin before leaving football for good to return to the tobacco industry. Contrary to the experiences of other members of the team, his appearance at the World Cup would serve him well in later life.

'There was this notoriety that we had, which has opened many doors,' said the midfielder. 'I worked at AZDA (Zaire's official distributors of Volkswagen motors), where I was Head of the Sales Department, at Motuka (another car company) and at TabaZaire.'

In 1988, Kilasu moved to Anglo to escape the chaos of Mobutu's regime, where he built a new life but remained in constant contact with his friend until the midfielder's death in June, 2020 after a long period of illness.

Kilasu's passing led to renewed calls for the DR Congo government to take better care of the veterans of the country's Cup winning teams. Both the Sports League for the Promotion and Defence of Human Rights (LISPED) and the Union of Footballers of Congo (UFC) have continued to highlight the fate of many of the players, not only of the class of '74 but also 1968, demanding improved medical care and financial support. Yet despite repeatedly sounding the alarm bells, successive administrations have done little to help, paying nothing more than lip service to the issue, a fact that was brought starkly into focus by the death of Kabasu Babo in 2022 when his body lay in the mortuary for two months because his family could not afford to bury him. Sadly, it has been an ongoing problem for a number of years.

Mwpeu Ilunga died in 2015 after a long battle with his health aged 66. Mwanza Mukombo, the diminutive left-back who played in all three games in West Germany, died in 2001 aged just 55. Winger Tshinabu Wa Munda succumbed to cancer a year later aged 56 and the classy defender Julien Kialunda, who returned to Zaire to spearhead their African Nations title bid in 1972, died prematurely from AIDS in 1987 (Unconnected to Kialunda's illness, the first case of the disease in West Germany was attributed to the visiting Zaire football team of 1974).

Yet such was the impact of the Leopards and the unprecedented success they achieved for Zaire on the football pitch that their memories live on, sometimes in the oddest of circumstances. In 2022, Spanish journalist Pablo Montanaro cursed Mukombo's name in jest because the defender was the one player missing from an ill-fated attempt to complete the 1974 Panini sticker album and the sticker of Mavuba Mafuila produced by the now defunct British firm FKS Publishing is equally in demand, if only because the player is pictured wearing a pair of thick-rimmed spectacles. Away from trading cards and sticker albums, the Leopards shirt is routinely voted one of the greatest of all-time and Mwepu's indiscretion is rolled out on a frequent basis typically ahead of the latest edition of the World Cup.

Attitudes towards the defender softened in later years however and such was his fame that his passing triggered a number of glowing tributes and flattering obituaries, including several from leading

European publications. On social media, there was an outpouring of grief from fans and admirers, including Crystal Palace and DR Congo winger Yannick Bolasie who thanked the former defender for the advice he had provided. A complex, sometimes contradictory figure, Mwepu held a grudge against Mobutu for many years but seemed to come to terms with the role he played in undermining the president's ambitions and his place in the game's history.

'I heard it rumoured that Mobutu reckoned the team had set the perception of African football back by 20 years,' he told author Jon Spurling in 2010. 'I suppose that if your sole purpose is to promote a more positive image of Africa then we had disgraced him.'

Mwepu eventually did succeed as a coach, training teams in DR Congo and overseas, ultimately working as the assistant to Florent Ibenge at the 2015 Africa Cup of Nations a year before his death. His life had been dominated by the game but the highpoint was still getting to West Germany.

'My best memory of football is the World Cup,' he confessed. 'It wasn't easy - only one team could represent Africa in the World Cup. Now there are five. Back then we were alone. We fought for a single place.'

It's a sentiment that Mana Mambwene, who made a living retreading tyres in the streets of Kinshasa, shares. 'It was great, all this love that our people showed us,' he said fondly. 'We were the most important men in the country. Received by the president who decorated us. It was truly pure bliss. One of my best memories. I stopped playing long ago, but people still appreciate me. They remember my past achievements. People still remember us,' he continued. 'But it was an incredible contrast between the return after the Africa Cup of Nations and the return after the World Cup. It was hard. Even if the results were not what we expected, we should still have been treated better than that but the ties I forged playing football helped me.'

Kibonge Mafu made a point of trying to correct the mistakes of the past. The oldest member of Vidinić's World Cup squad, he saw himself as the natural leader of the team and in 2006, twenty-six years after he last kicked a ball in anger with AS Vita Club, he returned from Belgium to stand for parliament in the country's first free elections with a personal mandate to secure financial recompense due to the side. Demonstrating a natural flair for politics, he unashamedly used a photo of himself with Pelé, taken before the Leopards' friendly against Santos in 1967, on all his campaigning paraphernalia but failed to get elected, finishing second to a rival candidate. However, his efforts were not in vain.

Kibonge's endeavours brought the plight of the Zaire team back into the public consciousness and led to the government promising a pension of $500 a month to each member of the team that was still alive. Although the payments eventually dried up, it was a financial boon for many of the squad, one that was gratefully received by those who needed help, including Zaire's very own Mr. Football, Nicodème Kabamba.

Kabamba holds a special place in the hearts of many in the game in his homeland. Captain of the 1968 AFCON winning team and assistant coach in 1974 in both Egypt and at the World Cup, he was one of the original *Belgicians* and went through his entire playing career without ever picking up a booking. Following events in West Germany, and having failed to agreed terms with FEZAFA with regards to taking over the role of coach with the national side, he plied his trade at domestic level, enjoying success with TP Mazembe, FC Lubumbashi Sport and FC Lupopo and even co-founded his own club, Scom Mikishi, who won the Linafoot title in 1991. In later years, in support of Kibonge's initiative, he helped form *l'Association des Léopards Champions d'Afrique des Nations de Football 68-74 et Mondialistes* in aid of those players that had represented the Leopards during the team's glory days, holding regular get togethers at his own home. Increasingly frail in later years, he was confined to a wheelchair but still actively promoted the players' cause. When he died in 2020 it was a mark of his popularity that his funeral was attended by a number of politicians, football administrators, those he coached and his former teammates. It was also a sign that attitudes in the country had changed since the passing of Kazadi Mwamba.

'The authorities of the country have understood that we must honour those who have honoured the country', reflected Alain Makengo, legal counsel to LIPSED. 'This is the reason why everyone has come to pay their respects to a champion.'

And what of Kabamba's boss, Blagoje Vidinić? Two years after stepping down from his role with Zaire, the enigmatic coach headed to South America to take up a similar position with Colombia who were due to hold the World Cup finals in 1986. The move was engineered by his good friend Horst Dassler who, having just struck a secret deal to take over French company Le Coq Sportif, was planning ahead and looking for sponsorship endorsements with potential finalists, believing his relationship with the new first team coach of the Colombians would help facilitate such an opportunity. Unfortunately for Dassler, his plan started to unravel when the country's economic problems began to jeopardise their ability to host the tournament. They eventually surrendered their right to stage the finals in 1982 but Vidinić at least secured the team's shirt sponsorship before he returned to Europe, having been unable to repeat his African success in South America.

The Yugoslav headed to France, where he turned his back on coaching and took a full-time job within Dassler's organisation, becoming an Ambassador for Le Coq Sportif, landing shirt deals with Algeria, Cameroon and Italy in time for the World Cup in Spain. In 1989, having enjoyed success in his new career, Vidinić set up International Soccer Marketing (ISM) with his daughter, Zorana, with the aim of buying and selling sponsorship rights within the game and together they would go on to secure exclusive marketing rights of the Copa Libertadores. He passed away at the end of 2006. There is no record of Vidinić having ever returned to Zaire, but it was probably no coincidence that the national team wore a kit manufactured by Le Coq Sportif in the 1980s.

Today, the Leopards are held in high regard in the Democratic Republic of Congo, where their victories at the African Cup of Nations are fondly recalled and at times revered. Contrary to expectation, the team's appearance at the World Cup underlines rather than undermines their status as footballing legends within the country and people are still proud of their achievement of being the first black African nation to qualify. Overseas, their legacy is slightly more problematic however.

Zaire finished their World Cup campaign with one of the worst records ever recorded in the competition. Played three, lost three, goals for zero, goals against fourteen. Only South Korea, who conceded sixteen in two games back in 1954, have a worst record for the opening round. El Salvador's 10-1 loss at the hands of Hungary in 1982 at least superseded their record of most goals conceded in a single match, one they shared with the Korean side who were unfortunate enough to come up against the great Magyar team of Puskas, Hidegkuti and Kocsis. Yet the Leopards defeat against Yugoslavia and Mwepu's antics against Brazil have somehow become ingrained into the psyche of football fans around the world and the name Zaire is now synonymous with the worst the World Cup has to offer while South Korea and El Salvador have somehow escaped the same ridicule.

At the time, however, they were not alone. Having given Italy a fright in their opening game, fellow minnows Haiti were brought crashing back down to earth by Poland the day after the calamity at the Parkstadion in a 7-0 defeat that encouraged further criticism regarding both team's involvement in the competition. Like the Leopards, the Haitians had experienced their own problems ahead of their second game. Midfielder Ernst Jean-Joseph failed a drugs test following the match against Italy, the first player to do so in the history of the competition, and was banned by FIFA. Having brought shame on the country, he was beaten up by members of the official delegation on the orders of Haiti's leader Baby Doc Duvalier in front of his teammates, which led to many of them having a sleepless night ahead of the game against Poland.

Regardless of the problems each faced away from the pitch, it was their performances on it that brought the question of future participation of teams from the Third World into sharp focus. Outgoing FIFA President Sir Stanley Rous, still bitter at his defeat to Dr João Havelange, who had been elected on a mandate to increase the presence of such nations at the World Cup, was quick to pour scorn on the results, which he felt devalued the competition. He was naturally supported by the media in England, France and Spain, whose indignation was fuelled by imperial sentiments of entitlement and racism rather than the failings and inabilities of their own teams during qualifying. Scottish journalist Malcolm Brodie's summing up was typical of the feeling of the day. 'Haiti and Zaire don't really belong in this grade of competition,' he wrote. '(they're) an embarrassment to a series endowed with so much talent.'

A large dose of racial prejudice helped set the tone and lowered the expectations around the footballing ability of both teams even before the competition started. The heavy defeats merely reinforced such prejudices, despite commendable performances against Italy and Scotland. Yet in the intervening years Haiti's reputation has recovered and their match against Poland barely registers a mention, partly thanks to Emmanuel Sanon's opener against the Italians that ended Dino Zoff's record breaking run of clean sheets but the narrative around Zaire has remained largely unchanged.

Although there has been a little more sensitivity towards the Leopards in recent years in light of the revelations around the missing bonuses, their creditable performances against the Scots and Brazil have been all but forgotten. The match against Scotland in particular has been blighted by a certain degree of revisionism, especially on the part of the Scottish squad themselves, who seem to hold a grudge against the Leopards and have been less than complimentary since that balmy evening in June, 1974. In a BBC documentary screened in 2010, winger Willie Morgan pulled no punches, describing Vidinić's side as a 'pub team that hadn't got a clue' while defender Gordon McQueen labelled the Zaire goalkeeper as 'hopeless'. Try as they might to convince themselves this to be true, neither statement holds much water following a repeat viewing of the game. As the match wore on, the Scots visibly struggled against the so-called 'pub team' from Africa and the Leopards made them work hard for their win, relying on David Harvey to keep them at bay. And try all they might, they were unable to find a way past Kazadi, who more than made amends for his first-half error with a string of outstanding saves. Indeed, *The Guardian* newspaper noted that Zaire possessed 'a number of players of outstanding speed and skill... (who) created enough chances to draw with Scotland' and later in the tournament defender Jim Holton freely admitted that the Leopards had provided a sterner test than Yugoslavia.

In truth, many of the Scotland team blame Zaire for their elimination and assert the scoreline would have been different had they played them in the second or third game. While it is hard not to feel a degree of sympathy for their plight, especially as they went home unbeaten, the truth of the matter is had they managed to beat Brazil or Yugoslavia their victory over the Leopards would have been a mere footnote in their history rather than a blot on the landscape.

Mwepu's rush of blood and the collective failure against Yugoslavia has led to a quadrennial fascination with Zaire that has kept the team in the spotlight for almost fifty years, not just for the wrong reasons either. With their colourful, iconic kits, initial care-free attitude and exotic mystery, the Leopards brightened up an otherwise drab, rain-sodden World Cup and played their part in the most fascinating and delicately poised groups in the opening round, leading to a vivid presence in the collective consciousness of many.

The politics of the day meant their 9-0 drubbing created an itch that many sought to scratch. Were Zaire one of the best teams in the world in 1974? No. But they had proven themselves to be the best team in Africa so had earned the right to sit at the top table while those that missed out licked their wounds in self-righteous indignation at the sheer nerve of such an upstart supposedly taking their place. Like many other players in West Germany, they had sacrificed much, maybe more, and shown grim determination to get there but the Leopards were ultimately defeated not by the more experienced pros of Scotland, Yugoslavia and Brazil but by the betrayal of the very man who had made the dream possible.

'We were poor kids. What did Mobutu want from us?' asked Mbungu Ekofo, before answering his own question. 'Prestige.'

Selected Bibliography

The Fight (1975) - Norman Mailer

The Puffin Book of Football (1979 edition) - Brian Glanville

Scotland's Quest for the World Cup: A Complete Record, 1950-86 (1986) - Clive Leatherdale

Football Against the Enemy (1994) - Simon Kuper

The World Cup - A Definitive History and Guide (2002) - Simon Shirley

Pitch Invasion: Adidas, Puma and the Making of Modern Sport (2006) - Barbara Smit

Complete Book of the World Cup (2006) - Cris Freddi

Foul! The Secret World of FIFA (2006) - Andrew Jennings

The Ball is Round (2007) - David Goldblatt

Stanley Rous's 'Own goal': football politics, South Africa and the contest for the Fifa presidency in 1974 (2008) - Paul Darby

Sneaker Wars: The Enemy Brothers Who Founded Adidas and Puma and the Family Feud That Forever Changed the Business of Sports (2009) - Barbara Smit

Feet of the Chameleon: The Story of African Football (2010) - Ian Hawkey

La Mort m'attendra - Ndaye Mulamba: le destin tragique de la star du foot africain brisée par Mobutu (2010) - Claire Raynaud

Death or Glory! The Dark History of the World Cup (2010) - Jon Spurling

Football imagery and colonial legacy: Zaire's disastrous campaign during the 1974 World Cup (2012) - Paul Dietschy

Scotland 74 - A World Cup Story (2014) - Richard Gordon

Zaire '74 - The Rise and Fall of Mobutu's Leopards

"Die schwärzeste Elf, die es je in Bayern gab": Haiti and Zaire at the 1974 FIFA World Cup and Growing Pains in World Football (2016) - Matt Robertshaw

The Politics of Football in Yugoslavia: Sport, Nationalism and the State (2018) - Richard Mills

Der Afrika-Cup: Geschichte und Geschichten vom größten Fußballfest des Afrikanischen Kontinents (2018) - Olaf Jansen

Index

Printed in Great Britain
by Amazon